THE APOCALYPTIC VISION IN

Paradise Lost

THE APOCALYPTIC VISION IN
Paradise Lost

LELAND RYKEN

Cornell University Press ITHACA AND LONDON

Standard Book Number 8014-0546-7
Library of Congress Catalog Card Number 72-95277

PRINTED IN THE UNITED STATES OF AMERICA
BY VAIL-BALLOU PRESS, INC.

To Mary

Acknowledgments

I owe gratitude to many persons who assisted me in writing this book. Two of my former teachers at the University of Oregon, Professor John Sherwood and the late Professor Kester Svendsen, made significant contributions to the manuscript in an earlier form. I am also grateful to Professor James R. Wilson, who is now at the University of Alaska, for the encouragement and guidance which he has given my academic career.

Grateful acknowledgment is due the editor of the *Huntington Library Quarterly* for permission to reprint, in substantially the same form, material which earlier appeared as an article in this journal. I wish to thank Columbia University Press for permission to quote from the Columbia Edition of *The Works of John Milton*, ed. Frank Allen Patterson *et al.* (New York, 1931–1938).

This study was assisted by a grant from the Rudolph Ernst Memorial Fellowship Fund, administered by the Department of English at the University of Oregon. I am also grateful for the assistance given by the English Department at Wheaton College in my preparation of the final manuscript.

Acknowledgments

I have dedicated the book to the one to whom my obliga-
tion is greatest.

L. R.

Wheaton College, Illinois
February 1969

Contents

Contents

Abbreviations

CE   *College English*
CL   *Comparative Literature*
ELH   *Journal of English Literary History*
HLQ   *Huntington Library Quarterly*
HTR   *Harvard Theological Review*
JEGP   *Journal of English and Germanic Philology*
JHI   *Journal of the History of Ideas*
MLN   *Modern Language Notes*
MP   *Modern Philology*
N&Q   *Notes and Queries*
PMLA   *Publications of the Modern Language Association of America*
PQ   *Philological Quarterly*
RES   *Review of English Studies*
SAQ   *South Atlantic Quarterly*
SEL   *Studies in English Literature, 1500–1900* (Rice University)
SP   *Studies in Philology*
TSLL   *Texas Studies in Literature and Language*
UTQ   *University of Toronto Quarterly*

THE APOCALYPTIC VISION IN

Paradise Lost

1

Introduction

When Milton chose the story of the Fall for his epic, he at once faced the problem of portraying in human terms an action and setting which are not directly accessible to human experience. By presenting not only the Fall of man but the entire celestial cycle—Creation, the war in Heaven, the Fall of man, and Redemption—Milton further increased the weight of the supernatural in his narrative. As a result, more than any other poem in the language, *Paradise Lost* is concerned with the invisible; Milton accurately describes it as a poem that relates "invisible exploits" (V, 565) and tells "Of things invisible to mortal sight" (III, 55).[1] Through thousands of lines supernatural agents are its only figures, and approximately two-thirds of its dialogue is spoken by God and his angels. Its two human characters, moreover, are removed from ordinary human experience by virtue of their unfallen condition through most of the epic.[2] And the subject matter is further

[1] All quotations from Milton's works have been taken from *The Works of John Milton*, ed. Frank Allen Patterson *et al.* (New York, 1931–1938).

[2] Milton's awareness of the difficulty of portraying perfect human beings is recorded in his plans for a drama on the topic of the Fall.

I

distanced from the reader by the poem's setting in the world of prehistory, before human experience as we know it existed.

This book discusses certain aspects of Milton's transcendental vision in *Paradise Lost,* aspects that I have called "apocalyptic." Although the latter term is a relatively recent addition to the vocabulary of literary criticism, it has long been used in reference to a species of writing, often religious in nature. The variety and range of its traditional uses are great. There are, however, some motifs which have been present in most situations where it has been used.

The word "apocalypse" is derived from the Greek word meaning "to reveal." Accordingly, it has traditionally been used to describe writing which purports to be a revelation of phenomena which transcend the world of ordinary reality. Apocalyptic writing has usually denoted prophetic writing —writing which is predictive of future events. Within this broad framework there are two main types of apocalyptic writing. One is concerned with a transcendental state, outside of time, which will follow history; such writing is eschatologically oriented. The other views the apocalyptic state as attainable on earth, and describes a future state that will occur within the order of nature and within the ordinary temporal succession. Apocalypses of this type are frequently social in emphasis, with the reformed social order which is envisioned constituting a warning to contemporary society. Whether the future state is considered as falling within or beyond time, it is viewed as an ideal state—a type of golden age in which there is an ultimate triumph of good over evil.

The apocalyptic concept, in its traditional meaning of a fu-

In the prologue of the third draft he has Moses tell the audience that they "cannot se Adam in the state of innocence by reason of thire sin" ("Milton's Outlines for Tragedies," *Works,* XVIII, 229).

ture ideal state, was of particular importance to the Puritan movement in the sixteenth and seventeenth centuries. Because of Milton's profound involvement in the Puritan Revolution, his relation to the apocalyptic ideal, often socially oriented, has been of widespread interest to his biographers and to historians of his ideas. Michael Fixler's book-length study *Milton and the Kingdoms of God* offers a full discussion of the unity of Milton's visionary endeavours and "their intimate relation to the visionary ideal of Puritanism." [3]

In this book I shall use the term "apocalyptic" in a manner at once broader and more limited than traditional uses of the word.[4] I shall use it to designate a transcendental state that is not located in history and the order of nature but that is placed either above or prior to ordinary time. The traditional concept of futurity, then, is not a part of my definition, although of course the eternal realm, since it always exists, will succeed history. As with the usual definitions of the term, the apocalyptic state which I describe is an ideal state which is infinitely desirable and which thus stands at an opposite pole from the demonic world, which is undesirable. In *Paradise Lost* the apocalyptic realm of transcendental, ideal experience includes Heaven and the prelapsarian Garden of Eden, and the agents which move within these areas (God, the angels, and Adam and Eve).

I call Milton's portrayal of apocalyptic reality a "vision" for several reasons. The archetypal metaphor of the vision implies that the content of the vision exists in the mind and is not experienced in a direct way in real life. A vision is some-

[3] Evanston, 1964.

[4] My concept of the apocalyptic is modeled on the critical system of Northrop Frye, *Anatomy of Criticism* (Princeton, 1957), especially pages 119, 125, 139–146, 155, 162, and 203–206.

thing perceived rather than directly experienced, something contemplated rather than actively participated in. Moreover, the concept of vision or dream is often associated with an envisioned experience which is ideal, with a "world of fulfilled desire emancipated from all anxieties and frustrations." [5] Milton's apocalypse is a vision in all these ways—in its remoteness from fallen reality, in its relation to a higher truth, and in its portrayal of an ideal state.

That the portrayal of apocalyptic experience presents special problems to a poet is evident, and the difficulties have led many a critic to condemn Milton out of hand for even attempting to write on such a subject. Samuel Johnson, for example, deprecates Milton's presentation of innocence when he writes, "The plan of *Paradise Lost* has this inconvenience, that it comprises neither human actions nor human manners. The man and woman who act and suffer are in a state which no other man or woman can ever know. The reader . . . has therefore little natural curiosity or sympathy." [6] Similar pronouncements have continued to the present day, as evidenced by a recent critic who believes that "the very nature" of Milton's themes removes "his poetry . . . from the ordinary concerns and common experience of men," and that "Milton's failure has been due largely to . . . his deliberate choice of topics which preclude recurrence to common experience." [7]

[5] Frye, *Anatomy of Criticism*, p. 119. On the general topic of the dream as an escape from the ordinary world of reality to a transcendental realm, I have also profited from Richard Wilbur's essays on Poe; cf. his introduction to Poe in *Major Writers of America*, ed. Perry Miller (New York, 1962), I, 369–383, and his article entitled "The House of Poe," in *Poe: A Collection of Critical Essays*, ed. Robert Regan (Englewood Cliffs, 1967), pp. 98–120.

[6] *Lives of the English Poets*, ed. L. Archer-Hind (London, 1946), I, 107.

[7] L. A. Cormican, "Milton's Religious Verse," in *From Donne to Marvell*, ed. Boris Ford (Baltimore, 1965), pp. 174, 180.

A common view, in short, is that "Milton's difficulties with the story of *Paradise Lost* are notorious." [8]

In its most extreme form this sort of criticism reduces itself into a dogmatic assertion that it is impossible to portray ideal perfection and that Milton is to be censured for having made the attempt. Thus we are told that "Milton was attempting the impossible—a huge mistake in art." [9] The same complaint is repeated by commentators who claim that "perfection, quite strictly, is unportrayable," [10] that Milton attempted to describe "what cannot be described," [11] and that Milton's "fault" was "that what he attempted was beyond the reach of human language." [12] There is a ready answer to such complaints, and it has been succinctly put forth by Joseph Summers: "By beginning with certain modern assumptions, we could easily 'prove' that what Milton has set out to do is impossible; to the embarrassment of our theories, however, we have the poem." [13]

The present study passes no *a priori* judgment on the nature of Milton's subject matter. My premise is that we must understand the nature of Milton's apocalyptic vision before we can evaluate it. If after analysis we find that Milton's subject was in every way an extremely difficult one to portray, it would seem that he deserves the greater praise for having created a visionary world removed from daily experience but open to the imaginative vision of the reader of the poem. The implied judgment that Milton's success in portraying apoca-

[8] T. W. Craik, *The Comic Tales of Chaucer* (New York, 1964), p. xiv.

[9] Mark Van Doren, *The Noble Voice* (New York, 1946), p. 136.

[10] A. J. A. Waldock, *Paradise Lost and Its Critics* (Cambridge, Eng., 1947), p. 97.

[11] Johnson, *Lives of the English Poets*, I, 108.

[12] Cormican, "Milton's Religious Verse," p. 174.

[13] *The Muse's Method* (Cambridge, Mass., 1962), p. 13.

lyptic reality in *Paradise Lost* was of the highest order underlies this entire study, but it is not a thesis that I attempt to
prove. My purpose is to determine the principles which constitute Milton's apocalyptic technique and to illustrate their
manifestation in the poem.

✎ 2

Theoretic Considerations

THE DOCTRINE OF ACCOMMODATION

Although any study of apocalyptic reality in *Paradise Lost* must ultimately be based on an analysis of the poem itself, it is first necessary to examine the theoretic considerations with which Milton approached his poem. The most important such consideration brought to bear on the problem of portraying the apocalyptic experience in humanly comprehensible terms was the doctrine of accommodation. This exegetical principle was one of the commonplaces of Medieval and Renaissance theology. While statements by individual writers varied in details, the central point of the doctrine remained the same: the representation of God in Scripture has been accommodated to man's understanding by being reduced to language which human intelligence can comprehend. This method of biblical exegesis was designed to provide an adequate explanation for the anthropomorphic portrayal of God in the Bible, particularly in the Old Testament. Statements of the doctrine usually centered on the representation of God, but the implications of the theory were often extended to biblical truth in general, with the result that spiritual truths of many kinds might be said to be accommodated in humanly understandable terms.

7

This principle of biblical interpretation had been stated definitely as early as Augustine. In commenting on an Old Testament passage which speaks of God's anger, Augustine explains, "The anger of God is not a disturbing emotion of His mind, but a judgment by which punishment is inflicted upon sin. His thought and reconsideration also are the unchangeable reason which changes things; for He does not, like man, repent of anything He has done. . . . But if Scripture were not to use such expressions as the above, it would not familiarly insinuate itself into the minds of all classes of men, whom it seeks access to for their good . . . ; and this it could not do, did it not first stoop, and in a manner descend, to them where they lie." [1]

An example of a Renaissance restatement of this doctrine is that by John Colet, founder of St. Paul's School, where Milton himself was later to receive his early education. Colet touches upon the subject repeatedly in his discussion of the Mosaic account of Creation in his four "Letters to Radulphus." Moses describes the Creation, writes Colet, "placing before the eye the arrangement of the world; which he does in this way . . . that he may seem to have regard to the understanding of the vulgar and rude multitude whom he taught." [2] Again, "So all things of God, when given to man, must needs lose somewhat of their sublimity, and be put in a form more palpable and more within the grasp of man. Accordingly, the high knowledge of Moses about God and Divine things and the creation of the world, when it came to be submitted to the vulgar apprehension, savoured altogether of

[1] *The City of God,* trans. Marcus Dods (New York, 1948), pp. 97–98.

[2] Selections from the "Letters to Radulphus," trans. Frederic Seebohm, *The Oxford Reformers: John Colet, Erasmus, and Thomas More,* 3d ed. (London, 1896), p. 50.

the humble and the rustic. . . . Thus, accommodating him-
elf to *their* comprehension, Moses endeavoured, by this most
honest and pious figure, at once to allure them and draw them
on to the worship of God." [3]

Protestant writers of the age showed no hesitation in adopting this doctrine of accommodation. The pronouncements of
John Calvin are of particular interest because of his influence
on the Protestant tradition in which Milton wrote. In commenting on the anthropomorphism of Isaiah 6:1–5, Calvin
writes, "We may ask how Isaiah could see God who is spirit
and is therefore not visible to bodily eyes. Since the minds of
men are incapable of mounting to the infinite height of God,
how can man apprehend God under any visible form? But we
must realize that whenever God revealed himself to be seen
by the fathers, he never appeared as he is in himself but as he
could be understood by human minds. . . . Therefore Isaiah
was shown a form of a kind which enabled him with his own
understanding to taste the inconceivable majesty of God. This
is the reason that he attributes a throne, a robe, and a bodily
appearance to God." [4] Unlike Colet, who stresses the social
and intellectual incapacities of those who receive accommodated spiritual truths, Calvin places the necessity of such accommodation in the universal human condition, without regard to distinctions of class or mental ability. "By this means,"
he writes, God "has consideration upon our weakness. For if
we were wholly spiritual like the angels, we should be able to

[3] *The Oxford Reformers*, pp. 56–57.
[4] *Calvin: Commentaries*, trans. and ed. Joseph Haroutunian (Philadelphia, 1958), p. 120. Other statements of the theory of accommodation can be found in Calvin's comments on Gen. 3:8; Ex. 3:2,4;
and Ezek. 9:3–4. All of these passages are conveniently quoted by
Edward A. Dowey, Jr., *The Knowledge of God in Calvin's
Theology* (New York, 1952), pp. 3–5.

see both him and his gifts. But as we are surrounded by this gross earthly body, we need symbols or mirrors, to exhibit to us the appearance of spiritual and heavenly things, in a kind of earthly way." [5] Calvin's formulation of the principle also evinces his Reformed theology in emphasizing that man should rest content with the representation which God has given of himself and should refrain from allegorical or mystical interpretations of the Bible. God has given us, he writes, "a description, not of what he is in himself, but of what he is to us, that our knowledge of him may consist rather in a lively perception than in vain and airy speculation." [6]

Statements of the theory of accommodation were not limited to theologians but were voiced by poets and men of letters as well. Dante makes poetic use of the concept in the *Paradiso*, where Beatrice explains to the poet,

> On this account the Scripture condescends
> Unto your faculties, and feet and hands
> To God attributes, and means something else. [7]

A seventeenth-century instance is John Dryden, who, in discussing "Heroic Poetry and Poetic Licence," writes, "For immaterial substances, we are authorized by Scripture in their description: and herein the text accommodates itself to vulgar apprehension, in giving angels the likeness of beautiful young men. Thus, after the pagan divinity, has Homer drawn his gods with human faces: and thus we have notions of things

[5] *Theological Treatises*, trans. and ed. J. K. S. Reid (Philadelphia, 1954), p. 131.

[6] *Institutes of the Christian Religion*, trans. John Allen (Philadelphia, 1930), I, 95. Another statement of the doctrine occurs in the same chapter, p. 99.

[7] *Paradiso*, IV, 43–45; *The Divine Comedy of Dante Alighieri*, trans. Henry W. Longfellow (New York, 1895).

above us, by describing them like other beings more within our knowledge." [8] Dryden's statement of the theory is particularly significant in that it indicates the facility with which the doctrine of accommodation was transferred from the area of biblical exegesis to that of poetic theory and practice. Interestingly, Dryden's remarks appear in an essay prefixed to *The State of Innocence,* his dramatic adaptation of Milton's epic.

As these statements suggest, the concept of the accommodation of spiritual truth to human understanding would have been a commonplace in the Renaissance to anyone familiar with current notions of biblical interpretation.[9] Milton, a

---

[8] *Of Dramatic Poesy and Other Critical Essays,* ed. George Watson (London, 1962), I, 204. The persistence with which the theory of accommodation appeared in literary contexts is suggested further by the following note which Pope attached to a passage in his edition of Book VIII of the *Iliad:* " . . . there are some Places in Scripture that in Compliance to human Understanding represent the Deity as acting by Motives like those of Men" (quoted from Reuben A. Brower, *Alexander Pope: The Poetry of Allusion* [Oxford, 1959], p. 125).

[9] The currency of the doctrine of accommodation in the Middle Ages and Renaissance is established more fully in several studies. C. A. Patrides, "*Paradise Lost* and the Theory of Accommodation," *TSLL,* V (1963), 58–63, quotes a total of eight Renaissance statements of the theory and lists five additional sources. The same writer offers the fullest bibliography to date of Renaissance references to the doctrine of accommodation in his book *Milton and the Christian Tradition* (Oxford, 1966), pp. 9–10. Frederic W. Farrar, *History of Interpretation* (London, 1886), p. 187, notes statements by five patristic writers, while Roland M. Frye, *God, Man, and Satan* (Princeton, 1960), pp. 9–13, quotes and discusses parallel passages from Aquinas, Calvin, Athanasius, and Knox. H. R. MacCallum, "Milton and Figurative Interpretation of the Bible," *UTQ,* XXXI (1961–62), 397–415, notes examples from Colet and Spinoza and makes significant and perceptive comments on Milton's formulation of the doctrine. Basil Willey, *The Seventeenth Century Background* (London, 1942), pp. 57–75, has a chapter on biblical interpretation, which includes a discussion of the theory of accommodation.

theologian in his own right, shows his knowledge and acceptance of this tradition in chapter ii of *De Doctrina Christiana*.
He begins by asserting axiomatically that man is incapable of
perfect comprehension of the Deity. "When we speak of
knowing God," he writes, "it must be understood with reference to the imperfect comprehension of man; for to know
God as he really is, far transcends the powers of man's
thoughts, much more of his perception" (*Works*, XIV, 31).
Because of his limited understanding, man is dependent for his
conception of God on the revelation which God has given of
himself: "No one . . . can have right thoughts of God, with
nature or reason alone as his guide, independent of the word,
or message of God. . . . God therefore has made as full a
revelation of himself as our minds can conceive, or the weakness of our nature can bear" (XIV, 31). In Milton's view,
then, the theory of accommodation is rooted in man's depend-
ence upon divine revelation for his knowledge of spiritual
truths.

Man's proper response to God's revelation of himself is to
receive the accommodated truth as it has been given to him
and to allow his conception of God to be formed by the details which he finds in Scripture. As Milton states, "Our safest
way is to form in our minds such a conception of God, as
shall correspond with his own delineation and representation
of himself in the sacred writings. For granting that both in the
literal and figurative descriptions of God, he is exhibited not
as he really is, but in such a manner as may be within the
scope of our comprehensions, yet we ought to entertain such
a conception of him, as he, in condescending to accommodate
himself to our capacities, has shown that he desires we should
conceive" (XIV, 31, 33).

In accepting the principle of accommodation, Milton is logically led to affirm the validity of an anthropomorphic picture of God. Regarding the outward appearance and form of God, for example, "If God be said 'to have made man in his own image, after his likeness,' Gen. i. 26. and that too not only as to his soul, but also as to his outward form . . . and if God habitually assign to himself the members and form of man, why should we be afraid of attributing to him what he attributes to himself, so long as what is imperfection and weakness when viewed in reference to ourselves be considered as most complete and excellent when imputed to God?" (XIV, 35). Not only human form but human emotions and actions as well are a legitimate part of our conception of God. Milton writes, "If after the work of six days it be said of God that 'he rested and was refreshed,' Exod. xxxi. 17. if it be said that 'he feared the wrath of the enemy,' Deut. xxxii. 27, let us believe that it is not beneath the dignity of God to . . . be refreshed in that which refresheth him, or to fear in that he feareth" (XIV, 35).

Along with this acceptance of a humanized conception of the Deity, Milton exhibits a distrust of the anthropomorphism which he finds in classical literature. "There is no need then," he writes, "that theologians should have recourse here to what they call anthropopathy, a figure invented by the grammarians to excuse the absurdities of the poets on the subject of the heathen divinities" (XIV, 33). The apparent contradiction results from a distinction which Milton wishes to make between human qualities which are attributed to God in Scripture and human qualities which are attached to him on the basis of man's own thinking and imagination. This distinction becomes clearer in his subsequent discussion, where he states, "It is better therefore to contemplate the Deity, and to conceive of him, not with reference to human passions, that is, after the manner of men, who are never weary of forming subtle imaginations respecting him, but after the manner of Scripture, that is, in the way wherein God has offered himself to our contemplation" (XIV, 33). The point would seem to be an elaboration of the idea, mentioned earlier, that accommodation begins with God and his revelation.[10] Man's conception of God must therefore find its limits not in his unchecked imagination but in the biblical revelation.

Milton's discussion is not without a degree of uncertainty and ambiguity. He is unwilling to state finally whether the representation of God in human terms is a literal or a figurative picture of the Deity. "In a word," he writes, "God either is, or is not, such as he represents himself to be. . . . If he be not such, on what authority do we say what God has not said" (XIV, 37)? Similarly, after insisting that man must rest content with the biblical representation of God in physical terms, Milton is quick to make the distinction that "in arguing thus, we do not say that God is in fashion like unto man in all

[10] This part of Milton's discussion is clarified if we remember that he is here writing in the mainstream of Reformed theology and wishes to underscore the main tenet of that tradition, namely, that Scripture alone is the authoritative source for religious belief. Milton's careful distinctions in the paragraph under consideration correspond to the following statement by Calvin: "For, since the human mind is unable, through its imbecility, to attain any knowledge of God without the assistance of his sacred word, all mankind, except the Jews, as they sought God without the word, must necessarily have been wandering in vanity and error" (*Institutes of the Christian Religion*, I, 75). In view of Milton's denunciation of accepting nonbiblical details concerning God as truth, the thesis that he regarded himself as adding to the revelation of God in writing *Paradise Lost* has received more attention than it deserves. William J. Grace, "Orthodoxy and Aesthetic Method in *Paradise Lost* and the *Divine Comedy*," *CL*, I (1949), 173–187, asserts but does not document that "Milton actually believed that he was adding historic details to the Scriptures."

his parts and members, but that as far as we are concerned to know, he is of that form which he attributes to himself in the sacred writings" (XIV, 37). As both passages reveal, Milton was unable to decide finally on the exact nature of the accommodated image.[11]

Like other writers on the subject, Milton in his discussion of the doctrine of accommodation displays certain characteristics which distinguish his formulation of the concept from others. In the first place, as MacCallum has noted,[12] Milton's acceptance of the anthropomorphic details of accommodated spiritual truth is unusually thoroughgoing. Comparison of Milton's version of the theory with other statements is instructive on this point. On the one hand, Milton's unhesitating acceptance of the physical details employed by biblical writers to describe God removes him from the allegorical view of accommodation. Dante's statement, for example, is made in the Catholic tradition of an allegorical, four-level method of biblical exegesis.[13] Accordingly he implies that it is incumbent

---

[11] Denis Saurat, in *Milton, Man and Thinker* (London, 1949), p. 100, misrepresents the statements of both Milton and David Masson when he states that, since in Milton's view God is completely unknowable, the accommodated image is only a figure and that "this is in no way, as Masson would have it, a proof of literal belief." Masson, *The Life of Milton* (London, 1880), VI, 819, correctly observes that for Milton the biblical representations "may or may not be figurative expressions."

[12] *UTQ*, XXXI, 402–3.

[13] For details of allegorical methods of biblical interpretation, see Farrar, *History of Interpretation*, passim; Seebohm, *The Oxford Reformers*, pp. 25–36; Henry Preserved Smith, *Essays in Biblical Interpretation* (Boston, 1921), pp. 33–58; Willey, *The Seventeenth Century Background*, pp. 61–67; Beryl Smalley, *The Study of the Bible in the Middle Ages* (Oxford, 1941), passim; and Harry A. Wolfson, *The Philosophy of the Church Fathers*, I (Cambridge, Mass., 1956), 24–72.

upon the reader of Scripture to rise from the physical vehicle of the metaphor to the spiritual mystery which lies beyond the realm of concrete details: Scripture "feet and hands / To God attributes, and means something else" (*Paradiso*, IV, 44–45). Milton's emphasis resists such a movement from the physical picture to a more spiritual conceptualization. According to his view, man has no need to acquire any other idea of spiritual truth than that which God has accommodated to him. "For it is on this very account," Milton asserts, "that he has lowered himself to our level, lest in our flights above the reach of human understanding, and beyond the written word of Scripture, we should be tempted to indulge in vague cogitations and subtleties" (XIV, 33).[14] To entertain any conception of God beyond the concrete particulars which he has given us is to "frustrate the purposes of God instead of rendering him submissive obedience" (XIV, 37). It is noteworthy that for Milton the anthropomorphic representation of God cannot be taken lightly, as it might be when interpreted allegorically.[15] Indeed, the physical details are true in so far as man is enabled to know.

[14] For discussion of Milton's adherence to the Protestant tradition of literal as opposed to allegorical interpretation of Scripture, see, in addition to MacCallum, George Newton Conklin, *Biblical Criticism and Heresy in Milton* (New York, 1949), p. 10, which describes the Protestant method of literal exegesis and states that "Milton in his examination of Scripture . . . followed consistently Calvin's dictum of interpretation which held that the first duty of an interpreter is to let his author say what he does say."

[15] Elbert N. S. Thompson's discussion of Milton's concept of accommodation in *Essays on Milton* (New Haven, 1914), pp. 111–115, is misleading in stating that for Milton the biblical "truths, rather than a literal statement of the revelation, are of vital concern to the human race" and that "ever the poet's thought is centered on the truth itself and not on its expression." Another example of an earlier misconception of Milton's ideas on accommodation is the discussion of Marjorie Nicolson, "Milton and the *Conjectura Cabbalistica*," *PQ*, VI

The emphasis of Milton on the literal interpretation of accommodated truth also differs from statements of the theory which stress the social and educational incapacity of the recipients of spiritual revelation. John Colet, as we have seen, takes the position that the Mosaic account of Creation was intended for "the vulgar and rude multitude." Accordingly, he is at pains to show that Moses, with his superior wisdom and insight into spiritual matters, did not have need of the same physical particulars with which he presented his story to the uneducated people: ". . . so that we perceive him to have spoken, not in keeping with his own intelligence, but so as to suit the conceptions of the multitude." [16] Milton's formulation makes no such distinctions between social classes and levels of intelligence. In his view, human nature without exception is incapable of a complete understanding of spiritual matters, "for to know God as he really is, far transcends the power of man's thoughts, much more of his perception" (XIV, 31). Milton's statement of the doctrine thus defines the limits of human understanding and asserts the necessity to rest content with the words and images of the Bible without attempting to penetrate behind them. Here he is similar to Calvin, who, as we have seen, also insists that man should accept the physical details of accommodation, "that our knowledge of him may consist rather in a lively perception than in vain and airy speculation." Yet Milton's very hesitation over the

(1927), 1–18, which assumes that Milton's understanding of the theory is similar to Henry More's and concludes too sweepingly that "Milton himself, it is safe to say, did not believe in an anthropomorphic deity seated on a throne, nor in a Second Cause with golden compasses. . . . In Milton, as in More, there is, besides the literal story, a philosophic interpretation . . . ; and there is a 'mystical or divinely moral' interpretation."

[16] Selections from "Letters to Radulphus," trans. J. H, Lupton, *A Life of John Colet* (London, 1887), p. 251.

question whether the physical representation of God is literal or figurative suggests a more materialistic attitude than that of Calvin, who states plainly that God "never appeared as he is in himself" and that he has given "a description, not of what he is in himself." Even in Milton's age, his version of the doctrine seems remarkable in its emphasis on the physical aspect of accommodation.

It is well to note that Milton's statement of the principle of accommodation is not as simple as a cursory reading of his discussion might suggest. Although we are enjoined to accept an easily grasped picture of divine truth, Milton would also insist that this picture be based on the details found in Scripture. By implication, one's conception of God will be more or less complete and accurate to the extent that his knowledge of the biblical account is full and correct. Moreover, the human attributes which are given to God in Scripture must be divested of some of their usual connotations before we can form a correct picture of the Deity. When we read that God repented himself, Milton writes, "let us believe that it did repent him, only taking care to remember that what is called repentance when applied to God, does not arise from inadvertency, as in men" (XIV, 33, 35). Similarly, we should not hesitate to attribute human qualities to God, "so long as what is imperfection and weakness when viewed in reference to ourselves be considered as most complete and excellent when imputed to God" (XIV, 35). The point which Milton apparently wishes to make is that although it is wrong to add allegorical meanings to physical representations of God, some kind of subtracting process is necessary in order to divest the representation of inappropriate human associations.[17]

[17] In view of Milton's insistence that when human qualities are attributed to God they must be divested of some of their usual con-

With Milton's use of the doctrine of accommodation in the area of biblical interpretation established, the question remains whether he regarded the doctrine as being equally applicable to matters of poetic theory and technique. Any conclusion which we reach must be made in the absence of explicit pronouncement by Milton, and since modern commentators have unanimously assumed that the theory of accommodation is as applicable to religious poetry as it is to biblical exegesis, it is perhaps salutary to be reminded that not all critics have agreed with this verdict. William Wilkie, writing in the middle of the eighteenth century, believed that in the early ages of the church God "thought fit to accommodate himself, by such a piece of condescension, to the notions and apprehensions of his creatures: but it would be indecent in any man to use the same freedom, and do that for God, which he only has a right to do for himself." [18] Wilkie goes on to assert that the poet who undertakes to portray God by means of accommodation "is justly chargeable with impiety, for presuming to represent the Divine Nature, and the mysteries of religion, according to the narrowness of human prejudice." Milton was

notations, serious objections should arise in regard to the thesis of Malcolm Ross that "Milton, writing as a bitter anti-royalist, drew heavily on the royalist literary tradition," and that "a contradiction between the symbol and the idea was inevitable" (*Milton's Royalism: A Study of the Conflict of Symbol and Idea in the Poems* [Ithaca, 1943], p. vii). Keeping in mind Milton's stipulation that "what is imperfection and weakness when viewed in reference to ourselves be considered as most complete and excellent when imputed to God," we are free to see that Milton could without contradiction use the royalist symbol to represent true spiritual perfection, despite the fact that he was hostile to the royalist image as it existed in the political situation in England.

[18] Preface to *Epigoniad* (Edinburgh, 1757); quoted in H. T. Swedenberg, Jr., *The Theory of the Epic in England, 1650–1880,* University of California Publications in English, XV (1944), 294.

of the contrary opinion, and he consciously used the theory of accommodation in portraying the supernatural parts of *Paradise Lost,* as modern critics have often noted.[19] We have already observed that poets such as Dante and Dryden found the theory congenial to their poetic technique. Dryden moreover, uses the doctrine in what might be called a prescriptive manner ("For immaterial substances, we are authorized by Scripture in their description. . . ."), implying that the method of Scripture serves as a kind of model for poets. Accordingly he proceeds to apply the theory to a consideration of Homer's portrayal of the gods.

There is evidence in *Paradise Lost* that Milton likewise looked upon the concept of accommodation as a legitimate poetic method. The *locus classicus* is Raphael's statement to Adam before describing the war in Heaven:

> and what surmounts the reach
> Of human sense, I shall delineate so,
> By lik'ning spiritual to corporal forms,
> As may express them best   [V, 571–574].

Raphael concludes his account of the war in Heaven with a parallel allusion to the doctrine of accommodation:

> Thus measuring things in Heav'n by things on Earth
> At thy request, and that thou maist beware
> By what is past, to thee I have reveal'd
> What might have else to human Race bin hid
>
>   [VI, 893–896].

[19] Critics affirming that Milton regarded the doctrine of accommodation as a legitimate poetic technique include Frye, *God, Man, and Satan,* p. 14; James H. Hanford, *A Milton Handbook,* 4th ed. (New York), p. 205; Patrides, *TSLL,* V, 62, and *Milton and the Christian Tradition,* pp. 9–10, 94; and Willey, *The Seventeenth Century Background,* p. 70.

Supplementing these statements are numerous other references
to the accommodation of spiritual truth. In his account of
Creation, for example, Raphael explains:

> Immediate are the Acts of God, more swift
> Then time or motion, but to human ears
> Cannot without process of speech be told,
> So told as earthly notion can receave
>
> [VII, 176–179].

In describing the fight between Satan and Michael, Raphael
again expresses the difficulty of finding an adequate earthly
medium to convey the magnitude of the struggle:

> They ended parle, and both addrest for fight
> Unspeakable; for who, though with the tongue
> Of Angels, can relate, or to what things
> Liken on Earth conspicuous, that may lift
> Human imagination to such highth
> Of Godlike Power   [VI, 296–301].

The accommodated nature of anthropomorphic details is
also suggested in less obvious ways. When we are told that
Satan wept "Tears such as Angels weep" (I, 620), the qualifying phrase is a reminder by the narrator that the narrative
exists on two planes and that the physical details are not true
in exactly the ordinary way. When we read that the angels
poured forth humor "such as Celestial Spirits may bleed" (VI,
333), we are again reminded that the action is being accommodated to our understanding. Adam's response to the story
of the war in Heaven, expressing the feeling that Raphael has
interpreted spiritual events which man could not with his own
abilities have understood, likewise falls within the frame of
reference provided by the doctrine of accommodation:

> Divine interpreter, by favour sent
> Down from the Empyrean to forewarne
> Us timely of what might else have bin our loss,
> Unknown, which human knowledg could not reach
>
> [VII, 72–75].

In particular, Adam's designation of Raphael as a "divine interpreter" becomes meaningful only when we realize that the story which he has told has been translated into the language of human experience. The same concept appears when Raphael, while speaking of the palace of Lucifer in Heaven, adds parenthetically,

> so call
> That Structure in the Dialect of men
> Interpreted   [V, 760–762].

Adam's words in thanking Raphael for having granted "This friendly condescention to relate / Things else by me unsearchable" (VIII, 9–10) again bring to mind the doctrine of accommodation, especially since statements of the doctrine by theologians sometimes used the term "condescension." [20]

From passages such as these one must conclude that the theory of accommodation was for Milton a basic premise in the portrayal of his apocalyptic vision. If this conclusion is correct, a context is provided for the apocalyptic elements in *Paradise Lost* and important critical implications follow. Milton's seventeenth-century reader, it must be remembered, would not have been surprised by the frank materialism in descriptions of spiritual events. He would not have been perplexed by the question, which modern criticism finds so vexing, how, if God is truly transcendent, he can be portrayed in

[20] Farrar, *History of Interpretation*, p. 187, quotes some examples.

physical terms.[21] For a reader acquainted with the doctrine of accommodation the answer is simple: the transcendent God accommodates himself to human understanding in visible images, and it is therefore neither inconsistent nor contradictory to maintain that God is incomprehensible and at the same time to portray him in human terms. Such a demanding seventeenth-century reader as Dryden was not offended, as readers from the time of Samuel Johnson forward have been, at the mixture of spirit and matter in the account of the war in Heaven. Milton's contemporaries were aware that Raphael's narrative was occurring at two levels, and therefore the poet could, without being guilty of confusion or failure to make up his mind, insist on the "otherness" of his story even while presenting the action in physical terms.[22]

Since Milton's poetic theory was based on the principle of accommodation, the reader must expect a preponderance of physical and human details in the apocalyptic parts of the narrative. Although modern critics may find the theory of accommodation unacceptable, it seems fruitless to assail Milton for describing spiritual reality in earthly terms when that was precisely what he intended to do and what his theory bound him to. For Milton's age, at least, the theory provided the necessary equipment to read with sympathy and understanding a humanistic story about spiritual mysteries. Later readers

[21] Marjorie Nicolson, echoing modern critical opinion, asks, "how can Infinity be expressed in finite terms, Spirit clothed in body and localized—even on a Throne in Heaven?" (*John Milton: A Reader's Guide to His Poetry* [New York, 1963], p. 223).

[22] The charge of inconsistency on Milton's part is made by A. J. A. Waldock, *Paradise Lost and Its Critics* (Cambridge, Eng., 1947), pp. 109–111, while John Peter, *A Critique of Paradise Lost* (New York, 1960), p. 22, asserts that "for poet and reader alike it is again chiefly a matter of indecision, of not knowing on what plane the poem's characters exist."

who ignore the doctrine of accommodation remove themselves from a sympathetic understanding of the poem.

THE PLATONIC THEORY OF IDEAS

The Platonic element in Milton's portrayal of apocalyptic reality is less pervasive and more problematical than the theory of accommodation. The usual point of departure for discussing the Platonic aspect is the question raised by Raphael in his preface to the account of the war in Heaven. After stating the doctrine of accommodation, Raphael adds: [23]

> though what if Earth
> Be but the shaddow of Heav'n and things therein
> Each to other like, more then on Earth is thought?
>
> [V, 574–576].

Raphael's suggestion that there may be an actual correspondence between Heaven and Earth, "the shaddow of Heav'n," has been interpreted by most critics as a formulation of Plato's theory of Ideas, which asserts that the world of empirical real-

[23] Raphael's query whether Earth in reality corresponds to Heaven is illogical in several ways. Since he has just come from Heaven and is thoroughly familiar with the heavenly landscape (witness his subsequent narrative), he should be able to state unequivocally whether Heaven is like the Earth where he is now situated. Raphael's indecision in this passage is also inconsistent with scattered remarks in his accounts of the war in Heaven and Creation asserting an actual correspondence between the earthly and transcendental realms (cf. V, 430–432; VI, 516–517, 640–641). One strongly suspects, in short, that Milton has here edited Raphael. Edwyn Bevan, *Symbolism and Belief* (Boston, 1957; first pub., 1938), p. 15, states that "it is Milton rather than Raphael" who asks the question in Book V, 574–576, though Bevan bases his conclusion on different grounds from those which I cite above: "by general opinion on earth the archangel could hardly have meant what was thought by a single human couple."

ity is an imperfect copy of the transcendental realm.[24] This prevalent view of the Platonic element in Milton's poetic theory has been formidably challenged by two scholars, and it is by way of these counterstatements that I can best approach my own assessment of the influence of the Platonic theory of Ideas in Milton's technique.

William G. Madsen has questioned the relevance of the Platonic theory of Ideas to an interpretation of *Paradise Lost* on the basis of the Renaissance practice of typological biblical exegesis.[25] Taking Raphael's statement about Earth as the shadow of Heaven as his point of departure, Madsen opposes the usual Platonic interpretation of the lines and proposes that "Milton is using 'shadow' here not in its Platonic or Neoplatonic sense but in its familiar Christian sense of 'foreshadowing' or 'adumbration'; and that the symbolism of *Paradise Lost* is typological rather than Platonic." In such an interpretation, the material images used by Raphael to describe the war in Heaven "are typological and prophetic, not Platonic; they speak of what lies ahead, not what lies above; they are a shadow of things to come." More specifically, Raphael's account of the battle in Heaven is not primarily a metaphorical description of some past event but "is a shadow of this last age of the world and of the Second Coming of Christ."

[24] Critical statements which give a Platonic interpretation to the passage include the following: Hanford, *A Milton Handbook*, p. 205; Merritt Y. Hughes, ed., *John Milton: Complete Poems and Major Prose* (New York, 1957), p. 315; M. M. Mahood, *Poetry and Humanism* (New Haven, 1950), p. 204; Marjorie Nicolson, "The Spirit World of Milton and More," *SP*, XXII (1925), 451; Irene Samuel, *Plato and Milton* (Ithaca, 1947), p. 145; George Wesley Whiting, *Milton's Literary Milieu* (Chapel Hill, 1939), p. 31; and Willey, *The Seventeenth Century Background*, p. 70.

[25] "Earth the Shadow of Heaven: Typological Symbolism in *Paradise Lost*," *PMLA*, LXXV (1960), 519–526.

Madsen's discussion adds a new dimension to our reading of *Paradise Lost* and supports a valid alternate or secondary interpretation of many passages in the poem. Details of the argument are open to question, however, and Madsen is wholly unconvincing in his major contention that a Platonic interpretation of Raphael's speech (V, 574–576) is "mistaken." His only basis for such a judgment is that the typological meaning of the word "shadow" was common in the seventeenth century and that a typological interpretation adequately explains much of the action in *Paradise Lost*. Analysis of the text of the poem will show that Madsen's assertion that the images do not speak of what lies above earthly reality is refuted by numerous passages in *Paradise Lost*.

It is important to note at the outset that Raphael's statement that Earth may be the shadow of Heaven occurs in answer to the specific question how to relate "To human sense th' invisible exploits / Of warring Spirits" (V, 565–566), how to "unfould / The secrets of another world" (V, 568–569). The immediate context of Raphael's statement, stressing different levels in the scale of being, thus points to a Platonic meaning, with its analogy between earthly and heavenly existence.

Statements made later in the poem by Adam, Raphael, and the epic narrator likewise emphasize that the events in Heaven represent a different level of being from that on Earth. Adam, for example, believes that the angel has described "Things above Earthly thought" (VII, 82), things "which human knowledg could not reach" (VII, 75). He tells Raphael, "Great things, and full of wonder in our eares, / Farr differing from this World, thou hast reveal'd" (VII, 70–71). When asking Raphael to move from the account of the war in Heaven to the story of the Creation of the world, Adam again makes the point that Earth is lower in the scale of being than the celestial realm where the battle had taken place: "Deign to descend now lower, and relate / . . . How first began this Heav'n which we behold" (VII, 84, 86). Even before Raphael's account of heavenly events we read that Adam's main concern in speaking with the angel is "to know / Of things above his World" (V, 454–455); he desires to learn of the heavenly beings, "whose excellence he saw / Transcend his own so farr" (V, 456–457) and "whose high Power so far / Exceeded human" (V, 458–459).

Both Raphael, the angelic narrator, and Milton, the epic narrator, also make it clear that the celestial parts of the narrative are concerned with a realm which lies above the earthly. Raphael states that his story is one which "surmounts the reach" of human understanding (V, 571), and he complains of the difficulty of finding things "on Earth conspicuous, that may lift / Human imagination to such highth / Of Godlike Power" (VI, 299–301). Similarly, the acts of God, although accomplished instantaneously, "to human ears / Cannot without process of speech be told, / So told as earthly notion can receave" (VII, 177–179). Milton, as epic narrator, speaks of the celestial battle as something which belongs to another world:

> Up led by thee
> Into the Heav'n of Heav'ns I have presum'd,
> An Earthlie Guest, and drawn Empyreal Aire,
> Thy tempring; with like safetie guided down
> Return me to my Native Element   [VII, 12–16].

After relating the war in Heaven the narrator states his intention to remain "Within the visible Diurnal Spheare; / Standing on Earth, not rapt above the Pole" (VII, 22–23).

27

In the poem, then, there is rather clear evidence that the celestial parts of the narrative are concerned with actions which transcend human comprehension. The repeated references to the strangeness and transcendence of the account must refer to a difference between two worlds, not simply between two separated points in time, for if the difference is only a temporal distinction, the account does not in fact deal with matter "Farr differing from this World." The symbolism of the poem is thus primarily Platonic, telling of what lies above in the scale of being, and the fact that some of the events which occur in Heaven foreshadow future events on Earth receives less emphasis in the poem than the fact that heavenly events transcend earthly experience.

It is perhaps significant that the clearest allusion to the typological method in *Paradise Lost*, where Michael tells Adam about proceeding "From shadowie Types to Truth, from Flesh to Spirit" (XII, 303), emphasizes the spiritual nature of the antitype as opposed to the physical nature of the type. Even if a typological interpretation of the battle in Heaven is accepted, the emphasis must remain on the opposition of spirit and body, not on the temporal opposition, for Raphael makes it clear that he will liken "spiritual to corporal forms" (V, 573). In much of the current concern with typological symbolism insufficient attention is given to the fact that the difference between a type and antitype is not a matter of time only but can also be a difference between the physical and the spiritual, between the external medium and the inner meaning. Like the doctrine of accommodation, typology is capable of different emphases by different writers. Since in *Paradise Lost* the theory of typology is said to concern the distinction between "Flesh" and "Spirit," we should perhaps question whether in every situation a type necessarily "looks forward in time, not upward through the scale of being." [26]

H. R. MacCallum has also used Renaissance theories of biblical exegesis to place qualifications on the critical approach which links Milton with the Renaissance tradition of Neoplatonism.[27] MacCallum notes that Milton's discussion of the theory of accommodation does not share common Neoplatonic characteristics. Instead of encouraging the reader of Scripture to penetrate beyond the concrete image to the spiritual reality which lies behind it, Milton stresses the necessity of resting content in the physical representation. His formulation does not permit an attempt to dissolve the poetic figure but insists that the reader accept it literally and deduce moral and doctrinal truth directly from it.

Although MacCallum's discussion provides a corrective to an unqualified emphasis on Milton's Platonism, I do not believe that his remarks invalidate the claim that the theory of Ideas formed a part of Milton's poetic theory. In the first place, Milton's deprecation of "vague cogitations and subleties" in the *De Doctrina Christiana* is directed against the Catholic and Scholastic method of allegorical interpretation of the Bible. Apparently Milton was not here thinking about Platonism at all, and it is therefore questionable whether his emphasis on a literal method of biblical exegesis implies anything about his attitude toward the Platonic theory of Ideas. Moreover, the theory of Ideas does not necessarily lead one to an attempt to penetrate beyond the physical image to the ideal

[26] Madsen lists this as one of the distinguishing characteristics of a type in his essay, "From Shadowy Types to Truth," in *The Lyric and Dramatic Milton,* ed. Joseph Summers (New York, 1965), p. 99.

[27] "Milton and Figurative Interpretation of the Bible," *UTQ,* XXXI (1961–62), 397–415.

archetype, as MacCallum assumes it does. Although many Platonists have been mystics, and although for Plato himself the earthly copy was less real than the archetypal Idea of that copy, the physical representation is still a genuine image of ultimate reality. As one commentator has perceptively written, "When despondent, the Platonist can reflect that this world is but a fleeting shadow of the real world of intelligible ideas; that the soul's home is not here, but in that other eternal world. When looking at the world more cheerfully, he remembers that it is, even if only a shadow, yet still a shadow of the eternal, of which it is a copy, however imperfect . . . ; and that all things are emanations of the divine." [28] Just as the doctrine of accommodation could be used to support either a literal or an allegorical method of biblical interpretation, the Platonic theory of Ideas is capable of leading either to an acceptance of the visible image or an attempt to dissolve the image and go beyond it. Milton's nonallegorical view of accommodation would not necessarily place him outside the pale of Platonism; it might simply establish him as a particular kind of Platonist. It is important to note that the statement of the theory of Ideas which appears in *Paradise Lost*, V, 574–576, asserts that the earthly copy is an accurate analogue of divine reality, not a vague image to be penetrated and transcended. We must conclude, I believe, that although Milton's version of the doctrine of accommodation does not display the same characteristics as statements of the doctrine by Renaissance Neoplatonists, it does not follow that Milton did not make use of certain Platonic concepts in his presentation of ultimate reality.

The most tenable interpretation of Raphael's statement that Earth may be "but the shaddow of Heav'n" is to regard it as

[28] Peter Butter, *Shelley's Idols of the Cave* (Edinburgh, 1954), p. 96.

an allusion to the Platonic theory of Ideas. Since the theory is voiced as part of the answer to the specific problem of how to express transcendental reality in humanly understandable language, it constitutes part of the poetic theory of symbolism which Milton brought to the apocalyptic portions of his poem. If Earth is really like Heaven, the latter can accurately be portrayed by using the images of the former. But if the theory of Ideas is part of Milton's poetic theory, there is not a great deal of insistence on this fact in the poem. Unlike the concept of accommodation, the idea that Earth is a copy of the transcendental realm is not pervasive in the epic.

The description in Book III of the "Kingly Palace Gate," along with the narrator's assertion that the scene cannot be adequately limned in earthly images, is perhaps a reference to the imperfect analogy between the heavenly archetype and its earthly copy:

> thick with sparkling orient Gemmes
> The Portal shon, inimitable on Earth
> By Model, or by shading Pencil drawn
>
> [III, 507–509].

In the account of Creation there are also passages which are at least consonant with the Platonic theory of the relationship between Earth and Heaven. The Creator looks upon his work and finds it good, "Answering his great Idea" (VII, 557),[29] and the Creation is said to be so perfect "That Earth now / Seemd like to Heav'n" (VII, 328–329). Similarly, the

[29] George Coffin Taylor, *Milton's Use of Du Bartas* (Cambridge, Mass., 1934), p. 92, regards the statement about God's "great Idea" as a clear allusion to the Platonic theory and notes several parallel instances in the Creation account of Du Bartas. Hughes, *John Milton: Complete Poems and Major Prose*, p. 360, finds both Christian and Platonic overtones in the statement.

31

epic narrator describes Paradise as "A Heav'n on Earth" (IV, 208); and Satan, finding Earth to be a "Terrestrial Heav'n" (IX, 103), is led to exclaim, "O Earth, how like to Heav'n" (IX, 99). Elsewhere God states, "Witness this new-made World, another Heav'n" (VII, 617), and in recounting the war in Heaven Raphael assures Adam that Heaven possesses hills, "For Earth hath this variety from Heav'n / Of pleasure situate in Hill and Dale" (VI, 640–641). On another occasion, Raphael, speaking of Paradise, asserts:

> yet God hath here
> Varied his bounty so with new delights,
> As may compare with Heaven   [V, 430–432].

And describing how the rebellious angels rifled Heaven's soil for minerals, Raphael notes the parallel between Heaven and Earth by telling Adam, "nor hath this Earth / Entrails unlike" those of Heaven (VI, 516–517).

Passages such as these, suggesting an actual correspondence between Heaven and Earth, imply an underlying principle which is at least consonant with the Platonic theory of Ideas. In most instances, however, there is no direct reference to the Platonic doctrine. It is perhaps well to note that Raphael's allusion to the theory in *Paradise Lost*, V, 574–576, appears in a subordinate clause and is phrased as a question rather than a declaration, thereby weakening the force of the statement. Raphael's formulation of the theory is designed to act as a buttress to the doctrine of accommodation. As we have seen, Milton in the *De Doctrina Christiana* could not decide whether the accommodated representation was literal or figurative. Raphael here uses the theory of Ideas to express the tentative conclusion that the physical images are a literal picture of spiritual reality. The most accurate conclusion would seem to be that the Platonic theory of Ideas fitted well with Milton's doctrine of accommodation, and that he used it to supplement that doctrine instead of insisting on it as the basic principle of his apocalyptic poetics.

In actual poetic technique the theory that earthly objects are the imperfect replicas of a transcendental realm would lead to much the same results as the doctrine of accommodation. On the one hand, the theory would form a philosophic justification for portraying ultimate reality by means of the tangible objects of earthly experience. But the earthly object is an imperfect copy, and a fundamental cleavage between the two worlds will always exist. The poetic narrative, while using physical objects and asserting the validity of the earthly analogue, might still claim that the action is "spiritual" and different from the "corporal" vehicle. The complex nature of the theory of Ideas would thus allow for a heavenly terrain filled with such earthly objects as "Hills . . . , Rocks, Waters, Woods" (VI, 644–645) without nullifying Adam's feeling that Raphael's account has, in some sense, presented "Great things, and full of wonder in our eares, / Farr differing from this World" (VII, 70–71). Like the doctrine of accommodation, the theory of Ideas does not lead to simple conclusions, but it does help to explain the rich diversities and paradoxes which we find in Milton's epic.

CHRISTIAN HUMANISM

The remaining philosophic assumptions which influenced Milton's treatment of the transcendental aspects of his story —such assumptions as the goodness of matter, monism, and the substantiality of angels—can best be discussed as separate manifestations of Milton's Christian humanism.[30] Seven-

[30] My definition of Christian humanism is based on M. M. Mahood's excellent discussion in *Poetry and Humanism*.

teenth-century Christian humanism recognized God as the proper center for man and the universe. Theocentric humanism, like humanism generally, emphasized the value of earthly life and the importance of striving to perfect all human possibilities. It differed from anthropocentric humanism in that, while affirming the value of worldly existence, it was nevertheless spiritualized and never lost the view of this world as *sub specie aeternitas.* Christian humanism differed from a more ascetic kind of Christianity in its enthusiastic acceptance of the physical universe and in its rejection of a dualism which claimed a sharp distinction between spirit and matter.

Even in its broad outlines, such a philosophy would have important implications for Milton's poetic technique, including his portrayal of apocalyptic reality. Mahood, for example, notes that "the imagery of Milton's poems, like their artistic shaping, springs from a Baroque consciousness of tension between the actual and the transcendental. In *Paradise Lost* especially, the images reflect the seventeenth-century faith in matter." [31] This faith in matter manifests itself in the poem in such details as the physical pleasures of the angels, the materialism of the celestial landscape, and the courtly trappings of the heavenly palace. A humanistic outlook would also have a deep influence on the poet's portrayal of life in Paradise. Milton's insistence on the beauty of unfallen sexuality is an obvious case in point. The materialism and human emphasis in *Paradise Lost* stem from Milton's general humanistic orientation as well as from such theories as accommodation and Platonism.

A specific aspect of Milton's Christian humanism is his acceptance of the philosophic doctrine of monism. Along with many other philosophers and theologians of his age, Milton

[31] *Poetry and Humanism,* p. 196.

believed that there was only one ultimate substance or principle in the created universe.[32] This philosophic tenet is expressed by Raphael in his well-known speech to Adam:

> O *Adam*, one Almightie is, from whom
> All things proceed, and up to him return,
> If not deprav'd from good, created all
> Such to perfection, one first matter all,
> Indu'd with various forms, various degrees
> Of substance, and in things that live, of life;
> But more refin'd, more spiritous, and pure,
> As neerer to him plac't or neerer tending
> Each in thir several Sphears assignd,
> Till Body up to Spirit work, in bounds
> Proportiond to each kind [V, 469–479].

This statement of the doctrine is followed by Raphael's simile of the tree with its various stages of refinement.

The concept of a single substance in varying degrees of purity does much to explain certain aspects of the imagery of *Paradise Lost*. Since all created things are of the same underlying substance, a material continuity is established between the visible and invisible worlds, and the way is opened for a portrayal of apocalyptic and earthly reality in identical terms. If Heaven is formed of the same substance as Earth, and the angels of the same material as men, it becomes perfectly logical to describe Heaven and its denizens in the same language used to depict the earthly scene. The only exception would be God himself, who is not, in Milton's Christian theology, a

[32] For the philosophic details of Milton's monism and his idea of the scale of nature, see Walter Clyde Curry, *Milton's Ontology, Cosmogony, and Physics* (Lexington, 1957), pp. 158–182; and William B. Hunter, Jr., "Milton's Power of Matter," *JHI*, XIII (1952), 551–562. Hunter's article is in part a revision of an earlier view stated in "Milton's Materialistic Life Principle," *JEGP*, XLV (1946), 68–76.

created being and therefore does not share the universal substance which his Creation does.[33] It must be remembered, however, that the universal substance exists in various stages of refinement, and it is therefore still possible to distinguish between the objects of Earth and the spiritual realm. Heaven is "more spiritous" than Earth despite their basic similarity. The two realms are both alike and different, depending on how one chooses to look at them. This concept of monism is of especial importance in two aspects of the imagistic technique of *Paradise Lost*.

[33] Details concerning God's separation from and relation to the material universe are discussed by Curry, *Milton's Ontology, Cosmogony, and Physics*, pp. 22–47 and passim; and by Hunter, *JHI*, XIII, 551–562, who concludes that in Milton's view God is an "eternal substance existing in pure actuality and containing no matter." A convenient bibliography of earlier discussions of the question of whether in Milton's view matter is a part of God is provided by Taylor, *Milton's Use of Du Bartas*, pp. 19–20. Peter F. Fisher, "Milton's Theodicy," *JHI*, XVII (1956), 37, believes that "Nature is, therefore, the body of God and is of the same substance. . . . Insofar as Milton stated that the original matter of the universe or substance was derived from God, 'the fountain of every substance,' he may be said to contain the pantheistic position within the framework of a Christian interpretation." This view runs counter to the conclusions, which I accept, of Hunter, quoted above, and Curry, who feels that God's "presence in all space is not pantheism" (p. 20) and that "God as pure spirit does not extend his divine nature or essence into the material world; he creates and supports by a communication of his virtue or power or influence" (p. 182). Since Curry's study is the most fully documented statement of the thesis that God is a spirit separate from the material universe, Barbara K. Lewalski, *Milton's Brief Epic* (Providence, 1966), p. 140, errs in listing Curry with those who argue the "ascription of materiality to God himself." Curry explicitly denies that Milton was "a rank materialist and a pantheist" (p. 35); and he speaks of Milton's God as "That incorporeal Spirit who is Light" (p. 18), "an incorporeal substance" (p. 40), and a "spiritual being" (p. 179). Michael F. Maloney, "Plato and Plotinus in Milton's Cosmogony," *PQ*, XL (1961), 34–43, is in substantial agreement with Curry on the question of Milton's alleged pantheism.

The first of these techniques consists of the system of comparison and relativism which underlies many of the images and terms in the poem. Raphael, for example, tells Adam that the physical food which God gives "to man in part / Spiritual, may of purest Spirits be found / No ingrateful food" (V, 405–407). Of particular interest in the passage is Raphael's reference to degrees of spirituality, and to the fact that even material things are partly spiritual. Within a monistic framework, matter itself is infused with spirit, and man differs from angels only in being less rarified. Since men and angels are composed of the same basic substance, Raphael's remark that in recounting the war in Heaven he will liken "spiritual to corporal forms" must not be interpreted as a denial of the corporality of angelic beings. As numerous passages in *Paradise Lost* make clear, Milton left no doubt as to the substantiality of angels. Raphael's statement that angels are "spiritual" forms is merely a recognition that in regard to the scale of being, angels are closer to God than men are, and hence they are spiritual only in a relative sense.[34] The many references in the poem to the angels as "spirits"[35] are based on a system of comparisons and are not inconsistent with Milton's assertions that angels have bodies and perform bodily functions. Similarly, when Raphael tells Adam that he may eventually "turn all to Spirit" and "wingd ascend / Ethereal, as wee" (V, 497–499), we must not interpret the term "spirit" in such a way as to mean that Adam will become immaterial. Raphael simply means that in his prelapsarian state Adam may ascend the dynamic scale of being and become a more refined crea-

[34] This reading of the passage is suggested by C. S. Lewis, *A Preface to Paradise Lost* (New York, 1961; first pub., 1942), pp. 111–112, and confirmed by Robert H. West, *Milton and the Angels* (Athens, 1955), p. 138.

[35] The Patterson-Fogle Index lists over fifty such references to the angels as spirits.

ture, nearer to God.[36] Passages such as those which I have noted are further examples of how Milton's philosophy, in this case monism, led him to conceive of apocalyptic reality in earthly terms while at the same time recognizing basic differences between various steps on the graduated scale of nature.

The other area where the concept of monism is important to the poetic technique of *Paradise Lost* is the area of light imagery. Renaissance monists believed that, like other physical things, light existed in a scale, increasing in brightness as it approached its divine source. God, from whom all physical and spiritual light emanated, was himself invisible, essential light.[37] Since for Milton and his age physical light was a symbol of God and spiritual reality, the image of light in its varying degrees of intensity and purity became a convenient medium for portraying transcendental experience. Although it cannot be shown conclusively that Milton regarded light as a material substance,[38] his materialistic bent makes it probable

[36] This interpretation is substantiated by Curry, *Milton's Ontology, Cosmogony, and Physics*, pp. 162–163.

[37] The Renaissance concept of physical and spiritual light as a graduated divine emanation is established by Don Cameron Allen, *The Harmonious Vision: Studies in Milton's Poetry* (Baltimore, 1954), pp. 100–102. Kester Svendsen, *Milton and Science* (Cambridge, Mass., 1956), pp. 64–72, also discusses the three-fold Renaissance concept of essential, physical, and spiritual light. Curry, *Milton's Ontology, Cosmogony, and Physics*, pp. 189–204, discusses the similarities between Milton's light imagery and the idea found in the *Zohar* that light proceeds from God in nine descending stages or degrees.

[38] Katherine B. Collier, *Cosmogonies of Our Fathers* (New York, 1934), pp. 338–341, shows that some seventeenth-century writers thought light to consist of material particles, some identified it with fire, and some merely affirmed its corporality. Alexander M. Witherspoon and Frank J. Warnke, eds., *Seventeenth-Century Prose and Poetry* (New York, 1963), p. 957, gloss lines 93–98 of Cowley's "Hymn to Light" with the statement, "The physicists of Cowley's

that he would have accepted the contemporary view of light's corporality and would have placed it in his monistic frame of reference. In any event, the concept of light existing in a chain with varying degrees of purity and refinement is so similar to the statement of monism in *Paradise Lost*, V, 469ff., that the relationship seems inevitable.

Within a monistic framework, light becomes a prime means of depicting transcendental reality, for it constitutes a literal link between the two realms of existence. As the seventeenth-century writer Samuel Purchas put it, light is "endowed with a double portion of earthly and heavenly Inheritance, shining in both . . . and lifting up the hearts of the godly to looke for a greater and more glorious light."[39] Although the human mind cannot comprehend something with which it has had no experience, it is completely capable of imagining varying intensities of such a common visible phenomenon as light, and portrayal of apocalyptic reality through light imagery becomes a most comprehensible way of presenting spiritual experience. Although the invisible fountain of light cannot be directly visualized by the angels (III, 375–382), much less by man, the light which man experiences is an emanation from God himself and is therefore in some sense a visible characteristic of the Deity. The use of a lower form of light to represent a higher, more spiritualized manifestation of it is one of the most common apocalyptic techniques in *Paradise Lost*.

A specific example of how Milton's monism enabled him to

day thought of light as a stream of material particles, which could penetrate air or water, but were unable to pass through a solid substance." Curry, *Milton's Ontology, Cosmogony, and Physics*, p. 131, rightly concludes that "the precise nature of Miltonic light—and its consistence, if any—remains somewhat of a mystery."

[39] Quoted in Whiting, *Milton's Literary Milieu*, p. 27.

use various degrees of light to represent in turn both physical and transcendental realities can be found in the invocation to light in Book III, 1–55.[40] Early in the passage there is a reference to the light which is God:

> God is light
> And never but in unapproached light
> Dwelt from Eternitie   [III, 3–5].

The invocation subsequently shifts without a clear transition to the physical light from which the poet, in his blindness, is cut off:

> but thou
> Revisit'st not these eyes, that rowle in vain
> To find thy piercing ray, and find no dawn
> [III, 22–24].

Later the poet again speaks of his physical blindness (lines 40–50) before addressing once more the "Celestial light" which shines "inward" (III, 51–52). As the critical controversy over the light symbolism in the invocation has demonstrated, the references to light cannot always be identified with complete confidence, but the passage reveals the facility with which a monistic philosophy enabled Milton to move from physical light to its more spiritual and divine aspects without making sharp distinctions. As one commentator has said of the element of monism in the invocation, "To Milton matter itself is divine and capable of infinite refinement toward

[40] The light imagery in these famous lines has received a wide variety of critical interpretations. For a comprehensive summary of how commentators have identified the references to light in the passage, see the study by Merritt Hughes, "Milton and the Symbol of Light," *SEL*, IV (1964), 1–33.

the Divine Essence itself, and physical light is essentially one with the light which proceeds from God Himself." [41] This kind of light imagery recurs throughout *Paradise Lost* and becomes a leading means by which the known can be used to portray unknown spiritual realities.

Robert West has observed that some of the details of Milton's portrayal of angels go beyond anything in the angelology of the age and derive from his broader belief in the goodness and universality of matter. It is not amiss, therefore, to discuss Milton's ideas regarding angels as part of his general humanistic orientation. Since scholarship has thoroughly defined the nature of Milton's angelology, I shall do no more than summarize the broad outlines of the topic. [42] Rejecting the Thomistic conception of angelic being, Milton aligned himself with the view that angels have substantial bodies. They are thus capable of performing all the physical activities common to men, including the assimilation of food and love-making. The bodies of angels are composed of a substance called "ether" or "empyrean." Like other writers who shared this view, Milton frequently speaks of these substantial angels as "spirits." His terminology in such situations is not inconsistent but merely serves to emphasize that the bodies of angels, though com-

---

[41] Charles G. Osgood, *Poetry as a Means of Grace* (Princeton, 1942), p. 94. Except for Osgood's paragraph-length discussion, Milton's light imagery has not been discussed in specific connection with his monism. This is surely an oversight on the part of critics.

[42] The definitive study of Milton's angelology is West's book, *Milton and the Angels* (Athens, 1955). For the limited topic of angelic substance it is perhaps more convenient to consult West's earlier article, "The Substance of Milton's Angels," *SAMLA Studies in Milton*, ed. J. Max Patrick (Gainesville, 1953), pp. 20–53. C. S. Lewis, *A Preface to Paradise Lost*, pp. 108–115, has a helpful and accurate chapter on "The Mistake about Milton's Angels."

posed of the same elements as human bodies, contain these components in a more refined state.[43] Finally, since the angels are substantial beings, they naturally inhabit a Heaven which possesses material characteristics.

Milton's ideas on this important scientific issue of his day obviously bear on his poetic technique. His angelology dictates his materialistic portrayal of the angels in *Paradise Lost*, and it explains the physical details of the heavenly scene. The bodies which the angels possess would lead the poet to portray them in human terms, while the more refined substance of which they are composed would lead him to emphasize the "spiritous" nature of angels in comparison to human beings. The final poetic effect of Milton's angelology is well summarized by West: "Angels are *presented* outwardly like men; they may, without contradiction, be *thought* of as spirits." [44]

Considered together, the doctrine of accommodation, the Platonic theory of Ideas, and Christian humanism constitute the theoretic underpinning of Milton's apocalyptic vision. If we integrate the various strands of philosophy and literary theory, we find that they correspond and reinforce one another to a remarkable extent. All of the theoretic aspects provide a foundation for a portrayal of apocalyptic reality in physical, human terms. At the same time, they do not minimize a very real difference between the visible and invisible worlds, and they show that the apocalyptic vision is, in impor-

---

[43] Curry, *Milton's Ontology, Cosmogony, and Physics*, p. 162, appropriately emphasizes that "Milton is not following that tradition which conceives of ether as a fifth essence differing in kind from all the four elements. He holds rather to the historical theory that ether is a matter sublimated from the four elements, or merely a purer form of air and fire." Svendsen, *Milton and Science*, p. 259, and West, *Milton and the Angels*, pp. 141, 204, accept Curry's conclusion.

[44] *Milton and the Angels*, p. 110.

tant ways, not directly accessible to human experience. An awareness of the theoretic background is helpful not only in establishing the assumptions with which Milton composed his epic and with which the reader of his generation interpreted the poem, but also in suggesting profitable critical approaches to *Paradise Lost*. The theoretic background establishes expectations which the poem fulfills.

❧ 3

Apocalypse through Contrast

One of the commonest techniques by which poets have portrayed apocalyptic reality is through contrast with ordinary human experience; the apocalyptic experience is "other" than that which we ordinarily experience, a distinction made explicit in the familiar designation "otherwordly." At its simplest level, the technique of contrast in *Paradise Lost* consists of explicit contrasts stated by the narrator.

As might be expected, there is a whole pattern of "then-now" temporal contrasts underlying the portrayal of prelapsarian perfection. Before the Fall, the vantage point is one which stresses the present perfection as opposed to subsequent evil. For example, when Satan, journeying to Eden, alights on what after the Fall became the Paradise of Fools, it is emphasized that the fiend walked

> Alone, for other Creature in this place
> Living or liveless to be found was none,
> None yet, but store hereafter from the earth
> Up hither like Aereal vapours flew

44

Of all things transitorie and vain, when Sin
With vanity had filld the works of men
[III, 442–447].

As the passage suggests, from the viewpoint of prelapsarian innocence the apocalyptic state is a present event which forms a
temporal contrast with later postlapsarian experience. The
same principle of temporal contrast underlies the statement
that before the Fall the golden stair leading from Heaven to
Earth formed "a passage wide, / Wider by farr then that of
aftertimes" (III, 528–529). Similarly, in the description of
Eden we read about "All Beasts of th' Earth, since wilde"
(IV, 341); and Adam and Eve, while in the prelapsarian garden, are "Our two first Parents, yet the onely two / Of mankind, in the happie Garden plac't" (III, 65–66). Perfection as
a present reality, opposed to eventual imperfection, appears
also in the reminder that Adam, in questioning Raphael
about the cosmos, was "yet sinless" (VII, 61), and in the identical statement about "*Eve* yet sinless" (IX, 659). Before the
Fall we read regarding the serpent that

Not yet in horrid Shade or dismal Den,
Nor nocent yet, but on the grassie Herbe
Fearless unfeard he slept   [IX, 185–187].

And in its prelapsarian condition the serpent walks erect, "not
with indented wave, / Prone on the ground, as since" (IX,
496–497).

Once the apocalyptic state has been dissipated by the Fall it
continues to be portrayed in terms of a temporal contrast
with postlapsarian experience. From a fallen viewpoint, however, the apocalyptic state is a past vision, with imperfection
now the present reality. The first examples of such a contrast
occur in the account of the fallen angels in Books I and II.

Satan, for instance, recalls to the minds of his cohorts the celestial condition "once yours, now lost" (I, 316). The epic narrator describes the demons as

> Powers that earst in Heaven sat on Thrones;
> Though of thir Names in heav'nly Records now
> Be no memorial   [I, 360–362].

In his scornful exchange with Satan, Zephon contrasts the rebel's present fallen state with his past apocalyptic condition:

> Think not, revolted Spirit, thy shape the same,
> Or undiminisht brightness, to be known
> As when thou stoodst in Heav'n upright and pure;
> That Glorie then, when thou no more wast good,
> Departed from thee, and thou resembl'st now
> Thy sin and place of doom obscure and foule
> [IV, 835–840].

In like manner, Michael accosts Satan during the war in Heaven with the words:

> how hast thou instill'd
> Thy malice into thousands, once upright
> And faithful, now prov'd false   [VI, 269–271].

The motif of apocalypse as a past state contrasting with present fallen reality appears again when Satan speaks of "paine, / Till now not known" (VI, 431–432), and when the rebel angels are said to have been "Purest at first, now gross by sinning grown" (VI, 661). Similarly, Raphael tells Adam that Lucifer, now fallen, was "brighter once amidst the Host / Of Angels" (VII, 132–133), while elsewhere he speaks of "The ruin of so many glorious once / And perfet while they stood" (V, 567–568).

The prelapsarian state of Adam and Eve in Paradise is likewise described, after the Fall, as a past condition different from that now known. Prelapsarian sexuality, for example, was wholly innocent, but from the vantage point of the fallen narrator and reader such innocence is a past vision, contrasting with present reality:

> Nor those mysterious parts were then conceald,
> Then was not guiltie shame   [IV, 312–313].

The same contrast is implied when the narrator, after describing prelapsarian love, asks, "O when meet now / Such pairs, in Love and mutual Honour joyn'd?" (VIII, 57–58). The "then-now" contrast between unfallen and fallen experience appears again when the narrator tells us that after the Fall Heaven is "Now alienated" from man (IX, 9). Again, in describing the fountain which flowed in Paradise, the narrator states, "There was a place, / Now not . . ." (IX, 69–70). Late in Book IX, after both Adam and Eve have eaten the forbidden fruit, the lost apocalyptic state is several times described in terms of temporal contrast. Adam asks:

> How shall I behold the face
> Henceforth of God or Angel, earst with joy
> And rapture so oft beheld? those heav'nly shapes
> Will dazle now this earthly   [IX, 1080–1083].

The epic narrator draws upon the same temporal contrast when he describes the postlapsarian passions of Adam and Eve which

> shook sore
> Thir inward State of Mind, calm Region once
> And full of Peace, now tost and turbulent:
> For Understanding rul'd not, and the Will
> Heard not her lore, but in subjection now
> To sensual Appetite   [IX, 1124–1129].

47

Adam, when chiding Eve, asserts that if they had not worked separately on the fatal day they

> had then
> Remaind still happie, not as now, despoild
> Of all our good   [IX, 1137–1139].

The "then-now" juxtaposition also appears in the Father's explanation that although "at first" (XI, 57) man had been perfect, the "pure immortal Elements" of Paradise "Eject him tainted now" (XI, 50, 52).

Temporal contrasts thus form the underlying principle in a number of descriptions of the apocalyptic vision. Another cluster of contrasts is based on a system of comparisons which is evident at many points in *Paradise Lost*. In such situations the apocalyptic state is contrasted, either quantitatively or qualitatively, with ordinary reality.

A typical example of the principle of using contrasting positions on a comparative scale occurs when, as Satan is progressing toward Paradise, we read that "of pure now purer aire / Meets his approach" (IV, 153–154). Paradise, in other words, is different from other regions by virtue of its superior purity, as we learn again later in the poem when Eve, lamenting the prospect of her expulsion from Paradise, asks, "how shall we breath in other Aire / Less pure . . . ?" (XI, 284–285). Similarly, after naming several earthly gardens, the narrator claims the superiority of Paradise with the statement, "in this pleasant soile / His farr more pleasant Garden God ordaind" (IV, 214–215). The same technique is repeated when the narrator catalogs the famous gardens of mythology and legend only to assert that Paradise is better than them all—that none of them "might with this Paradise / Of *Eden* strive" (IV, 274–275). Adam also affirms the comparative superiority of the Garden of Eden to other regions when, in describing how God had transported him to Paradise after his creation, he recalls that when he first saw the garden "what I saw / Of Earth before scarce pleasant seemd" (VIII, 305–306).

The perfect human beings who inhabit Paradise are, like the garden itself, portrayed by contrasting them to inferior creatures. Eve, for instance, is "in naked beauty more adorn'd / More lovely then Pandora" (IV, 713–714). Eve is also said to be

> more lovely fair
> Then Wood-Nymph, or the fairest Goddess feign'd
> Of three that in Mount *Ida* naked strove   [V, 380–382].

In similar manner, when Adam meets Raphael accompanied by his train of "compleat perfections," we are told that his state is "More solemn then the tedious pomp that waits / On Princes" (V, 354–355).

Heaven and its agents are likewise contrasted to lesser states. Moloch describes God as being "higher" (II, 72) and "stronger" (II, 83) than the other celestial beings. The stairs of Heaven were before the Fall "Wider by farr" (III, 529) than the stairs used by God's angels in fallen history. The glorious region which Satan finds on the sun is "beyond expression bright, / Compar'd with aught on Earth" (III, 591–592), and the air is there "No where so cleer" (III, 620). Adam contrasts the glory of Heaven to all other areas when he says regarding Raphael that "other place / None can then Heav'n such glorious shape contain" (V, 361–362); and Adam is anxious to learn from Raphael

> Of things above his World, and of thir being
> Who dwell in Heav'n, whose excellence he saw

> Transcend his own so farr, whose radiant forms
> Divine effulgence, whose high Power so far
> Exceeded human   [V, 455–459].

This contrast between celestial and terrestrial beings appears again in Raphael's formulation of the "various degrees" in the chain of existence, in which heavenly beings form a contrast with earthly creatures by being "more refin'd, more spiritous, and pure, / As neerer to him plac't or neerer tending" (V, 475–476). Raphael elsewhere makes other comparative contrasts between Heaven and Earth, as when he describes the heavenly

> Regions to which
> All thy Dominion, *Adam*, is no more
> Then what this Garden is to all the Earth,
> And all the Sea   [V, 750–753].

Raphael's procedure is, in his own words, "to set forth / Great things by small" (VI, 310–311). A similar assertion about the superiority of Heaven to Earth appears when Raphael, speaking of love among the angels, assures Adam that

> Whatever pure thou in the body enjoy'st
> (And pure thou wert created) we enjoy
> In eminence   [VIII, 622–624].

The apocalyptic state which succeeds history is likewise superior to earthly experience, since it will constitute a "far happier place / Then this of Eden, and far happier daies" (XII, 464–465). As we would expect, the Deity is also portrayed through a technique of contrast. The Father affirms that the Son's power is "In Heav'n and Hell . . . above compare" (VI, 705); and Adam, recalling his dialogue with God, states:

My earthly by his Heav'nly overpower'd,
Which it had long stood under, streind to the highth
In that celestial Colloquie sublime,
As with an object that excels the sense   [VIII, 453–456].

As all of these passages indicate, at numerous points the apocalyptic vision is presented through a technique of contrasts, with the comparative superiority of the apocalyptic realm making it different from the order of fallen nature.

A nearly identical kind of contrast emerges from descriptions of the apocalyptic state in superlative terms. These place the apocalyptic realm at the top of a comparative scale and imply a contrast between it and all other items on the scale. Descriptions of Paradise in superlatives abound. The garden is surrounded by woods "Of stateliest view" (IV, 142), and it includes within it "goodliest Trees loaden with fairest Fruit" (IV, 147). In Paradise are found "All Trees of noblest kind for sight, smell, taste" (IV, 217). When Adam is first placed in the garden he finds that it is "with goodliest Trees / Planted" (VIII, 304–305), and he finds "Each Tree / Load'n with fairest Fruit" (VIII, 307). Adam and Eve in their prelapsarian condition constitute "the loveliest pair / That ever since in loves imbraces met" (IV, 321–322); and as individuals they likewise surpass all ordinary human beings:

> *Adam* the goodliest man of men since borne
> His Sons, the fairest of her Daughters Eve
>
> [IV, 323–324].

And Satan, although his motive is evil, describes Eve before the Fall as "Fairest resemblance of thy Maker faire" (IX, 538). This cluster of superlatives associated with the garden and its inhabitants yields a composite picture of a realm qualitatively different from, and superior to, the world of empirical reality.

Heaven and it agents are likewise presented in superlative terms which imply a contrast with lower forms of existence. Raphael, for example, reinforces the contrast between angels and men by calling the former "purest Spirits" (V, 406), even though he insists that angels are comprised of the same substance and enjoy the same food as men do. Heaven is not simply bright but "brightest" (V, 644), and we read also of "highest Heav'n" (VI, 13; X, 889), inhabited by "Spirits of purest light" (VI, 660). Within Heaven, God, the supreme apocalyptic being, is "Heav'ns purest Light" (II, 137), and his highest position in the scale of existence is reiterated when we are told that he is "High Thron'd above all highth" (III, 58). Similarly, "Beyond compare the Son of God was seen / Most glorious" (III, 138–139), and Christ is elsewhere described as being "Thron'd in highest bliss" (III, 305). God is called "Heav'ns matchless King" (IV, 41), while the quality of his being supreme, hence removed from all other beings, is mentioned at least nine times.[1] The Son attributes superlative qualities to the Father when he calls him "First, Highest, Holiest, Best" (VI, 724); and Christ himself, after the final conquest of Satan, will be "exalted high / Above all names in Heav'n" (XII, 457–458). Other superlatives used to describe God include "mightiest" (I, 99), "highest," [2] "most high," [3] and "worthiest." [4] Each time such a superlative description appears, whether it is applied to Heaven and its agents or to Paradise and its inhabitants, we are reminded of the contrast which exists between the apocalyptic state and the earthly existence which we know.

[1] IV, 956; V, 670; VI, 723, 814; VII, 142; IX, 125; X, 28, 70; XI, 82.
[2] I, 667; II, 479; VI, 114, 205.
[3] VI, 906; XI, 705; XII, 120, 369, 382.
[4] III, 310; VI, 177, 185, 707, 888.

EMPIRICISM MODIFIED

There is validity to the conclusion, stated by a number of commentators, that apocalyptic poetry always relies on some form of analogy to human experience. If the apocalyptic vision is not amenable to description in terms of empirical reality, it ceases to be humanly comprehensible. At the same time, however, the apocalyptic realm differs from ordinary reality in significant ways. The presence of this "similar-dissimilar" tension in apocalyptic experience underlies one critic's definition of mystical poetry as poetry which "endeavors to render an experience . . . which is by definition foreign to all human experience, and yet to render it in terms of a modified human experience." [5] This formulation describes accurately a technique, recurrent in *Paradise Lost*, by which Milton qualifies empirical reality in such a way that the apocalyptic experience thus portrayed is contrasted with experience as we know it.

Modifying terms appear several times in descriptions of the angels. When, for example, we read that angels possess "the strength of Gods" (I, 116), the qualifying phrase implies that their strength is different from human strength. The superhuman quality of angelic strength is reiterated when Beelzebub, after mentioning the destruction which the fallen angels have suffered, qualifies the destruction by adding, "As far as Gods and Heav'nly Essences / Can perish" (I, 138–139); the implication is that destruction among angels, unlike that among men, is not total, a fact which becomes explicit later

[5] Yvor Winters, "Emily Dickinson and the Limits of Judgment," in *Emily Dickinson: A Collection of Critical Essays*, ed. Richard B. Sewall (Englewood Cliffs, 1963), pp. 31–32.

in the poem when we read that angels, in contrast to "frail man" (VI, 345), "Cannot . . . die" (VI, 347). In Heaven the tables are "pil'd / With Angels Food" (V, 632–633), the result again being a modified empirical image. In the account of the war in Heaven we learn that wounded angels bleed, but that the situation differs from our earthly experience is intimated by Raphael's statement that the angels issue humor "such as Celestial Spirits may bleed" (VI, 333).

Heaven, like its inhabitants, is described in terms of qualified human experience. Heaven has its night, but Raphael is careful to explain to Adam that night in the celestial region differs from night on Earth, "for Night comes not there / In darker veile" (V, 645–646). In Heaven, indeed, night is so different from earthly night that "darkness there might well / Seem twilight here" (VI, 11–12). Even the reason for the existence of night in Heaven differs from the cause underlying the interchange of day and night on Earth, for Raphael states, "wee have also our Eevning and our Morn, / Wee ours for change delectable, not need" (V, 628–629). In Raphael's narrative of the celestial battle, God the Father informs the Son that two days of battle are past, "Two dayes, as we compute the dayes of Heav'n" (VI, 685), and we again draw the inference that heavenly days are in some way different from the days of our earthly experience. Similarly, the "Flours worthy of Paradise" (IV, 241) represent a slight alteration of empirical reality, since it is implied that the Paradisal flowers exceed in worth the flowers of our experience.

For the poet who is describing an apocalyptic vision by a technique of modified empiricism there exists a whole set of ready-made apocalyptic adjectives which can be used to modify a noun naming an empirical phenomenon. This technique is, indeed, as habitual for a poet describing apocalyptic reality as the epic simile, let us say, is for a poet writing an epic. When, for instance, the epic narrator speaks of God's "supernal Power" (I, 241), the adjective linking the power to the transcendental realm qualifies the empirical concept "power." In similar manner, the term "Elisian" in the phrase "*Elisian* Flours" (III, 359) signalizes a modification of our empirical expectations, just as in the descriptions of "transcendent brightness" (I, 86) and God's "Transcendent Seat" (X, 614) the adjective qualifies the noun by placing it in an apocalyptic context, outside the order of nature.

A number of such apocalyptic adjectives are repeated throughout the poem and form individual motifs within the general pattern of modified empiricism. The adjective "ethereal" is a typical example. We read that God hurled the rebellious angels "from th' Ethereal Skie" (I, 45), and Belial speaks of "th' Ethereal mould" of God (II, 139). God is "th' Ethereal King" (II, 978), and the light in which he dwells is an "Ethereal stream" (III, 7). God calls the angels "Ethereal Powers" (III, 100), and we are told later by Raphael that the angels are composed of "Ethereal substance" (VI, 330). A military trumpet calls the angels to battle in the war in Heaven, but the contrast between that trumpet and the trumpets of our experience is implied by the phrase "Ethereal Trumpet" (VI, 60). Raphael, too, is not an ordinary messenger, but an "Ethereal Messenger" (VIII, 646), while the inhabitants of Heaven are "ethereal people" (X, 27). In all of these instances, the descriptive word "ethereal" functions as a stock epithet which qualifies the thing being described and places it in an apocalyptic context.

A similar motif of modified empiricism centers around the term "heavenly." The angels are called "Heav'nly Essences" (I, 138), "heav'nly mindes" (IV, 118), and "heav'nly Quires"

(IV, 711). Raphael, by shaking his plumes, emits "Heav'nly fragrance" (V, 286), and he is called a "Heav'nly stranger" (V, 316) and a "Heav'nly Guest" (VII, 69) by Adam. Similarly, Adam addresses God as "Heav'nly Power" (VIII, 379) and Michael as "Heav'nly instructer" (XI, 871). The Paradise in Eden is contrasted by Raphael to "Heav'nly Paradises" (V, 500), and we hear also of "heav'nly Thrones" (VI, 723) and "heav'nly ground" (VII, 210).

The terms "ambrosial" and "empyreal" are likewise used repeatedly to modify and qualify empirical objects. God's altar in Heaven "breathes / Ambrosial Odours and Ambrosial Flowers" (II, 244–245). When God speaks "ambrosial fragrance" fills Heaven (III, 135), and "in Heav'n the Trees / Of life ambrosial frutage bear" (V, 426–427). Night in Heaven is different from night on Earth, as suggested by the phrase "ambrosial Night" (V, 642), and Heaven is adorned with "Flour Ambrosial" (VI, 475). Eden, too, possesses "Ambrosial Fruit" (IV, 219) and "ambrosial Fount" (XI, 279). Parallel instances of modification occur with the term "empyreal." We read at various points about "Empyreal substance" (I, 117), "Empyreal Minister" (V, 460), "Empyreal Mansion" (III, 699), and "th' Empyreal road" (V, 253). Other passages speak of "Gold / Empyreal" (VI, 13–14), "Empyreal form" (VI, 433), and "Empyreal Aire" (VII, 14). In such passages the presence of the adjective in conjunction with an empirical noun yields a modified human experience—an experience which is analogous to ordinary experience and at the same time different from it.

The qualifying word most frequently used in descriptions of apocalyptic reality is "celestial." Heaven is characterized by "celestial light" (I, 245; III, 51) and possesses "Celestial soile" (VI, 510). In Heaven we also find "Celestial Roses"

(III, 364) and "Celestial Armourie" (IV, 553). The angels possess "Celestial vertues" (II, 15), "Celestial voices" (IV, 682), and "Celestial temper" (IV, 812); and they are called, as we would expect, "Celestial Spirits" (VI, 333). The heavenly scene includes within it "Celestial Tabernacles" (V, 654). In the account of the battle in Heaven we read about "Celestial Armies" (VI, 44) and the "Celestial Panoplie" of Christ (VI, 760); and in the Creation scene we encounter "Celestial Equipage" (VII, 203) and "Celestial Quires" (VII, 254). God is the "Celestial Father" (V, 403), while the epic poet's divine inspirer is called his "Celestial Patroness" (IX, 21). The angels in Heaven have "Celestial visages" (X, 24), and Michael sheds "his shape Celestial" (XI, 239) in order to speak to Adam as a man. To Adam, however, it is clear that Michael is a "Celestial Guide" (XI, 785).

As this discussion has demonstrated, the application of adjectives denoting apocalyptic characteristics to empirical nouns represents a consistent principle underlying the presentation of Milton's apocalyptic vision. Other instances of such modifiers include the terms "spiritual," [6] "eternal," [7] "ethereous," [8] "divine," [9] and "immortal." [10] Each time such modifiers appear, they transform the empirical image into something different from ordinary reality. It is part of the grand

[6] "Spiritual substance" (IV, 585), "spiritual Creatures" (IV, 677), "spiritual Natures" (V, 402), and "spiritual Armour" (XII, 491).

[7] "Eternal Father" (V, 246), "Eternal Empire" (VII, 96), "Gods Eternal store" (VII, 226), and "Gods Eternal house" (VII, 576).

[8] "Ethereous mould" (VI, 473).

[9] "Love divine" (III, 225), "lineaments Divine" (V, 278), "Divine instructer" (V, 546), "Vigour Divine" (IV, 158), "Divine / Hystorian" (VIII, 6–7), "shape Divine" (VIII, 295), and "objects divine" (XII, 9).

[10] "Immortal fruits" (III, 67), "immortal love" (III, 267), "immortal bliss" (IX, 1166), and "immortal Elements" (XI, 50).

system of contrasts which Milton uses to portray his apocalyptic vision.

It has long been the critical custom to raise the topic of Milton's Latinate and archaic diction in connection with the matter of epic style. We have been conditioned to view Milton's adherence to the dictum that the language of the age is never the language of poetry as his method of fulfilling the epic demand of a high style—of signalizing to the reader that he is observing a great event, as C. S. Lewis puts it. More recently we have been alerted to the way in which some of the examples of Latinate diction in the middle books of *Paradise Lost* answer the grand masterpiece of decorum in yet another way. Several critics have observed that a number of the words used to describe the apocalyptic vision are words which in current usage carry negative connotations but which in their original meanings were free from such associations.[11] The principle involved here has been definitively described by Christopher Ricks, who explains that such Latinate words take us "back to a time when there were no infected words because there were no infected actions. . . . Many of the Latinisms" show Milton "reaching back to an earlier purity—which we are to contrast with what has happened to the word, and the world, since." [12]

[11] The first critic to observe this effect in some of Milton's terms was Arnold Stein, *Answerable Style* (Minneapolis, 1953), pp. 66–67. Fuller studies of the topic are those by Christopher Ricks, *Milton's Grand Style* (Oxford, 1963), pp. 109–117; Anne Ferry, *Milton's Epic Voice* (Cambridge, Mass., 1963), pp. 36–41; and Stanley Fish, *Surprised by Sin* (New York, 1967), pp. 92–157.

[12] *Milton's Grand Style*, pp. 110, 111.

58

There has been a tendency to view Milton's employment of this etymological technique as a somewhat accidental concomitant of his frequent use of words which have been derived from Latin and which in Milton's idiom often bear Latin force. In the present discussion I wish to suggest that Milton's technique of placing certain words so firmly in a specific context that they must be regarded as deviations from normal meaning is not unique to Milton's style but is rather a particular manifestation of a principle which is common to most literature.

The view that poetic language is continually qualified by its context in a poem forms the basis of the literary theory of Cleanth Brooks, one of the leading critics of the mid-twentieth century. It is the thesis of Brooks that in order to understand any poem we must be aware of "the importance of the total context of the poem as the area in which the terms of the poem work and have their meaning." [13] Each part of a poem, according to the contextual theory, "helps build the total meaning and is itself qualified by the whole context. In many poems the qualification amounts to a significant shading and, in some cases, even to a complete reversal of the ordinary meaning." [14] The term which Brooks used and popularized as the key term in his theory was "irony," which he defines simply as "the kind of qualification which the various elements in a context receive from the context." [15] The universality of the contextual qualification of language in poetry has been amply demonstrated by Brooks, by the essays in *The Well Wrought Urn* alone; and although Milton's use of the contex-

[13] "The Poem as Organism: Modern Critical Procedure," *English Institute Annual, 1940* (New York, 1941), p. 37.

[14] "Irony and 'Ironic' Poetry," *CE*, IX (1948), 237.

[15] *The Well Wrought Urn* (New York, 1947), p. 209.

tual principle in his portrayal of innocence is certainly an unusual and original manifestation of the principle, it is salutary
to remind ourselves that the principle itself is widespread in
literature.

Another relevant critical consideration is what Paul Goodman has identified as the conceptual background that operates
in a work of literature.[16] According to Goodman, "Thoughts
in a poem may be immediately presented or mediately opera-
tive as background sources of probability." Thus in *Oedipus
Rex*, for example, the judgment "The Oracle demands a mur-
der" is immediately presented in only one episode, but it operates as a conceptual background and explanation for the action throughout the play. The judgment, in short, becomes
the context within which the action unfolds and against
which we are to measure what is happening at any given mo-
ment.

The conceptual background for the apocalyptic scenes in
Paradise Lost might be formulated by the proposition "The
apocalyptic state is one of complete goodness, perfection, and
innocence." This background is part of the context which
qualifies the words used to describe the apocalyptic vision. As
a result, when we are confronted by the presence of a word
which today has negative associations, our awareness of the
context informs us that the usual meaning of the word must
be reversed.

I wish to insist that the background assumption of perfection is one which the reader should be willing to grant as an *a
priori* axiom. In writing his poem doctrinal to his nation Milton was using as his material an established story and theological system. He did not have to prove that God is good and

[16] *The Structure of Literature* (Chicago, 1962; first publ., 1954),
p. 199.

that Satan is evil. Nor was it incumbent on him to prove that the apocalyptic scenes in Heaven and Paradise pictured perfection and innocence; they did so by definition, and the epic writer of Christian story knew that his readers were aware of the common presuppositions of the account. Milton himself states the need for allowing an apocalyptic context to qualify what in fallen experience has negative connotations when, in his discussion of the doctrine of accommodation in *De Doctrina Christiana*, he insists that it is good to attribute human qualities to God, "so long as what is imperfection and weakness when viewed in reference to ourselves be considered as most complete and excellent when imputed to God" (*Works*, XIV, 35). Milton, it is clear, would not agree with the critical view that "if God is to be shown acting in a story, we have something better to do than take his status for granted." [17] Criticism which refuses to grant validity to the conceptual context of the poem disregards a basic premise of Milton's apocalyptic technique.

As we read the account of the apocalyptic scenes in *Paradise Lost* we are repeatedly reminded of the conceptual background and context of the events. Early in Book IV, before we have been introduced to life in Paradise, we are told that Satan intends to ruin "innocent" man (IV, 11), with the adjective serving as a reminder of the conceptual background which envelopes the idyllic scenes in Eden. "Then was not guiltie shame" (IV, 313), the epic narrator informs us; "spotless innocence" had not yet been eradicated from human experience (IV, 318). The human couple "thought no ill" (IV,

[17] William Empson, *Milton's God* (Norfolk, 1961), p. 94. Empson's view is shared by John Peter, *A Critique of Paradise Lost* (New York, 1960), p. 160, who believes that one of Milton's "unfounded artistic assumptions" is that the figure of God in the poem "can be taken over intact from its context in the Bible or in Christian belief."

320), and even Satan, bent on the destruction of human perfection, is aware of the context of "harmless innocence" (IV, 388) surrounding the Paradisal state.

After the initial presentation of prelapsarian life in Book IV we continue to be reminded consistently of the conceptual context of innocence and perfection. Adam tells Eve that no evil can harbor in her because she has been "Created pure" (V, 100), and we read later that "no thought infirme" entered Eve's consciousness as she waited on Raphael (V, 384). The narrator concludes Adam and Eve's morning hymn with the formula, "So pray'd they innocent" (V, 209), while several hundred lines later he interrupts the narrative to apostrophize their "innocence / Deserving Paradise" (V, 445–446). Later in the same book Raphael reminds Adam—and the reader— that God has made man "perfet" (V, 524); and the angel's final words to Adam before returning to Heaven reiterate that Adam has been created "pure" (VIII, 623) and is yet "Perfet within" (VIII, 642). Similarly, Adam, "yet sinless" (VII, 61), questions Raphael about the Creation of the world, and he in turn describes to the angel how he won Eve when she was "pure of sinful thought" (VIII, 506).

In Book IX, as the Paradisal state becomes increasingly precarious, the reminders of continuing innocence and perfection are still frequent. Adam bids farewell to Eve by telling her to go in her "native innocence" (IX, 373). Satan, too, takes pleasure in observing Eve's "graceful Innocence" (IX, 459), even though he is intent on sending her back to Adam "Despoild of Innocence" (IX, 411). During the temptation itself the serpent is answered by "*Eve* yet sinless" (IX, 659). And when Adam first views the fallen Eve he asks, "How art thou lost, how on a sudden lost . . . ?" (IX, 900), reminding us once again that all which has preceded has been unfallen perfection.

Passages such as these suggest the care and consistency with which Milton reminds the reader of the conceptual background and context of innocence within which the apocalyptic vision takes place. The reader has every reason to heed these reminders by the epic narrator. For one thing, as Wayne Booth has remarked, the epic narrator has traditionally mixed commentary and dramatic presentation, and his comments are intended to carry the same authority as his demonstration does.[18] In addition to the usual authority with which the epic narrator speaks, the narrator of *Paradise Lost* speaks with special prerogative because he is, within the dramatic logic of the poem, the inspired seer whose transcendental vision extends beyond the limited, fallen experience of the reader.[19]

Both the nature of the Christian story itself and the reminders by the narrator, then, function to establish a context of perfection and innocence within which the apocalyptic scenes of *Paradise Lost* occur. Let us now observe how an awareness of this context leads us to attribute positive, unfallen meanings to words which in our fallen experience have acquired negative associations.

In his description of Paradise the epic narrator states that the brooks ran "With mazie error under pendant shades" (IV, 239). The concepts of the maze and error both have negative associations in fallen experience, and Milton makes such connotations explicit elsewhere in the poem. The fallen angels in Hell, for example, argue in vain about philosophic questions,

---

[18] *The Rhetoric of Fiction* (Chicago, 1961), pp. 3–9. Cf. also Fish, *Surprised by Sin*, p. 46.

[19] This is the chief thesis of Anne Ferry's book, *Milton's Epic Voice*. John Diekhoff, *Milton's Paradise Lost: A Commentary on the Argument* (New York, 1946), also says some good things about the epic narrator, observing, for example, that the invocations in which the poet claims divine inspiration serve the dramatic function of establishing the narrator as someone who speaks with special authority.

"in wandring mazes lost" (II, 561), and Adam, in his soliloquy after the Fall, admits, "all my evasions vain, / And reasonings, though through Mazes, lead me still / But to my own conviction" (X, 829–831). Similarly, the word "error" in normal usage denotes a mistake or untruth; and it is used in such a pejorative sense later in the poem when Adam, speaking of his earlier decision to allow Eve to work alone, states that he regrets "That errour now, which is become my crime" (IX, 1181), and when Eve speaks slightingly of her words, which have been "Found so erroneous" (X, 969). What we find in the description of Eden, then, is the presence of two words which normally bear derogatory overtones, both in our own experience and in the postlapsarian portions of *Paradise Lost*. The conceptual background, which I have summarized in the formulation, "The apocalyptic state is one of complete goodness, perfection, and innocence," reminds us of the need to qualify the usual meanings of the words, and we realize that the "error" of the streams is merely innocent wandering (that is the Latin meaning of the root) and that the modifier "mazie" denotes only that the wandering involves intricate winding. It is part of the larger technique of contrast, with the double meanings of the words reflecting two states, one fallen and the other unfallen.

A very similar situation occurs in the account of the Creation. When God commands that the land and water be separated, some of the streams of water "under ground, or circuit wide / With Serpent errour wandring, found thir way" (VII, 301–302). Here the word "error" is flanked by two words which often bear negative connotations. The term "serpent" ordinarily carries strong overtones of treachery and danger, both in human experience and in numerous instances in *Paradise Lost*. The word is derived from the Latin word meaning "to creep," and in the description of the streams it should be interpreted with only its Latin force. The sharp contrast between such an interpretation and the ordinary negative interpretation of the word is a measure of the difference between fallen and unfallen experience. The same principle applies to the "wandring" of the water. In fallen experience wandering often implies aimless movement or straying from an approved moral or intellectual standard, as when the demons become lost in "wandring mazes" (II, 561) as they argue about foreknowledge and free will, or when Eve, contemplating her leaving of Eden, the place of perfection, laments that she must "wander down / Into a lower World" (XI, 282–283). In the account of Creation, however, the concept of wandering denotes only a meandering movement through an irregular course. When we are told that at the time of Creation the rivers flowed "With Serpent errour wandring," then, we can read the phrase correctly only if we realize that the three words which in ordinary usage often have negative associations are so firmly embedded in an apocalyptic context that they must be divested of the usual pejorative meanings.

There are numerous other instances in which we must reject the derogatory overtones of a vocabulary which bears the taint of sin in ordinary usage but which in the prelapsarian state was only positive. The concept of luxury, for example, can be a negative quality, as Adam learns in the prophetic vision of fallen history late in the poem when he is instructed by Michael concerning the wicked who live in "luxurious wealth" (XI, 788) and the evil times when all is turned "To luxurie and riot" (XI, 715). In an apocalyptic context, however, the description of the vine which "gently creeps / Luxuriant" (IV, 259–260) and of the plants in the garden which grow "Luxurious by restraint" (IX, 209) is a reminder of the contrast between innocence and sin, between luxury as perfect fertility and luxury as immoral excess.

Another example of a word which has acquired negative associations with the development of the language is the word "vicissitude." In customary usage the word connotes an uncontrollable and malevolent change of fortune, but in its original Latinate meaning the term signified only change or alteration. When describing the heavenly condition Milton uses the earlier meaning in telling us that variation in Heaven is "Grateful vicissitude" (VI, 8), with the modifying term reinforcing the contrast implicit in the noun between pure and impure meanings. The same contrast is repeated during the Creation scene, where we read that God made the stars "To illuminate the Earth, and rule the Day / In thir vicissitude" (VII, 350–351).

A number of words used to describe the newly created world of nature yield the same contrast between prelapsarian and postlapsarian experience, as reflected in untainted and tainted meanings of the same words. When the epic narrator tells us about "All Beasts of th' Earth, since wilde" (IV, 341), we make the equation of wildness with fallen experience. This equation is reinforced later in the poem when Adam, contemplating the effects of the Fall (although he is still innocent), laments the prospect of living "in these wilde Woods forlorn" (IX, 910), and when Eve, upon learning of her banishment from Paradise, bemoans that she must leave Eden and go "Into a lower World, . . . obscure / And wilde" (XI, 283–284). Because of these negative connotations associated with wildness we are somewhat surprised when the concept is also connected with life before the Fall. During the act of Creation "Innumerous living Creatures, perfet formes" (VII, 455) rise from the ground "As from his Laire the wilde Beast where he wonns / In Forrest wilde" (VII, 457–458). Although the quality of wildness is attributed to the newly created animals by way of comparison and simile only, wildness becomes one of their identifying characteristics by a technique of transference. Furthermore, we know that the sides of the mountain of which Paradise forms the crown are "With thicket overgrown, grottesque and wilde" (IV, 136). Even the vegetation in the garden is "Tending to wilde" (IX, 212), and nature in Paradise is "Wilde above Rule or Art" (V, 297). If we heed the narrator's reminder of the conceptual background when he tells us that all of God's Creation before the Fall is comprised of "perfet formes" (VII, 455), we will have no difficulty in distinguishing between tainted and untainted meanings of the word "wild." Before the Fall wildness describes a state of nature untouched by human cultivation and control, while after the Fall the condition of wildness implies a state which is predatory and violent.[20]

The descriptions of animals at Creation yield additional instances of the principle of contrasting meanings of words. The creeping animals are said to streak "the ground with sinuous trace" (VII, 481), and the snakes display "Thir Snakie foulds" (VII, 484). Such adjectives, although in ordinary ex-

---

[20] The eulogistic and pejorative attitudes toward wildness and the state of nature are bound up with the philosophic debate, especially prevalent in the Renaissance, between nature and art. Edward Tayler, *Nature and Art in Renaissance Literature* (New York, 1964), pp. 36–37, provides a good summary of the intellectual milieu which forms the context of Milton's distinction between wildness as a positive and negative quality: "When Art is viewed eulogistically . . . , Nature usually signifies the unformed, the inchoate, the imperfect, or even the corrupt. . . . In this view Nature is that which has been more or less impaired by original sin. . . . When, on the other hand, Art is viewed pejoratively . . . Nature signifies the original, the unspoiled, the transcendent, or even the perfect."

perience implying treachery, are, as we know from the apocalyptic context, devoid of such negative overtones when applied to the creatures which God has just created perfect. The dislike of snakes, so common in fallen experience, appears to be linked with that animal even before the Fall, since we are told that the serpent was "Suttlest Beast of all the Field" (IX, 86, 560) and was therefore considered by Satan "Fit Vessel, fittest Imp of fraud" (IX, 89) to perpetrate the temptation. Later Satan finds the snake asleep, "well stor'd with suttle wiles" (IX, 184). We are reminded also of the passage in Book IV where we read that

> the Serpent sly
> Insinuating, wove with Gordian twine
> His breaded train, and of his fatal guile
> Gave proof unheeded   [IV, 347–350].

What are we to make of the prelapsarian attribution of subtlety, slyness, and guile to the snake? According to the present argument, the answer depends on the degree of our awareness of the apocalyptic background against which we are to measure the prelapsarian scenes of *Paradise Lost*. Slyness and subtlety in our thinking denote achieving an end by devious means, but surely delicate artfulness can be a good quality when achieving a good end; we should, therefore, divest these descriptive words of pejorative associations in order to make the description accord with the innocence which we know existed before the Fall. If the terms linked with the serpent seem difficult to interpret with positive meanings only, it is perhaps a measure of the distance between the fallen reader and the apocalyptic vision.

The concept of wantonness is employed so often in the poem, both in prelapsarian and postlapsarian contexts, that it becomes a particularly obvious case of Milton's use of the principle of allowing the context to determine the meaning of a word.[21] In ordinary usage wantoness implies lewdness and sensuality, but we are forced to qualify this meaning when we find the term used repeatedly in the descriptions of Eden and its innocent inhabitants. Eve, for example, wore her golden hair "in wanton ringlets wav'd" (IV, 306). Adam believes that the plants of the garden require "More hands than ours to lop thir wanton growth" (IV, 629), and Eve likewise expresses concern over the "wanton growth" of the vegetation in Paradise (IX, 211). The narrator assures us that before the Fall nature "Wantoned as in her prime" (V, 295). Even the serpent, in his attempt to attract the attention of Eve in the prelude to the temptation, "Curld many a wanton wreath in sight of Eve" (IX, 517). In an apocalyptic context, then, we find the concept of wantonness referred to five times, twice denoting the quality of being visually pleasant and attractive and three times denoting untrammeled growth.[22] Not until after the Fall does the word acquire the bad connotations which we associate with it. Postlapsarian sexuality is lustful,

[21] The word "wanton" represents a slight variation from other words discussed above, since the *Oxford English Dictionary* indicates that the word's original meaning was ambivalent. As used in *Paradise Lost*, however, the term adheres to the general pattern of the other words which I note: its meaning depends on its context in the poem, with its positive meaning giving way to pejorative meanings only after the Fall has occurred.

[22] Ricks, *Milton's Grand Style*, p. 112, considers the "wanton wreaths" which the serpent curls before Eve an example of the negative use of the word. Such a reading is thoroughly plausible. It seems to me, however, that the word here describes the same kind of visually attractive waves which also characterize Eve's hair. Since both uses of the term denote the same quality, it seems preferable to regard both situations as innocent and to attribute the wantonness to the unfallen snake rather than to the fallen Satan.

and in describing it the narrator uses the word "wanton" in conjunction with other negative terms denoting sensuality: Adam

> on Eve
> Began to cast lascivious Eyes, she him
> As wantonly repaid; in Lust they burne
> [IX, 1013–1015].

Similarly, in his preview of fallen history Adam sees "wantonness and pride / Raise out of friendship hostil deeds in Peace" (XI, 795–796). Considered together, these references to wantonness in *Paradise Lost* constitute another of Milton's etymological arguments, with the development of the word's meanings from something positive to something negative intended to mirror a parallel movement in human experience from innocence to evil.

The same contrast between good and bad manifestations of a phenomenon can be observed in Milton's handling of a cluster of terms and images having to do with magnificent appearance, often of a regal nature. The word "pomp" is customarily used to designate an undesirable ostentation of wealth and pageantry, and Milton uses it thus several times in the epic. Satan sits as "Hells dread Emperour with pomp Supream" (II, 510), while Adam's welcome of his angelic visitor Raphael is "More solemn then the tedious pomp that waits / On Princes" (V, 354–355). Similarly, the flood which God sent upon the Earth in Noah's time is said to have overwhelmed the evildoers "with all their pomp" (XI, 748). But there is also an innocent, wholesome kind of pomp, according to the epic narrator. "A pomp of winning Graces waited" on Eve (VIII, 61), and after God's completion of the Creation of the world we read that "the bright Pomp ascended jubilant" (VII, 564). In such instances we are being asked to compare opposed meanings of a word and the opposed conditions which they imply, with the context determining the meaning of the word. Similarly, when we hear Eve commended for yielding to her husband "all her shows" (VIII, 575) we must recognize that the word "shows" does not carry any suggestion of the "meer shews" (IV, 316) which we associate with fallen experience, where the term implies empty ostentation and morally sterile magnificence. The whole motif of royalty, which is as profoundly a part of Heaven and Paradise as it is of Hell, is to be subjected to the principle of contextual qualification. That Milton devoted twenty years of his life, and his eyesight, to disparaging seventeenth-century English monarchy is well known; and Malcolm Ross has amply demonstrated Milton's antipathy to royalism.[23] But Ross errs in his failure to distinguish, as Milton clearly intends that we should, between kingship in an apocalyptic state and in a demonic state. Before the Fall kingship was a positive, uncontaminated force, and as such it differed from monarchies which succeeded the Fall.

Examples of the contextual qualification of language could be multiplied. The word "lapse" is used to refer to the Fall itself when Michael speaks to Adam of "thy original lapse" (XII, 83), but when we read about the "liquid Lapse" of water in Paradise (VIII, 263), the apocalyptic context signalizes that the word means simply "fall." When God the Father calls the Son his "sole complacence" (III, 276), the context qualifies the term so as to make it mean contentment and righteous satisfaction, not smug self-satisfaction. Before the existence of sin "absolution" could not denote the remission of sin or guilt, as it does when referring to fallen experience in Book III, 291, so that when we read that the work of Crea-

[23] *Milton's Royalism* (Ithaca, 1943).

71

tion was "soon / Absolved" by the Creator (VII, 93–94), we must adjust the meaning of the word to denote freedom from further activity rather than freedom from pollution.

Throughout the description of his apocalyptic vision, then, Milton uses contrasts between positive and negative meanings of words to reflect contrasts between an unfallen and fallen world. In doing so he was drawing upon a time-honored tradition of biblical commentary, a tradition which Arnold Williams summarizes in this way: "In the beginning man was given a perfect language to go with the perfect nature in which he was created. Then, as a result of sin, this perfect language was, like human nature, corrupted." [24] Such correspondence between unfallen language and unfallen experience is made explicit in *Paradise Lost*. Adam, when naming the animals, made the name accord with the nature of the animal; as he tells Raphael, "I nam'd them, as they pass'd, and understood / Thir nature, with such knowledg God endu'd / My sudden apprehension" (VIII, 352–354). Similarly, when praising Adam for his eloquence, Raphael asserts that Adam's outward speech is a reflection of the wholesomeness of his inner condition:

> Nor are thy lips ungraceful, Sire of men,
> Nor tongue ineloquent; for God on thee
> Abundantly his gifts hath also pour'd
> Inward and outward both, his image faire
>
> [VIII, 218–221].

And after the Fall, as Sin and Death are preparing to infuse their corruption into the entire world, Sin states her intention to reside in man and to "infect" all "His thoughts, his looks, words, actions" (X, 608). The equation of words and actions

[24] *The Common Expositor* (Chapel Hill, 1948), p. 228.

thus becomes a central consideration of both theory and practice in the poem, and it is part of the general pattern of contrasts by which Milton portrays apocalyptic reality. Such a technique of contrasting the unfallen use of a word with its contaminated use keeps the reader constantly aware of the doomed nature of prelapsarian innocence, and thus reinforces the impression of a precariousness which we all sense in reading the middle books of the epic. But to be reminded of the transience of the prelapsarian state is not, as some commentators would contend, to destroy the apocalyptic vision.

Several critics have advanced the view that Milton did not, in fact, present a vision of perfection, and that Adam and Eve are fallen human beings before they eat the forbidden fruit.[25] These critics have centered their contention on such episodes as Eve's love of her reflection in the water, her dream of eating the forbidden fruit, Adam's uxoriousness, and the argument between Adam and Eve over working separately. A number of Miltonists have argued against the view that Milton failed to give us a picture of prelapsarian innocence on the valid grounds that such a view constitutes "an insupportable construction of Milton's intention," [26] that Milton was operating within a theological framework in which sin existed only when human agents, by an act of conscious volition, chose to do an evil act,[27] that although certain events before

[25] This view has been argued by E. M. W. Tillyard, *Studies in Milton* (New York, 1951), pp. 10–13; Millicent Bell, "The Fallacy of the Fall in *Paradise Lost*," *PMLA*, LXVIII (1953), 863–883, and LXX (1955), 1187–1197, 1203; and A. J. A. Waldock, *Paradise Lost and Its Critics* (Cambridge, Eng., 1947), p. 61.

[26] Kester Svendsen, *Milton and Science* (Cambridge, Mass., 1956), p. 280. See also the article by Wayne Shumaker, below, note 27.

[27] Critics who argue this view include Wayne Shumaker, "The Fallacy of the Fall in *Paradise Lost*," *PMLA*, LXX (1955), 1185–87, 1197–1202; H. V. S. Ogden, "The Crisis of *Paradise Lost* Recon-

73

the Fall in *Paradise Lost* establish signs of danger the portrayal of innocence is not impaired by its being rendered increasingly precarious,[28] and that any symptoms of evil which
we attach to Adam and Eve before their actual disobedience
are a measure of our fallen viewpoint rather than any flaws in
the apocalyptic state.[29] The observation which I wish to
make regarding these statements is that the principle of contextual qualification provides a sound rationale for each of
them. Narrative events, as well as individual words, are subject to qualification in an apocalyptic context. Eve's supposed
vanity and pride, and Adam's alleged sensuality, should be ad-
justed to the conceptual background of apocalyptic innocence, and as the studies of the commentators cited demonstrate, such adjustments are wholly consonant with the text.
To some, allowing a conceptual context to direct our interpretation of the poet's dramatic presentation will seem simplis-
tic, but if, as I have argued, such contextual qualification is a
universal literary technique, it would be anomalous indeed not
to apply the principle to the apocalyptic parts of *Paradise
Lost.*

sidered," *PQ*, XXXVI (1957), 1–19; B. A. Wright, *Milton's Paradise
Lost* (New York, 1962), p. 159ff.; Irene Samuel, "*Purgatorio* and the
Dream of Eve," *JEGP*, LXIII (1964), 446; A. S. P. Woodhouse, *The
Poet and His Faith* (Chicago, 1965), pp. 113–114; and Dennis H.
Burden, *The Logical Epic* (Cambridge, Mass., 1967), p. 132 and
passim.

[28] This is essentially the view of the following critics: Stein, *Answerable Style*, p. 90ff.; J. B. Broadbent, *Some Graver Subject* (London, 1960), pp. 197–9; Douglas Day, "Adam and Eve in *Paradise
Lost, IV*," *TSLL*, III (1962), 369–381; Davis P. Harding, *The Club
of Hercules* (Urbana, 1962), p. 68ff.; and A. Bartlett Giamatti, *The
Earthly Paradise and the Renaissance Epic* (Princeton, 1966), pp.
299–330.

[29] This is the main thesis, applied in a variety of contexts, of Fish's
book, *Surprised by Sin.*

ENAMELED IMAGERY

The use of images taken from the realms of jewels, minerals, and human artifice is an archetypal technique for depicting the apocalyptic state. As an apocalyptic technique it extends from the beginnings of literature to the present day. It occurs in the biblical descriptions of the heavenly city, with its jasper, clear glass, streets of pure gold, gates of pearl, and "all manner of precious stones." [30] The same technique underlies the presentation of Heaven in the Middle English poem *The Pearl*, just as it forms a dominant motif in John Bunyan's description of the celestial city in *The Pilgrim's Progress*. The luxurious vegetation of Renaissance pastoral poetry is also conventionally hardened by enameled imagery; typical examples are the silver sand, orient pearl, precious stone, and ivory which characterize the pastoral paradise portrayed in Michael Drayton's "Endimion and Phoebe," and the silver rivers, enameled meadows, and mosaical floor of flowers in Philip Sidney's description of the pastoral land of Arcadia.[31] William Butler Yeats thus sums up a long apocalyptic tradition when he contrasts the cyclical biological world to "the artifice of eternity," which includes among its salient images "holy fire," "gold mosaic," "hammered gold and gold enameling," and "the glory of changeless metal." [32]

Milton's frequent use of images naming objects of immobile, marmoreal hardness has been noted by several commentators. One of the best documentations of this characteristic of

[30] There is a concentration of such images in the description of the New Jerusalem in Revelation 21.

[31] "Endimion and Phoebe," lines 50, 71, 145; *Arcadia*, Book I, ch. ii and iii.

[32] Quotations are from "Sailing to Byzantium" and "Byzantium."

Milton's imagery is G. Wilson Knight's essay entitled "The Frozen Labyrinth," where he comments on "the static and sculptural quality of Milton's nature imagery," the "stony, carven immobility" of the descriptions of Eden, the Miltonic tendency to translate "the natural into terms of human artistry" and "to capture and eternalize each essence in statuesque permanence," and the "polished, burnished, almost brazen universe" and "cosmic or Heavenly brilliance" which we find in *Paradise Lost*.[33] All of this is very well stated, but the apocalyptic function of the enameled imagery is wasted on Knight, who uses the evidence to support a wholesale condemnation of Milton's supposed lack of sensitivity to the natural and vital. J. B. Broadbent attempts a rectification of Knight's pejorative conclusions by arguing that Milton's use of the convention of enameled imagery is based on the Renaissance commonplace that nature is God's art and on the necessity which Milton faced of "countering . . . geographical realism" with features which would make the Garden of Eden "more than earthly and out of time and place." [34] The most satisfactory analysis of the apocalyptic principle involved in enameled imagery is given by Wendell Stacy Johnson in his study of the structure of imagery in *The Pearl*.[35] What Johnson says about that poem is relevant to *Paradise Lost* as well: "The imagery of the poem can in the main be divided into two groups: on the one hand, images out of the

[33] *The Burning Oracle* (London, 1939), pp. 59–113. Quotations are from pages 80, 83, 89, and 90. Knight makes some of the same observations in *Chariot of Wrath* (London, 1942), though with a more sympathetic attitude.

[34] "Milton's Paradise," *MP*, LI (1954), 160–176; *Some Graver Subject*, pp. 173–185.

[35] "The Imagery and Diction of *The Pearl*: Toward an Interpretation," *ELH*, XX (1953), 161–180.

world of growing things . . . which are associated with the dust of the earth; on the other, images of light and of brilliant, light-reflecting, gems, free of any spot (dust). . . . The two groups are directly and explicitly opposed to each other. . . . Thus the distinction between the *erbere* and the land of light and of brilliant gems is . . . the antithesis . . . between mundane and spiritual realms."

The term "enameled" was conventional in Medieval and Renaissance poetry, and Milton uses it in *Paradise Lost* when he speaks of the "gay enameld colours" in Paradise (IV, 149). Although Broadbent argues that the word "enameled" referred primarily to color rather than to hardness of texture,[36] it is not completely clear that this was the only meaning which the word was intended to carry in *Paradise Lost*.[37] In any event, I wish to use the term "enameled imagery" to refer to a composite image which includes both visual brilliance and hardness of texture, and in which brightness, immobility, and

[36] According to Broadbent, the term "enameled," "which today suggests the hard whiteness of bathrooms and saucepans, meant to the seventeenth century the brilliant color used in miniatures and jewelry —it was the color rather than the hardness which took effect" (*MP*, LI, 165).

[37] Reliance on images of color is not very extensive in the apocalyptic portions of *Paradise Lost*. One critic states, "The beautiful description of Eden in book iv of *Paradise Lost* contains only seven color words, three of which are forms of *gold*. Not much can be said, then, for Milton's use of color in description" (Walter Graham, "Sensuousness in the Poetry of Milton and Keats," *SAQ*, XVI [1917], 347). Don Cameron Allen makes a similar observation about the lack of variety of color in descriptions of Heaven and explains this scarcity of color on the basis of Renaissance Neoplatonic thought, which equated perfection with pure, essential light; as a result, "in *Paradise Lost* we are being led through a world that is still bathed in essential light, so we shall have to think in metaphors of white splendor . . . , not in those of color and sharp edges, the figures of a post-lapsarian cosmos" (*The Harmonious Vision* [Baltimore, 1954]), p. 102.

artifice all combine to suggest a world of transcendent permanence which contrasts with the ordinary world of cyclical change and decay. It will be my argument that Milton frequently mingles the textural and visual aspects of enameled imagery, and that when he uses names of jewels to refer to colors, for example, we should respond imaginatively to the whole range of sensations which form the composite enameled world of the apocalyptic vision.

Dazzling light, with a surface splendor which goes beyond the light of common day, is particularly a characteristic of the Heaven of *Paradise Lost*. God himself is the "Fountain of Light . . . invisible / Amidst the glorious brightness" (III, 375–376). God's brightness, in fact, is so intense "that brightest Seraphim / Approach not" (III, 381–382). Christ, too, is "the effulgence" of God's brightness (III, 388), and he is "with Radiance crown'd" (VII, 194).[38] The angels are likewise brilliant in their visual brightness. They are variously called "Spirits of purest light" (VI, 660), "Guardians bright" (III, 512), "heav'nly Spirits bright" (IV, 361), and "th' An-

[38] The exact nature and extent of the equation of light with the Son is currently a matter of dispute among Miltonists. The thesis, which I do not find conclusive, that Milton in the invocation to Book III uses "holy Light" as a metaphor under which he addresses the Son has been argued in these studies: Denis Saurat, *Milton, Man and Thinker* (London, 1944), pp. 262–3; William B. Hunter, Jr., "The Meaning of 'Holy Light' in *Paradise Lost* III," *MLN*, LXXIV (1959), 589–92, and "Holy Light in *Paradise Lost*," *Rice Institute Pamphlet*, XLVI (1960), 1–14; J. H. Adamson, "Milton's Arianism," *HTR*, LIII (1960), 269–276; and Jackson Cope, *The Metaphoric Structure of Paradise Lost* (Baltimore, 1962), p. 150. A more valid approach is represented by the analysis of David W. D. Dickson, "Milton's 'Son of God': A Study in Imagery and Orthodoxy," *Papers of the Michigan Academy of Science, Arts, and Letters*, XXXVI (1950), 275–281, which demonstrates the ways in which biblical and conventional Christian light symbolism is applied to the Son.

gelic Squadron bright" (IV, 977). These "Progenie of Light" (V, 600) inhabit "glittering Tents" (V, 291); and in the celestial war the scene is described in images of unearthly brightness:

> the Plain
> Coverd with thick embatteld Squadrons bright,
> Chariots and flaming Armes, and fierie Steeds
> Reflecting blaze on blaze . . . [VI, 15–18].

In such a description even the objects which are analogous to earthly experience are hardened by the more than earthly intensity of the light and reflection. Heaven's dazzling brightness is, along with its height, its most consistently mentioned characteristic, and no further documentation is needed here.[39] The dominance of light as an apocalyptic image in *Paradise Lost* is sufficiently attested to by the conclusion of Josephine Miles that after Milton the adjective "bright" became markedly more important in English poetry as a representative descriptive adjective denoting moral goodness.[40]

In addition to the hardened brilliance of light, enameled imagery in *Paradise Lost* consists of a whole complex of images naming jewels, minerals, and qualities of human artifice.

[39] Critical analyses of light imagery in *Paradise Lost* are numerous. Perhaps the most thorough discussion is that by Cope, *The Metaphoric Structure of Paradise Lost*, pp. 72–148. Also excellent are Isabel MacCaffrey's remarks in *Paradise Lost as "Myth"* (Cambridge, Mass., 1959), passim. D. C. Allen, in *The Harmonious Vision*, pp. 95–109, relates Milton's light imagery to Renaissance thought and makes the point, very relevant to the present discussion, that in *Paradise Lost* the light of Heaven is "essential" light, differing in intensity and effect from the earthly light which we know. Merritt Hughes, "Milton and the Symbol of Light," *SEL*, IV (1964), 1–33, offers a comprehensive history of commentary on light imagery in Milton.

[40] "From Good to Bright: A Note in Poetic History," *PMLA*, LX (1945), 766–774.

These images are as characteristic of Eden as they are of Heaven, and a discussion of the relevant passages as they emerge in the poem will demonstrate the manner in which the enameled apocalyptic world becomes established in our imaginative vision.

The first picture of Heaven in terms of enameled artifice occurs when Satan, on his way to Eden, sees

> Opal Towrs and Battlements adorn'd
> Of living Saphire, once his native Seat;
> And fast by hanging in a golden Chain
> This pendant world [II, 1049–1052].

We glimpse the enameled aspects of Heaven at closer range when, as the angels bow in adoration before God in Book III, we observe them "cast / Thir Crowns inwove with Amarant and Gold" (III, 351–352). In the same scene our imaginative view includes Heaven's "Amber stream" (III, 359), "the bright / Pavement that like a Sea of Jasper shon" (III, 362–363), and the "gold'n Harps" of the angels which hang "glittering by thir side" (III, 365–366). Even the intangible aspects of Heaven partake of the permanence imparted by artifice, as evidenced by the fact that the "resplendent locks" of the angels are "inwreath'd with beams" (III, 361). And in the angels' hymn to Christ we are given a preview of the apocalyptic chariot which overthrew the rebel angels, a chariot possessing "flaming Chariot wheels" (III, 394). The first extended scene in which Heaven is the setting thus establishes the heavenly region as a place where enameled qualities lend a statuesque permanence to the realm.

After the opening scene in Book III, the perspective shifts back to that of Satan's approach to Eden. The distant view of Heaven again stresses its brilliance and hardness, as Satan sees

a Kingly Palace Gate
With Frontispice of Diamond and Gold
Imbellisht, thick with sparkling orient Gemmes
The Portal shon   [III, 505-508].

And that this burnished scene represents a world which transcends our earthly experience is made explicit by the narrator's assertion that the heavenly gate is "inimitable on
Earth / By Model, or by shading Pencil drawn" (III,
508-509). As Satan journeys on he comes to the stairway
leading from Earth to Heaven and discovers, as we do, that all
of the steps are "steps of Gold" (III, 541). The narrator further informs us that on occasions when the golden stairs are
drawn up to Heaven, "underneath a bright Sea flow'd / Of
Jasper, or of liquid Pearle" (III, 518-519). The paradoxes involved in such an enameled description are repeated when, a
few lines later, we read that Satan "windes with
ease / Through the pure marble Air his oblique way" (III,
563-564). The "marble" quality of the air means primarily
"shining," but by using the term which he does the poet infuses a quality of crystallized permanence into the description.

When Satan lands on "The golden Sun in splendor likest
Heaven" (III, 572), he finds an apocalyptic realm which is
portrayed in a rhetoric as enameled as Milton had at his command. We are told:

The place he found beyond expression bright,
Compar'd with aught on Earth, Medal or Stone;
Not all parts like, but all alike informed
With radiant light, as glowing Iron with fire;
If mettal, part seemd Gold, part Silver cleer;
If stone, Carbuncle most or Chrysolite,
Rubie or Topaz, to the Twelve that shon
In *Aarons* Brest-plate   [III, 591-598].

81

As the narrator continues the description, he asks:

> What wonder then if fields and regions here
> Breathe forth *Elixir* pure, and Rivers run
> Potable Gold . . . ?   [III, 606–608].

After viewing the scene, Satan observes the "glorious Angel" Uriel (III, 622), who wears "a golden tiar" of "beaming sunnie Raies" (III, 625). And Satan, in adapting his disguise to this enameled scene, dons wings "Of many a colour'd plume sprinkl'd with Gold" (III, 642), and he carries "a Silver wand" (III, 644).

When the reader comes to the descriptions of Paradise in Book IV, he finds a strand of enameled qualities along with the lush vegetation and profuse life of Eden. The "golden hue" (IV, 148) of the blossoms and fruit appears "with gay enameld colours mixt" (IV, 149), the effect of the description being one of visual brilliance beyond the world of nature which we know. In the garden we also find fruit "Of vegetable Gold" (IV, 220),[41] as well as trees bearing "fruit burnisht with Golden Rinde / . . . , *Hesperian* Fables true" (IV, 249–250). The streams of Paradise are as enameled as those in Heaven and on the sun, as we discover when we read that "crisped Brooks" run from the "Saphire Fount" (IV, 237), and that the streams pass "Rowling on Orient Pearl and sands of Gold" (IV, 238). In such a description associations both of

---

[41] This is one of the more talked about images in the poem. F. R. Leavis, *Revaluation* (New York, 1936, 1947), p. 50, singles out the image for comment in his denigration of Milton's style, arguing that although such an image conveys "a vague sense of opulence, . . . this is not what we mean by 'sensuous richness.' " In a reply, Douglas Bush ably presents the case for Milton's intention to portray, not a garden such as the ones which we know in everyday life, but "a golden age more perfect than even the classical poets had imagined. He is gathering us . . . into the artifice of eternity" (*Paradise Lost in Our Time* [Ithaca, 1945]), pp. 96–97.

color and texture combine to form a composite enameled image. The streams of Paradise, in reflecting the vegetation growing on their banks, act as a "chrystal mirror" (IV, 263), and the permanence which we associate with human artifice becomes linked with the vegetation of the garden when we read of "the soft downie Bank damaskt with flours" (IV, 334).

Outside the Garden of Eden is the "Gate of Paradise," which is "a Rock / Of Alablaster, pil'd up to the Clouds" (IV, 543–544), and Gabriel, guarding the entrance to the garden, sits "Betwixt . . . rockie Pillars" (IV, 549). Near at hand is the "Celestial Armourie," which is "Hung high with Diamond flaming, and with Gold" (IV, 553–554); and later we learn that the Cherubim inhabit an "Ivorie Port" (IV, 778). Similar enameled effects emerge when we read that, at twilight time in the garden, "now glow'd the Firmament / With living Saphirs" (IV, 604–605), and again when we hear the stars described as "the Gemms of Heav'n" (IV, 649), emitting "glittering Starr-light" (IV, 656). The bower of Adam and Eve is also portrayed under the aspect of artifice, which lends a quality of static permanence to it despite its vital greenery. The roof of the bower is called "inwoven shade" (IV, 693). Various flowers "wrought / Mosaic" (IV, 699–700) and

> with rich inlay
> Broiderd the ground, more colour'd then with stone
> Of costliest Emblem   [IV, 701–703].

The same kind of description of vegetation under the aspect of artifice occurs later in the poem when we read about the "thick-wov'n Arborets and Flours / Imborderd on each Bank" (IX, 437–438).

With Raphael's dispatch from Heaven to Earth, and in his

subsequent accounts of the war in Heaven and the Creation, the scene shifts from Paradise back to Heaven, and enameled imagery continues to form an important apocalyptic motif in the poem. As Raphael departs from Heaven on his mission, the gate of Heaven opens, "On golden Hinges turning" (V, 255). One of the pairs of wings which Raphael wears possesses "regal Ornament" (V, 280), while

> the middle pair
> Girt like a Starrie Zone his waste, and round
> Skirted his loines and thighes with downie Gold
> And colours dipt in Heav'n   [V, 280–283].

Raphael tells Adam that in Heaven each morning the angels "find the ground / Cover'd with pearly grain" (V, 429–430), and he describes how, when the angels eat, "rubied Nectar flows / In Pearl, in Diamond, and massie Gold" (V, 633–634). "Golden Lamps" (V, 713) burn nightly around God, and God wields a "Golden Scepter" (V, 886). Satan, as he prefaces his suggestion to rifle Heaven's soil for weapons during the celestial battle, limns a picture of the heavenly scene in enameled terms:

> Which of us who beholds the bright surface
> Of this Ethereous mould whereon we stand,
> This continent of spacious Heav'n, adornd
> With Plant, Fruit, Flour Ambrosial, Gemms & Gold . . .
>
> [VI, 472–475].

Visual splendor and textural rigidity combine in such an enameled description. Another picture of surface brilliance is described when, with the coming of "fair Morn Orient in Heav'n" (VI, 524), the warrior angels are said to stand "in Arms . . . / Of Golden Panoplie, refulgent Host" (VI,

526–527). Christ's chariot of conquest is also replete with enameled qualities: [42]

> the wheels
> Of Beril, and careering Fires between;
> Over thir heads a chrystal Firmament,
> Whereon a Saphir Throne, inlaid with pure
> Amber, and colours of the showrie Arch
>
> [VI, 755–759].

Christ rides "sublime / On the Chrystallin Skie, in Saphir
Thron'd" (VI, 772), while the rebel angels are thrown over
the "Chrystal wall of Heav'n" (VI, 860). With each description of this kind, another detail is added to the view of
Heaven as a place possessing all the permanence which can be
suggested by images of marmoreal hardness.

More enameled descriptions emerge from the account of
Creation. We are told about the myriads of heavenly hosts
who stand "between two brazen Mountains" (VII, 201), and
also about the "golden Hinges" (VII, 207) of Heaven's gates
and the "golden Compasses" (VII, 225) with which God cir-
cumscribes the universe. "Golden Harps" (VII, 258) are also
a part of the scene; and after the Creation the heavenly train
returns to the "blazing Portals" of Heaven (VII, 575), trav-
ersing there the heavenly road "whose dust is Gold" (VII,
577). This reference to Heaven's golden pavement is not the
first mention of this characteristic of the heavenly city, for already in Book I we learned of "The riches of Heav'ns pavement, trod'n Gold" (I, 682). After the account of Creation
we hear about Heaven's "Golden Altar" (XI, 18), "Golden
Censers" (VII, 600), and "Glassie Sea" (VII, 619).

[42] James H. Sims, *The Bible in Milton's Epics* (Gainesville, 1962),
p. 32, demonstrates the way in which the description of Christ's
chariot is based on details of Ezekiel's vision in the Old Testament.

If one considers the large number of references to heavenly light in *Paradise Lost*, the use of enameled imagery emerges as one of the dominant apocalyptic techniques in the poem. My analysis of the nature and function of this imagery does not represent the standard approach among Milton critics. I have seen no commentary on the poem which claims a composite image including both visual and textural dimensions, with brilliance of light or color and hardness of surface reinforcing each other and often indistinguishable from each other. The apocalyptic function which I assign to mineral images would be disputed by some commentators. G. Wilson Knight, as already noted, regards such imagery as an undesirable idiosyncrasy of Milton's poetic style. Isabel MacCaffrey, convinced that Milton's attitude toward "art" was pejorative and that after the building of Pandemonium early in the poem gold has been established as something evil, believes that in apocalyptic contexts Milton's general practice is to mellow his enameled descriptions by surrounding them with organic imagery.[43] Even Douglas Bush speaks of "the idea of unhealthy artifice and evil which in Paradise Lost is associated with gold." [44] This critical climate regarding images of artifice and jewels is, I believe, a result of the now universal awareness that Spenser in describing the Bower of Bliss in the *Faerie Queene* used images of jeweled artifice to symbolize moral sterility.[45] The tacit assumption of critics has been that Spenser represents the dominant tradition. The truth is that he does not. As I sug-

[43] *Paradise Lost as "Myth,"* pp. 160–161.

[44] *Paradise Lost in Our Time*, p. 95.

[45] Giamatti, *The Earthly Paradise and the Renaissance Epic*, pp. 310–312, has applied the pejorative overtones associated with artifice in Spenser to Milton's Paradise, concluding, incorrectly as it seems to me, that "we cannot ignore the implied similarity" between Paradise and the Bower of Bliss.

gested in my introductory remarks to this topic, the use of images of jewels, minerals, and artifice has been a major technique in portraying apocalyptic reality from the Bible through Yeats. Despite the evil associated with gold in Hell in *Paradise Lost,* we will have no difficulty in accepting gold and mineral images as good when they appear in apocalyptic situations if we allow the principle of contextual qualification its proper due.[46]

There is disagreement not only about the function of enameled imagery, but also about whether there even is a static quality present in *Paradise Lost.* Joseph Summers, in an excellent discussion of motifs of motion and variety in the poem, argues that, despite the archetypal human longing for a "vision of static being," Milton "specifically rejected such an ideal, both morally and aesthetically," with the result that "his subject and art are not marmoreal enough" to satisfy the reader's desire for stasis.[47] The present analysis affords evidence that such a conclusion requires qualification. Without questioning that Milton's apocalyptic universe is in many respects a vital one, I feel that it is evident that Milton drew upon the tradition which pictures ideal perfection through enameled images, and that in *Paradise Lost* such images, combining visual and textural hardness of surface, depict a transcendental realm whose permanence forms a contrast with the transient world of earthly experience.

[46] The need to allow the context, whether apocalyptic or demonic, to control the connotations which we attribute to words and images is urged by William Madsen, who notes that gold is found in both Hell and Heaven and that "it is not hard to see that the value of gold or any other material thing depends on one's attitude toward it" ("The Idea of Nature in Milton's Poetry," in *Three Studies in the Renaissance: Sidney, Jonson, Milton* [New Haven, 1958], p. 232).

[47] *The Muse's Method* (Cambridge, Mass., 1962), pp. 85–86.

MYSTIC OXYMORON

The conventional presence of the rhetorical figure of paradox in descriptions of apocalyptic reality has been discussed
by several writers. Father Walter J. Ong, in a widely known
study, argued that the use of paradox and wit in Medieval
Latin liturgical poetry served the function of portraying the
transcendental mysteries of the Christian religion, and he concluded that there is "a relevance to wit poetry quite special to
Christianity." [48] The relationship between paradox and apocalypse is also suggested by the title of Bernard Bolzano's nine-
teenth-century treatise called *Paradoxes of the Infinite*,[49] and
the whole topic as it relates to Renaissance literature has been
definitively studied in Rosalie Colie's monolithic work entitled
*Paradoxia Epidemica: The Renaissance Tradition of Para-
dox.*[50]

Despite this agreement on the presence of paradox in apocalyptic contexts, there has not been total agreement on the
exact nature of such paradoxes. A distinction must be made,
of course, between a paradox whose apparent contradictions
can be resolved on rational, empirical grounds and an oxymoron, whose contradiction is real and cannot be resolved in
terms of ordinary experience. I wish to limit the present discussion to the more narrowly defined area of oxymoron. One
writer, critical of the loose way in which the term "paradox"

[48] "Wit and Mystery: A Revaluation in Mediaeval Latin Hym-
nody," *Speculum*, XXII (1947), 310–341.

[49] Trans. Fr. Prihonsky (London, 1950).

[50] Princeton, 1966. In addition to containing a chapter on Milton's
use of paradox in *Paradise Lost*, this book discusses such topics related
to the present discussion as "the rhetoric of transcendence" and
"paradoxes in divine ontology."

is used today by theologians and language theorists, is sceptical of the possibility that oxymoron can be a meaningful vehicle for portraying ultimate reality. He argues, "Contradictory statements are not meaningful. They affirm two senses—one of which negates the other. In such a situation, a person is left with a statement whose meaning is vacuous. . . . It would be impossible to know whether the affirmation or its negation should seriously be considered—and it is impossible seriously to consider both as meaningful." [51] An alternate view, and one which I find acceptable, is suggested by Kenneth Burke in his analysis of the "mystic oxymoron" as it appears in Keats's "Ode on a Grecian Urn." Burke theorizes that a poet who is presenting a transcendental experience can portray the transcendental realm by combining two items which in empirical reality contradict each other. According to Burke, the "transcendent scene is the level at which the earthly laws of contradiction no longer prevail." [52] The apocalyptic world which transcends the world of temporal contradictions represents a contrast to our own experience, but since the two terms of the oxymoron, when taken individually, are empirical phenomena, their fusion in the figure of the mystic oxymoron yields a meaningful and intelligible picture of the apocalyptic world, despite its obvious difference from our own experience.

The figure of mystic oxymoron does not appear frequently in the apocalyptic portions of *Paradise Lost*, but its occurrences are among the more famous passages in the poem, suggesting that as a rhetorical device mystic oxymoron produces

[51] Ben F. Kimpel, *Language and Religion: A Semantic Preface to a Philosophy of Religion* (New York, 1957), p. 123.

[52] *A Grammar of Motives and A Rhetoric of Motives* (Cleveland, 1962), p. 462.

greater imaginative impact than its rate of occurrence indicates. Oxymoron is present in the statement of the angels that God is "Dark with excessive bright" (III, 380). Such an image cannot be totally understood on an empirical level, and the effect is to suggest a realm where the contradictory qualities of light and darkness can coexist. A similar oxymoron is applied to the Son when the Father addresses him with the words, "Son in whose face invisible is beheld / Visibly, what by Deitie I am" (VI, 681–682). God the Father's omnipresence is expressed in the oxymoronic statement that during the act of Creation on Earth the Father, seated on his throne in Heaven, "also went / Invisible, yet staid" (VII, 588–589).

The greatest number of mystic oxymorons in *Paradise Lost* involve a fusion of a solid, enameled image with a vegetative image. While some of these paradoxes can be resolved by taking the enameled term as a reference to color only, it seems to me that a substantial number of these phrases combine qualities of marmoreal hardness and vegetative vitality in such a way that we are forced to postulate an apocalyptic world exempt from the contradictions which exist in the order of nature which we know. Satan's distant view of Heaven, for example, includes "Battlements adorn'd / Of living Saphir" (II, 1049–1050). We read elsewhere about the "Sea of Jasper" (III, 363) which Heaven's pavement resembles, and we are told that when the heavenly stairway is raised to Heaven, "underneath a bright Sea flow'd / of Jasper, or of liquid Pearle" (III, 518–519). Although in such passages it is possible to view the jasper and pearl as color images, it is hardly possible not to be reminded of the mineral qualities of these words, the result being another instance of mystic oxymoron. A similar example of the same principle occurs with the description of the "Ambrosial Fruit / Of vegetable Gold" (IV,

219–20) found in Paradise. Qualities of pliability and stasis may exist together in the image of the "liquid Plain" (IV, 455), as they most certainly do when Heaven's gates of gold are called "living dores" (VII, 566). This fusion of enameled and vegetative images in a mystic oxymoron applies not only to individual phrases but also to large motifs in the poem. I have already demonstrated how enameled images form a continuous pattern throughout the poem, lending a quality of sculptured permanence to both Heaven and Paradise. At the same time, however, both regions possess an abundance of life and motion. The result is a picture of contradictions, since in earthly experience something cannot be simultaneously fluid and static in its essential nature. The solution to the contradiction is to recognize that these contradictory motifs share the same principle which underlies individual mystic oxymorons, the principle of combining two empirical phenomena to suggest a transcendental realm in which the sum is greater than the parts.

Milton's handling of the matter of day and night in Heaven furnishes another motif of mystic oxymoron in the poem. During his account of the war in Heaven Raphael tells Adam that "Eevning now approach'd" (V, 627) in Heaven, and he goes on to assure Adam that "wee have also our Eevning and our Morn" (V, 628). Night in Heaven, however, differs considerably from night on Earth, according to the angel. Heavenly night is more like "Twilight (for Night comes not there / In darker veile)" (V, 645–646), a description which accords with the later mention of "the duskie houre" in Heaven (V, 667). We read also that Satan led the rebellious angels from God's throne "ere yet dim Night / Her shadowie Cloud withdraws" (V, 685–686), and "ere dim Night had disincumberd Heav'n" (V, 700). The same picture of celestial

night as a kind of dimness rather than darkness emerges when
Raphael describes how the partial darkness proceeded "To
veile the Heav'n, though darkness there might well / Seem
twilight here" (VI, 11–12). Raphael's assertions that night in
Heaven does not bring real darkness are later controverted by
the statements that "Now Night her course began, . . . over
Heav'n / Inducing darkness" (VI, 406–407), and that "*Satan*
with his rebellious disappeerd, / Far in the dark dislodg'd"
(VI, 414–415). And the sense of contradiction becomes complete when we compare the reference to the angels who stand
in God's presence continually and "Melodious Hymns about
the sovran Throne / Alternate all night long" (V, 656–657)
with the unequivocal assertion elsewhere that there are angels
who

> with songs
> And choral symphonies, Day without Night,
> Circle his Throne rejoycing [V, 161–163].

The entire complex of passages variously describing night in
Heaven as being dark, merely dim, and nonexistent constitutes
a pattern of mystic oxymoron and suggests a higher realm
where the contradictions of human experience are somehow
no longer contradictions.

Another general pattern of oxymoron in the poem involves
the simultaneous presence of spring and autumn in Paradise.
On the one hand, the Garden of Eden is a place of the bur-
geoning life which we associate with spring, as evidenced by
numerous references in the poem to blossoms (e.g., IV, 148,
630) and flowers (e.g., IV, 241, 256). Springtime in Paradise
is also established by the mention of "th' Eternal Spring" (IV,
268) which exists there and by the narrator's statement that
except for Adam's sin spring would have "Perpetual smil'd on
Earth with vernant Flours" (X, 679). At the same time, how-

ever, the garden is a place of harvest and fruition, as evidenced by the many references to fruits and their consumption by Adam and Eve (e.g., IV, 219, 331–332, 422). The same impression of autumn fruition is conveyed by the narrator's description of how the dinner table of Adam and Eve was with "All *Autumn* pil'd" (V, 394), as well as by Eve's statement about their abundance in Paradise, "where store, / All seasons, ripe for use hangs on the stalk" (V, 322–323). The paradoxical union of spring and autumn which emerges from the various descriptions of Paradise is made explicit by the narrator's statement that "*Spring* and *Autumn* here / Danc'd hand in hand" (V, 394–395).[53] The sense of contradiction regarding the seasons becomes reinforced when, despite the talk about eternal spring, Eve tells Adam that in his presence "All seasons and thir change, all please alike" (IV, 640). The entire contradictory fusion of spring and harvest is best understood as an attempt to portray apocalyptic reality through a technique of mystic oxymoron.

Yet another motif of mystic oxymoron centers in the dichotomy, common in the Renaissance, between "art" and "nature," between order and irregularity. As noted earlier, there are some descriptions of Paradise which draw upon images of human artifice, such as the "inwoven" roof of the bower (IV, 693), the embroidered "inlay" and "Mosaic" of flowers (IV, 699–704), and the "Arborets and Flours / Imborderd on each Bank" (IX, 437–438). The garden's adherence to a principle of order and civilized regularity is also established by the "Walks, and Bowers" found within it (VIII, 305), as well as by the constant labors which Adam and Eve apply toward

---

[53] Mary Irma Corcoran, *Milton's Paradise with Reference to the Hexameral Background* (Washington, D.C., 1945), p. 21, notes the hexameral tradition that in Paradise there was "flower and fruit together on the bough."

keeping the garden pruned (IV, 624–632; IX, 205–219, 244–247). At the same time, this principle of art and regularity seems to be controverted by some of the descriptions of Eden's abundance. Paradise is "Wilde above Rule or Art" (V, 297), and Eve expresses concern that

> the work under our labour grows,
> Luxurious by restraint; what we by day
> Lop overgrown, or prune, or prop, or bind,
> One night or two with wanton growth derides
> Tending to wilde   [IX, 208–212].

In Paradise "Nature . . . plaid at will" (V, 294–295), and the flowers of Paradise, instead of being arranged in the "Beds and curious Knots" (IV, 242) which imply human cultivation and control, are "Powrd forth profuse on Hill and Dale and Plaine" (IV, 243). In Paradise, then, we find the presence of those two great Renaissance opposites, art and nature,[54] and we observe that "Eden is ruled jointly by order and abundance, which in our fallen experience often clash."[55] Although some readers might feel that Milton inadvertently bungled the description of Paradise, a more tenable view would be one which places this contradiction, along with others, in a pattern of mystic oxymoron in which the poet suggests a world which transcends the world of contradictions which we know.

[54] Marjorie Nicolson, *John Milton: A Reader's Guide to His Poetry* (New York, 1963), pp. 237–9, relates Milton's description of Eden to the Renaissance debate over art and nature and concludes that Milton's Paradise partakes of both qualities.

[55] MacCaffrey, *Paradise Lost as "Myth"*, p. 153. Stein, *Answerable Style*, p. 63, likewise notes that in addition to "the rightness of the marvelous order" in the garden there exists "its richness, its authorized excess." Jeffrey Hart, *"Paradise Lost* and Order," *CE*, XXV (1964), 578–80, stresses the order which pervades the prelapsarian garden.

4

Apocalypse through Negation

EMPIRICISM DENIED

The equation of perfection and inactivity, and the corresponding technique of using a negation of empirical phenomena to suggest the otherworldly, belong to a long philosophical and theological tradition. The tradition has classical roots [1] and has been prevalent in many forms of Christian thought, especially among mystics.[2] The "negative way" of approach to God has been described by one of the most famous Christian mystics as the process in which one, "by the very fact of

[1] The Platonic and Aristotelian linking of immobility and perfection, and their related view that "motion and change belong to the imperfect sensible world," are noted by Lawrence W. Hyman, *Andrew Marvell* (New York, 1964), p. 41.

[2] Background and analysis of the theological tradition of negation are contained in these studies: Evelyn Underhill, *Mysticism*, rev. ed. (Cleveland, 1955; first pub., 1930), pp. 380–412; Robert Leet Patterson, *The Conception of God in the Philosophy of Aquinas* (London, 1933), pp. 101–223; Edwyn Bevan, *Symbolism and Belief* (Boston, 1957; first pub., 1938), pp. 18–25; Rosalie Colie, *Paradoxia Epidemica: The Renaissance Tradition of Paradox* (Princeton, 1966), pp. 23–26; and C. A. Patrides, *Milton and the Christian Tradition* (Oxford, 1966), p. 9.

not seeing and not knowing, truly enters into Him who is beyond sight and knowledge." [3] Translating this apocalyptic tradition into dialectical terms, Kenneth Burke speaks of the principle of " 'negative theology,' which finds it necessary to define the 'Allness' of God in terms synonymous with 'nothing' ('infinite,' 'unending,' 'incomprehensible,' 'inexpressible,' 'invisible,' 'unknowable,' and the like). . . . On the simplest dialectical level, the 'First Principle' . . . would be something beyond the description of all human experience; we could only say that it does *not* have color, it does *not* have weight, it does *not* have size or shape." [4]

Milton's relationship to the theological tradition of negation is clearly established by his comments in *De Doctrina Christiana*. In discussing the attributes of God, Milton writes, "Hitherto those attributes only have been mentioned which describe the nature of God, partly in an affirmative, partly in a negative sense, inasmuch as they deny the existence of those imperfections in the Deity, which belong to created things; as, for instance, when we speak of his immensity, his infinity, his incorruptibility" (*Works*, XIV, 53, 55). This principle of describing the divine through a renunciation of empirical qualities underlies several aspects of Milton's poetic portrayal of apocalyptic reality in *Paradise Lost*.

In its least complex manifestation, the technique of negation consists of individual words and phrases which combine an empirical noun with a term denoting the absence of the very thing which has been named. As we would expect, such words and phrases are frequently applied to God. The angels'

[3] Saint Dionysius Areopagitica, *The Theologia Mystica of Saint Dionysius,* trans. Alan W. Watts (West Park, New York, 1944), p. 35.
[4] *A Grammar of Motives and A Rhetoric of Motives* (Cleveland, 1962), pp. 87, 295.

hymn to the Father in Book III contains several negative terms. The angels praise God as "Immutable, Immortal, Infinite" (III, 373). God, they state, is Himself "invisible" (III, 375), and He sits "Thron'd inaccessible" (III, 377). Similar negations occur in the morning hymn of Adam and Eve, who sing of God as being "Unspeakable" (V, 156), and "To us invisible" (V, 157). In the same hymn we hear of God's "goodness beyond thought" (V, 159), and about the way in which all creatures "extoll / Him . . . without end" (V, 165). Adam later calls God "the infinitely Good" (VII, 76), to whom he and Eve owe "Immortal thanks" (VII, 77) and whose sovereign will they "observe / Immutably" (VII, 78–79). Elsewhere Adam assures Eve that God is "infinitly good, and of his good / As liberal and free as infinite" (IV, 414–415), while Adam and Eve together praise God's "goodness infinite" (IV, 734). When Adam asks God for a mate he contrasts his own condition to that of God, who has no need to propagate, being "already infinite" (VIII, 420). Adam attributes another negation to God when he states that after Eve's creation she was "Led by her Heav'nly Maker, though unseen" (VIII, 485), while Eve, recalling the same event, uses the same kind of negative idiom when she states that she was led "invisibly" (IV, 476).

More epithets based on a denial of empirical qualities are applied to God by Raphael when he speaks of "the Father infinite" (V, 596) and of how the Father "all his Father full expresst / Ineffably into" the Son's face (VI, 720–721). Elsewhere Raphael draws upon the principle of negative transcendence with his mention of "th' invisible King" (VII, 122), and with his account of how during the Creation of the world the Father "went / Invisible" (VII, 588–589). Similarly, Michael informs Adam that God "oft descends to visit

97

men / Unseen" (XII, 48–49). The fallen angels, too, conceive of God in terms which deny empiricism, as evidenced by Moloch's acknowledgment that God is "inaccessible" (II, 104), and by Belial's assertion, phrased in negatives, that despite any war of revenge which the demons might wage against God

> yet our great Enemy
> All incorruptible would on his Throne
> Sit unpolluted, and th' Ethereal mould
> Incapable of stain would soon expel
> Her mischief, and purge off the baser fire
>
> [II, 137–141].

Mammon likewise calls to mind God's "Glory unobscur'd" (II, 265) in his speech during the infernal council.

God, like the other characters in the poem, attributes negatives to himself. The Father, in asserting to the Son that his foreknowledge does not impair man's freedom of choice, states that the Fall is "by me immutably foreseen" (III, 121). Several lines later the Father again speaks of his "high Decree / Unchangeable" (III, 126–127). The Father also speaks of his "inaccessible high strength" (VII, 141), and he implies his own infinity when he states that he fills "Infinitude" (VII, 169).

The formula of negative transcendence is as much a part of the idiom of the epic narrator as it is of the characters in the narrative. In the invocation to Book III he speaks of the "unapproached light" (III, 4) in which God dwells. He extends the principle of negation to the entire story of his epic by identifying it as one which tells "Of things invisible to mortal sight" (III, 55). In his narrative descriptions, too, the narrator employs negative theology, as when he tells of God's speech filling Heaven with "joy ineffable" (III, 137). Similarly, the narrator informs us that Satan's malice "serv'd but to bring forth / Infinite goodness, grace and mercy" on God's part (I, 217–218); and before giving the roll call of fallen angels he tells how in subsequent history they led idolaters to forsake "th' invisible / Glory" of God (I, 369–370).

Empiricism is also denied in a number of passages describing the angels. The angels, for example, are identified as spirits "that never fade" (III, 360), and they "walk the Earth / Unseen" (IV, 677–678). The angels who praise God in Heaven are "numbers without number" (III, 346), while Zephon, in rebuking Satan, is said to possess "grace / Invincible" (IV, 845–846). Raphael prefaces his account of the war in Heaven by calling the actions of the angels "invisible exploits" (V, 565), and the accuracy of the negation conveyed by the word "invisible" is attested to by the frequency with which negative terms appear in the subsequent narrative. The angelic hosts are "Innumerable" (V, 585), and they stand "in Orbes / Of circuit inexpressible" (V, 594–595). God tells Gabriel to lead to battle his "Sons / Invincible" (VI, 46–47), who perform "infinite" deeds (VI, 241). In describing the "fight / Unspeakable" (VI, 296–297) between Satan and Gabriel, Raphael is perplexed, logically enough, by the problem of finding humanly comprehensible terms in which to phrase the description of the encounter. More negations of empirical reality are used to describe the "inviolable Saints" (VI, 398) who remain faithful to God and who as a result are "invulnerable, impenitrably arm'd" (VI, 400). In the same passage the very state of innocence of the unfallen angels is couched in negatives: their essential identity is "not to have sinnd, / Not to have disobei'd" (VI, 402–403). As a result, in battle "they stood / Unwearied, unobnoxious to be pain'd" (VI, 403–404). Angels "number-less" (VII, 197) surround Christ's chariot, and the celestial beings inhabit "Pavilions numberless" (V, 653). In view of the many negative terms used in descriptions of the angels, it is not surprising that Adam responds to Raphael's story in kind, calling it an account of things "by me unsearchable" (VIII, 10).

Descriptions of the prelapsarian garden also draw upon the principle of denying empirical qualities to suggest a realm where only transcendental qualities exist. The garden's seclu-sion is insured by a surrounding thicket of "Insuperable highth" (IV, 138), and the perfection of the prelapsarian rose is depicted as an absence of fallen qualities when the narrator tells about "Flours of all hue, and without Thorn the Rose" (IV, 256).[5] In the garden Adam and Eve have "choice / Unlimited of manifold delights" (IV, 434–435). More negatives occur when we read that the human pair re-ceives from God "All perfet good unmeasur'd" (V, 399), and that the Earth yields "Varietie without end" (VII, 542). Para-dise is comprised of "pure immortal Elements that know / No gross, no unharmoneous mixture foule" (XI, 50–51), and it is "incorrupt" (XI, 56). The animals of Paradise, too, are char-acterized by an explicit absence of fallen qualities. Thus we read that the snake was not "nocent yet" (IX, 186), that he slept "unfear'd" (IX, 187), and that he was to Adam "Not noxious" (VII, 498).

The perfection of Adam and Eve, like that of the garden, is frequently described in terms denying imperfections. One of

[5] The theological tradition behind Milton's use of the thornless rose as a symbol of prelapsarian perfection is noted by Grant Mc-Colley, *Paradise Lost: An Account of Its Growth and Major Origins* (Chicago, 1940), p. 147; and George W. Whiting, " 'And Without Thorn the Rose,' " *RES*, X (1959), 60–62.

the first references to the human pair describes them as "Reaping immortal fruits of joy and love, / Uninterrupted joy, unrivald love" (III, 67–68). Eve is both "immortal" (IX, 291) and "from sin and blame entire" (IX, 292), while Adam's discourse is "unblam'd" (IX, 5). In asserting Eve's freedom from evil Adam tells her that "in thee can harbour none" (V, 99). The moral perfection of Adam and Eve is repeatedly couched in words and phrases which denote the absence of sin: "they thought no ill" (IV, 320); "no thought infirme" entered Eve's consciousness (V, 384); "in those hearts / Love unlibidinous reign'd, nor jealousie / Was understood" (V, 448–450); Adam is "Led on, yet sinless" (VII, 61); "*Eve* yet sinless" (IX, 659) is "pure of sinful thought" (VIII, 506). The unfallen sexuality of Adam and Eve "is undefil'd" (IV, 761); and it is said to consist "Not in the bought smile / Of Harlots" and other perversions of fallen experience (IV, 765–770). We read also "Of conjugal attraction unreprov'd" (IV, 493), as well as that "Then was not guiltie shame" (IV, 313). From one point of view the entire innocence of Adam and Eve is summed up in a single negation, which Adam phrases as the condition "not to taste that onely Tree / Of knowledge" (IV, 423–424).

As the foregoing discussion has shown, the principle of negation underlies a number of individual words and phrases used to describe the various aspects of the apocalyptic world of *Paradise Lost*. Of the arts, literature alone can use a technique of negation. Such a nonverbal art form as a painting, for example, can portray a cloudless sky, but it has no means of explicitly denoting to the viewer—of forcing him to note specifically—the fact, "There was not a cloud in the sky." Nor does painting have any means of even suggesting the absence of such intangible qualities as mortality or sin, which the verbal art form denotes by the terms "immortality" and "sinlessness." When negations appear in poetry, they have the paradoxical effect of evoking the very phenomena which they deny. Thus when Milton in *Paradise Lost* describes the apocalyptic state as an absence of ordinary reality, the reader not only catches a glimpse of the apocalyptic realm but is also reminded of the limitations which remove the natural and fallen state from transcendental perfection.

PATTERNS OF REJECTION

The technique of describing the apocalyptic experience through a negation of empirical qualities is present in large patterns found in *Paradise Lost* as well as in the individual words and phrases already discussed. Since many of these motifs of rejection are built into the poem itself and depend on the sequential progression of the narrative, a consideration of these patterns is most profitable if the discussion remains close to the linear development of the poem. It is important to note also that an over-all pattern of negation may be a relative absence of empirical phenomena and need not be a total denial of empiricism, such as we find in the word "invisible." Mystics of the negative way, for example, describe the ascent to God in images of night and darkness. Such images constitute analogies to human experience, not a complete absence of ordinary experience. But images of darkness still convey a sense of the relative elimination of finite experience, and they thus constitute a pattern of relative negation. Similarly, many of the motifs with which I shall be concerned evince a principle of relative renunciation rather than a total denial of empirical reality.

Paradise Lost begins with the depiction of Satan and his fallen cohorts in Hell. The dominant values and emotions portrayed in Books I and II are those associated with human experience, especially human experience as embodied in the heroic tradition of classical epic and medieval romance. These heroic qualities include physical prowess, military aspirations, desire for personal glory, and an impulse to build the impressive physical structures of Pandemonium.[6] The varieties of hatred and revenge exhibited by the demons during their infernal council are rooted in fallen human experience.[7] The style in which this action is presented belongs likewise to the tradition of classical heroic epic. Epic similes and allusions to mythology and history appear here with greater frequency than anywhere else in the poem, and Satan and his followers are all masters of oratory and rhetoric. The opening two books of *Paradise Lost*, in short, are concerned mainly with portraying heroic energy by means of a heroic idiom.[8]

With the opening of Book III we reach the first extended scene set in Heaven, and one of the dominant apocalyptic techniques underlying the scene is a pattern of negation. Basi-

[6] Arnold Stein, *Answerable Style* (Minneapolis, 1953), pp. 17–37, has a good discussion of the debased emphasis of the fallen angels on physical and material power.

[7] C. S. Lewis, in *A Preface to Paradise Lost* (New York, 1961; first pub., 1942), pp. 104–107, has an engaging analysis of the human emotions at work in the various fallen angels.

[8] For a more extensive discussion and documentation than I attempt here of the heroic values and style found in the passages dealing with the fallen angels in Hell, see these studies: C. M. Bowra, *From Virgil to Milton* (London, 1945), pp. 194–246; Kingsley Widmer, "The Iconography of Renunciation: The Miltonic Simile," *ELH*, XXV (1958), 258–269; Davis P. Harding, *The Club of Hercules* (Urbana, 1962), passim; and John M. Steadman, *Milton and the Renaissance Hero* (Oxford, 1967), passim. E. M. W. Tillyard, in his book *Milton* (London, 1930), pp. 276–9, attributed "heroic energy" to Satan and drew the conclusion, standard in 1930 but in rather complete disrepute among Miltonists today, that Milton unconsciously admired such heroic energy.

cally what we find is an absence of the very qualities and poetic style which have been established as the norms in the infernal scenes in Books I and II. B. Rajan's observations sum up the situation aptly: the heavenly style is "a style stripped of simile and ornament, reduced as nearly as possible to the plain truth of scripture, devoid of the resources of literature and mythology. . . . 2,140 lines of *Paradise Lost* are set in Heaven. Yet in all these lines there is not a single complex or multiple simile, only one simile which involves a literary allusion, and only one place name, Biblical or Classical." [9] Even the syntax of God's speeches is simpler and more direct than that which we find in the oratorical flourishes of the fallen angels.

That God's speeches do not show a total lack of rhetoric has been indisputably demonstrated by analyses of the patterns of verbal rhetoric and figures of sound at work in these passages.[10] But even the rhetorical patterns of schematic repe-

[9] *Paradise Lost and the Seventeenth Century Reader* (New York, 1948), pp. 128, 163–4. D. C. Allen, *The Harmonious Vision* (Baltimore, 1954), p. xi, similarly finds that "only once does God slip into a poetic figure." For other discussions of the now customary distinction between infernal and celestial styles in *Paradise Lost,* see, in addition to the works of Bowra, Widmer, Harding, and Steadman cited in the preceding note, the following studies: Phyllis MacKenzie, "Milton's Visual Imagination: An Answer to T. S. Eliot," *UTQ,* XVI (1946–7), 25; Stein, *Answerable Style,* pp. 127–9; Irene Samuel, "The Dialogue in Heaven: A Reconsideration of *Paradise Lost,* III, 1–147," *PMLA,* LXXII (1957), 601–611; B. A. Wright, *Milton's Paradise Lost* (New York, 1962), p. 120; Anne Ferry, *Milton's Epic Voice* (Cambridge, Mass., 1963), pp. 69–73; Thomas Greene, *The Descent from Heaven* (New Haven, 1963), pp. 383–4; Helen Gardner, *A Reading of Paradise Lost* (Oxford, 1965), p. 55; and Stanley Fish, *Surprised by Sin* (New York, 1967), pp. 57–91.

[10] See J. B. Broadbent, "Milton's Rhetoric," *MP,* LVI (1959), 224–242; and Jackson Cope, *The Metaphoric Structure of Paradise Lost* (Baltimore, 1962), pp. 164–176.

tition in the celestial dialogue do not alter the tonelessness and impersonality which commentators have attributed to God's speeches. One critic has observed in connection with the dialogue in Heaven that "no passage in Milton is verbally more highly developed; in other words, no passage more depends for its effect on reading aloud." [11] The rhetoric, in other words, can be viewed as confirming our impression of God as a transcendent voice which stands behind the entire action of *Paradise Lost* and which in Book III pronounces on the nature of things. In a later section I shall have opportunity to demonstrate the presence in the poem of a motif which portrays God simply and explicitly as a voice rather than as a person. The rhetoric of the celestial dialogue in Book III, based on verbal repetitions, can be viewed as a dramatization of the principle that God is a voice rather than a visualized person possessing human emotions and other human characteristics. Although the opening lines of Book III do not represent a total retreat from rhetoric, then, the absence of metaphor and reliance on figures of sound constitute a relative negation of certain aspects of human experience. The poetic style, unadorned by simile and allusion, is based on the "tacit recognition that God, who is the source of proper poetry, is above verse-making," [12] while the portrayal of God as a transcendent voice adheres to the principle of conceiving of the divine as "the negation of personality." [13]

Other patterns of negation are also evident in the depiction of Heaven. Commentators have often noted the relative inac-

[11] Allan Gilbert, "Form and Matter in *Paradise Lost*, Book III," *JEGP*, LX (1961), 659.

[12] Allen, *The Harmonious Vision*, p. xi.

[13] The principle of defining God as an absence of human personality is discussed by Burke, *A Grammar of Motives and A Rhetoric of Motives*, pp. 35, 80.

tivity of Heaven, and although the thesis could be qualified by reference to a number of details in the poem, the technique of presenting the apocalyptic as the negation of activity and motion is an important one in the celestial scenes in *Paradise Lost*. Again the negation is partly a matter of the absence of qualities attributed to the fallen angels. Throughout the poem, for example, the essential nature of Satan consists of ceaseless motion, beginning with his rising from the burning lake and continuing through the many events and assumed disguises which characterize his quest from Hell to the temptation of man in Paradise. So complete are the changes in Satan during the poem that some commentators have even been led to conclude that his characterization in the poem is not unified.[14]

Such flux is totally absent from the portrayal of God, whose fixed position is habitually presented in the poem by having movement occur around him and be directed toward him. In Book III (lines 349ff.) the angels bow in adoration toward God and cast their crowns toward the still center which is God. Later in the poem our impression of God as a changeless being is reinforced by the description of him as "fixt for ever firm and sure" (VII, 586). The impression of angelic movement around an immobile Deity is created by the reference to the angels as God's

> Eyes
> That run through all the Heav'ns, or down to th' Earth
> Bear his swift errands over moist and dry,
> O're Sea and Land   [III, 650-653].

---

[14] Cf. Allan Gilbert, *On the Composition of Paradise Lost* (Chapel Hill, 1947), pp. 52–57; and A. J. A. Waldock, *Paradise Lost and Its Critics* (Cambridge, Eng., 1947), pp. 81–87.

The same kind of delegation of action by the unmoved Father
to a secondary agent occurs when the act of Creation is spoken of as

> the work
> Of secondarie hands, by task transferd
> From Father to his Son   [V, 853–855].

During the war in Heaven, too, God maintains a fixed position amidst the agitation of warring spirits, and we read that
while "horrid confusion heapt / Upon confusion rose" (VI,
668–669) the Father sat "Shrin'd in his Sanctuarie of Heav'n
secure, / Consulting on the sum of things" (VI, 672–673).
Only on the third day does the Son, as the active agent within
the Godhead, go forth to drive the rebel angels from Heaven
while the Father, still the contemplative, immobile divine
agent, looks on.

The contrast between ceaseless flux and transcendent still-
ness which we find in the portrayal of Satan and God is repeated in the presentation of the fallen demons and the faithful angels. One of the most persistent themes of the fallen
angels in Hell is the change which they have recently under-
gone. Satan exclaims his dismay regarding "how chang'd" (I,
84) Beelzebub is as a result of his fall from bliss, and even
while asserting his refusal to relent in his hatred toward God,
Satan is forced to acknowledge that he is "chang'd in outward
lustre" (I, 97) from his original state. Later Satan asks his followers in Hell, "Is this the Region . . . / That we must
change for Heav'n . . ." (I, 242–244)? The repeated emphasis on the "fall" of the demons serves to underscore a
change which has occurred in their situation, as does Satan's
constantly diminishing brightness. The essential issue pervad-
ing the speeches in the council in Hell is the matter of how

the demons can best change their present state of misery, just as "the atmosphere of busy planning" [15] which permeates Books I and II finds its chief motive in the demons' desire to alter their present condition. Even the plan to effect man's fall is predicated on the concept of change—man's change from perfection to a condition of "faded bliss, / Faded so soon" (II, 375–376).

Heaven, we are told, possesses "change delectable" (V, 629), but when compared with the changes which we have observed in Hell the variation is limited indeed. The perfection of the angels in Heaven consists of standing instead of falling, of continuing in their obedience to God's will instead of changing from their devotion to the Deity. The thing which distinguishes the unfallen angels from Satan's followers "is not different activity than that of Hell, but the will and the faith beyond all activity." [16] Moreover, the characteristic changes which occur in Heaven, such as the interchange of night and day, tend to be recurrent and ritualistic in nature; and as several commentators have stated, such cyclical, repetitive action itself assumes a kind of changeless quality.[17]

Even some of the cosmological details of the universe of *Paradise Lost* contribute to the inactivity of Heaven. The elements and minerals of Heaven are inactive until the demonic

[15] Waldock, *Paradise Lost and Its Critics,* p. 94, correctly notes "the atmosphere of busy planning, of life nearly as lively as ever, of energies unquenched" in Hell, drawing the erroneous conclusion that such activity represents a positive quality in the poem.

[16] Widmer, *ELH,* XXV, 267.

[17] Ferry, *Milton's Epic Voice,* p. 31, makes the point that the cyclical pattern of prelapsarian experience is "a cycle whose constant renewal was an assurance of permanence." See also Isabel MacCaffrey, *Paradise Lost as "Myth"* (Cambridge, Mass., 1959), pp. 73–81; and William G. Madsen, "Earth the Shadow of Heaven: Typological Symbolism in *Paradise Lost,*" PMLA, LXXV (1960), 523.

angels mingle and concoct them (VI, 507ff.). Raphael's description of the great chain of being is notable for the dynamic activity which pervades it, with all lower forms of being on the scale aspiring upward "Till body up to spirit work" (V, 478). Implicit in the statement, however, is the notion that the ascending scale culminates in a static spiritualized condition of permanently arrested development, and that not only God but also the angels are in this condition past change can be inferred from Raphael's statement to Adam that man's body

> may at last turn all to Spirit,
> Improv'd by tract of time, and wingd ascend
> Ethereal, as wee   [V, 497–499].

Cosmology also contributes to the impression of inactivity which emerges from the descriptions of Eden in the middle books of *Paradise Lost*. In the Ptolemaic astronomy which pervaded Renaissance thought as it did Milton's epic, the Earth represented the still center of the revolving cosmos. Robert Recorde, writing on the topic in the mid-sixteenth century, summarizes the traditional view in this way: "The earth is in the middle of the world, as the center of it. . . . The earth hath no motion of itself, no more than a stone, but restest quietly." [18] How does Milton manage to dramatize this cosmological idea in his poem? The answer lies again in the sequential placing of scenes in the poem. The action begins in Hell, whose essential identity is flux and change. The opening lines of Book III are set in Heaven, where there is relative rest. By the middle of Book III, how-

---

[18] *The Castle of Knowledge*, in *Prose of the English Renaissance*, ed. J. William Hebel *et al.* (New York, 1952), p. 138.

ever, the focus has shifted back to the ever-changing landscape of Satan's journey through space to the Earth. The whole shift from Hell to Heaven and back to Satan's advance past the various revolving planets constitutes, as M. M. Mahood has stated, "an outer circle where all is in agitation." [19] As we follow Satan's advance toward Paradise we move away from the violently moving periphery "into the centre of this vortex-like cosmos," with Satan's flight representing "a progress away from violent motion into complete calm." [20] The effect of inactivity produced by the formal structure of the poem is reinforced by the description of Paradise after Satan arrives there. A sense of arrested motion is conveyed by the account of how Satan meets "gentle gales / Fanning thir odoriferous wings" (IV, 156–157) as he "journied on, pensive and slow" (IV, 173). The extended account of the odorous spices of the garden (IV, 156–167) contributes "to a certain lulling heaviness in the atmosphere of Paradise," and descriptions in the following lines are slightly ennervating in effect.[21] Descriptions of Eden as a place of continual spring (IV, 268; X, 679) also lend a quality of static inactivity to our impressions of the garden.

If the cosmology of *Paradise Lost*, as embodied in the narrative structure of the poem, is one source of Eden's lack of action, a second cause is the pastoral convention which is at the heart of the Paradisal vision. There have been many approaches to the pastoral garden as it appears in Milton's epic. The traditional elements in Milton's Paradise have been

[19] *Poetry and Humanism* (New Haven, 1950), p. 178. My entire discussion of the cosmological inactivity of Earth is indebted to Mahood's excellent treatment of the topic.

[20] Mahood, *Poetry and Humanism*, p. 179.

[21] These observations are made by Greene, *The Descent from Heaven*, pp. 401–2.

thoroughly examined.[22] Criticism in the first half of this century was preoccupied with the aesthetically irrelevant thesis that Milton did not actually believe in a lost pastoral garden,[23] while Paul Elmer More, following the same impressionistic approach, argued that Milton's belief in Paradise was a vital one and that, in fact, "the true theme" of *Paradise Lost* "is Paradise itself; not Paradise lost, but the reality of that 'happy rural seat'. . . ."[24]

[22] The definitive study of the relation of the Renaissance pastoral garden, including Milton's, to its tradition is A. Bartlett Giamatti's study, *The Earthly Paradise and the Renaissance Epic* (Princeton, 1966). Other studies concerned with the relation of Milton's Paradise to traditional descriptions include these: Grant McColley, *Paradise Lost: An Account of Its Growth and Major Origins* (Chicago, 1940), pp. 128–157; Mary Irma Corcoran, *Milton's Paradise with Reference to the Hexameral Background* (Washington, D.C., 1945); Evert Mordecai Clark, "Milton's Abyssinian Paradise," *University of Texas Studies in English*, XXIX (1950), 129–150; J. B. Broadbent, "Milton's Paradise," *MP*, LI (1954), 160–176; and Frank Kermode, "Adam Unparadised," in *The Living Milton* (London, 1960), pp. 85–123.

For general discussions of conventions in descriptions of the earthly Paradise, see Sabine Baring-Gould, *Curious Myths of the Middle Ages* (London, 1914), pp. 250–265; Robert R. Cawley, *Unpathed Waters: Studies in the Influence of the Voyagers on Elizabethan Literature* (Princeton, 1940), pp. 3–31; Arnold Williams, *The Common Expositor* (Chapel Hill, 1948), pp. 95–111; Howard Rollin Patch, *The Other World According to Descriptions in Medieval Literature* (Cambridge, Mass., 1950); and Ernst Robert Curtius, *European Literature and the Latin Middle Ages* (New York, 1953), pp. 195–200.

[23] For typical statements of the view see Tillyard, *Milton*, pp. 282–4; Arthur Sewell, *A Study in Milton's Christian Doctrine* (London, 1939), p. 144; Basil Willey, *The Seventeenth Century Background* (London, 1942), pp. 147–8; John S. Diekhoff, *Milton's Paradise Lost: A Commentary on the Argument* (New York, 1946), p. 93; Waldock, *Paradise Lost and Its Critics*, p. 125; and David Daiches, *Milton* (New York, 1966), p. 191.

[24] "The Theme of 'Paradise Lost,'" *Shelburne Essays*, Fourth Series (Cambridge, Mass., 1922), pp. 239–253.

I propose to approach the pastoral garden in *Paradise Lost* in terms of its conformity to the general pattern of negation which I have been considering. That pastoral is a kind of negation has been suggested by Hallett Smith, who believes that "in pastoral . . . virtue is demonstrated negatively, by showing how many of the evils of active life are avoided in the retired, obscure life of shepherds." [25] The pastoral life of Adam and Eve in Paradise is, of course, only relatively free from human experiences; the garden presents many analogies to ordinary experience. There is vegetation and animal life, as well as interchange of day and night, in Eden. Moreover, as many critics have observed, there is abundant motion within the prelapsarian cosmos, with all forms of being ascending the dynamic scale of being. Adam and Eve have their daily work to perform, too, and the seriousness with which they regard their calling is made clear in numerous passages.

Wherein, then, lies the negation which I have claimed as part of the pastoral garden? It consists chiefly of the absence of the qualities and institutions of the civilized life which is our lot. Adam and Eve are involved in a spiritual relationship toward God, a marital relationship toward each other, and a relationship involving authority over the rest of the Creation; but besides these basic roles there is a total absence of the complex institutional roles which characterize civilized life. There is neither state nor church in Paradise. Moreover, while Renaissance pastoral poetry is usually motivated by the impulse to retreat from the city to the country, by an awareness of the "sharp difference between two ways of life, the rustic and the urban," [26] in the world of *Paradise Lost* there is

---

[25] *Elizabethan Poetry* (Cambridge, Mass., 1952), p. 301.
[26] Frank Kermode calls this "the first condition" of Renaissance pastoral poetry, in *English Pastoral Poetry from the Beginnings to Marvell* (New York, 1952), p. 14.

nothing urban from which to retreat. The self-contained scope of the action which occurs within the walls of the garden is an index to its lack of civilized institutions: this is an existence where sailing the seas, building cities, and traveling from one locale to another are conspicuously lacking. Pastoral literature traditionally presented its characters under the guise of the shepherd's life, but even the role of the shepherd, primitive as it is, is something which came after the simplicity of Paradise had been broken into a number of identifiable roles. Adam and Eve are simply man and woman inhabiting the garden, and although they perform the function of tending the garden, that role reflects a less specialized world than one which contains the separate categories of shepherd and other vocations. The nakedness of Adam and Eve, much emphasized in *Paradise Lost*, is another aspect of the absence of civilized accoutrements. Even the cultivated appearance of the garden is not exactly what it seems to be. The plants which form the bower of Adam and Eve are woven together in the manner of artifice, but this artifice is a product of God's craftsmanship, not of human art,

> for blissful Paradise
> Of God the Garden was, by him in the East
> Of *Eden* planted   [IV, 208–210].

And despite Adam and Eve's pruning of the plants in the garden, the flowers of Paradise are explicitly declared to be exempt from human art in the narrator's description of the

> Flours worthy of Paradise which not nice Art
> In Beds and curious Knots, but Nature boon
> Powrd forth profuse on Hill and Dale and Plaine
>
> > [IV, 241–243].

In a variety of ways, then, the pastoral Garden of Eden represents an absence of the qualities which we know as part of our civilized existence, with the poet portraying "a position *above* his created world—dealing with a world more simple than his own." [27]

The general pattern of negation in *Paradise Lost* includes two additional motifs. One of these consists of the manner in which the Fall of Adam and Eve is described as an opening of their eyes, suggesting that the prelapsarian state consisted of an absence of certain things which became a part of human existence after the Fall. In Eve's first encounter with Adam after having eaten the forbidden fruit she asserts that the fruit possesses "Divine effect / To open Eyes" (IX, 865–866), and that she now finds her eyes "opener . . . , / Dimm erst" (IX, 875–876). In urging Adam to eat of the fruit Eve again claims that she has acquired "op'nd Eyes" (IX, 985), and after both Adam and Eve have disobeyed the prohibition they "found thir Eyes . . . op'ned" (IX, 1053). Later Adam reproaches Eve with the words:

> since our Eyes
> Op'ned we find indeed, and find we know
> Both Good and Evil, Good lost, and Evil got
>   [IX, 1070–1072].

The whole motif of the Fall as eye-opener adheres to a principle of negation by retrospectively portraying the state of innocence as the absence of experience initiated by the Fall.

[27] This view of pastoral poetry is stated by Cleanth Brooks and John Edward Hardy, in *Poems of Mr. John Milton* (London, 1957), p. 267. This represents their modification of the widely accepted thesis of William Empson, developed in *Some Versions of Pastoral* (London, 1935), that pastoral projects the complex civilized world onto a simpler plane; as distinguished from Brooks and Hardy, Empson believes that the pastoral world is both superior and inferior to our world, and that Milton displays "the double feeling of pastoral, that he is both inferior and superior to Adam" (p. 189).

A final pattern of rejection in the poem consists of the series of protestations by various narrators in the epic to the effect that the apocalyptic realm is one which cannot be described in terms of ordinary human experience. In describing the angels who stand in God's presence, for example, the epic narrator states that the angels "from his sight receiv'd / Beatitude past utterance" (III, 61–62). Similarly, the scene which Satan views on the sun is "beyond expression" (III, 591); and Uriel, in speaking about God's created works, asks:

> what created mind can comprehend
> Thir number, or the wisdom infinite
> That brought them forth, but hid thir causes deep
>
> [III, 705–707].

The impossibility of finding anything comparable to the apocalyptic realm on Earth is repeated when the epic narrator, after describing Heaven's portal, states that it is "inimitable on Earth / By Model, or by shading Pencil drawn" (III, 508–509). The narrator strains to find words to describe Paradise, and he would describe all "if Art could tell" (IV, 236), the implication being that his art is inadequate to portray the apocalyptic. Adam admits the futility of finding adequate comparisons between heavenly and earthly feasts with the question, "yet what compare" (V, 467)? Similarly, the angels who praise God after the Creation of the world ask, "what thought can measure thee or tongue / Relate thee" (VII, 603–604)?

Raphael's narrative of the celestial battle and of Creation contains a number of similar assertions that the apocalyptic vision cannot be portrayed in earthly terms. Raphael begins his account of the war in Heaven by asking:

> how shall I relate
> To human sense th' invisible exploits
> Of warring Spirits . . . /
> how last unfould
> The secrets of another world . . . ?
>
> [V, 564–566; 568–569].

The same difficulty arises later when Raphael attempts to describe the fight between Satan and Michael:

> They ended parle, and both addrest for fight
> Unseakable; for who, though with the tongue
> Of Angels, can relate, or to what things
> Liken on Earth conspicuous, that may lift
> Human imagination to such highth
> Of Godlike Power   [VI, 296–301].

At another point Raphael asks:

> to recount Almightie works
> What words or tongue of Seraph can suffice,
> Or heart of man suffice to comprehend?
>
> [VII, 112–114].

The apocalyptic world which Raphael is describing is in some ways not amenable to description in terms of human experience, and it can be suggested negatively only by asserting that it consists of things not found in empirical reality.

Patterns of rejection, it is clear, constitute an important apocalyptic technique in *Paradise Lost*. Critics have usually judged ill of the aesthetic success of the technique of negation. Thus we read about the "monotony of the situation" in Eden,[28] about the "emptiness and tedium of existence in that garden," [29] and about the "eternity of boredom" which con-

---

[28] Walter Raleigh, *Milton* (London, 1909), p. 105.

[29] Laurence Binyon, "A Note on Milton's Imagery and Rhythm," in *Seventeenth Century Studies Presented to Sir Herbert Grierson* (Oxford, 1938), p. 189.

stitutes life in Paradise.[30] Other critics argue that "the quietistic adoration and leisure in heaven and on earth" contrast unfavorably with the teeming activity in Hell,[31] that "Milton hardly succeeded in making the heavenly host . . . interesting," [32] and that the descriptions of Heaven and Eden are "not alluring to us." [33] One commentator condemns the whole convention of portraying perfection as rest, stating that "a perfect state is by nature static and it is not easy to make it attractive" and that "The changeless comfort of Heaven itself" is "uninteresting." [34] Without attempting to prejudge the question of the aesthetic effectiveness of the apocalyptic technique of negation, I wish to conclude the present analysis with two observations. For one thing, patterns of negation do not by themselves constitute the apocalyptic vision of *Paradise Lost*. Renunciation is balanced by a variety of other techniques, as other chapters in this study demonstrate. To speak only of the inactivity of the apocalyptic realm is thus misleading. Secondly, the technique of rejection of empiricism involves more dramatic conflict than is usually recognized. Apocalyptic negation implies the absence of something else, and there is always an implicit dramatic tension between the quality being denied and its denial. Negation of empiricism, whether it involves a single word or a large motif, should be viewed as part of a large dramatic conflict which juxtaposes things and their absence, nature and transcendence.

[30] Waldock, *Paradise Lost and Its Critics*, p. 125.

[31] R. J. Zwi Werblowsky, *Lucifer and Prometheus* (London, 1952), p. 70.

[32] Charles Williams, *The English Poetic Mind* (Oxford, 1932), p. 128.

[33] Diekhoff, *Milton's Paradise Lost: A Commentary on the Argument*, p. 96.

[34] Curt A. Zimansky, "Gulliver, Yahoos, and Critics," *CE*, XXVII (1965), 47.

5

Apocalypse through Analogy

ANALOGIES OF SCENE

Theorists concerned with the portrayal of apocalyptic reality in poetry commonly assert that the principle of analogy underlies all such writing.[1] One writer, for example, theorizes that religious poetry must express the transcendental in earthly terms, must "convey one thing in terms of another thing . . . if it is ever to reach our minds, which, after all, are tuned-in to the wave-lengths of the visible world." [2] Cleanth Brooks states the same view when he writes that Milton's apocalyptic world, which "is by definition one which no reader of the poem could possibly have experienced," must be

[1] In the present discussion "analogy" denotes "aspects of similarity between apocalyptic reality and ordinary reality." My impression is that critics have wasted a good deal of ink on such topics as the idea that metaphor is the opposite from simile (since it asserts identity rather than comparison) and the argument about whether the main point of Milton's epic similes is the similarity or contrast between the phenomena joined in the simile. In my discussion it makes no difference if the analogy (similarity) between apocalypse and experience is expressed in simile, metaphor, or direct, literal statement.

[2] Evelyn Underhill, "The Philosophy of Contemplation," in *Mixed Pasture* (New York, 1933), p. 16.

"rooted (like any metaphor) in known experience." [3] Similarly, a theorist of religious language emphasizes, quite legitimately, that any conception of apocalyptic reality which we may have is perforce a conception conditioned by human experience: "Man may well know divine reality; but whatever he knows about its nature is not 'divine knowledge.' It is human knowledge about divine reality. Man likewise is familiar with human language, and with no other. . . . No symbol employed in religious life is supernatural. Only the referent of religious life is 'supernatural.' " [4]

That Milton employs various means to modify the elements of ordinary experience which he uses in portraying apocalyptic reality has been evident from the preceding discussion of techniques of contrast and negation in *Paradise Lost*. Yet it is equally obvious that Milton consistently depicts apocalyptic experience in terms of human experience. If at many points various speakers in the poem stress the difficulty and impossibility of finding earthly analogues to apocalyptic reality, it is also important to note that there are many passages in which speakers assert the principle of analogy as the basis of their accounts. As observed in the earlier analysis of the theoretic considerations underlying Milton's apocalyptic vision, this kind of duality, stressing the simultaneous similarity and difference between apocalyptic and earthly experience, is exactly what we would expect from a theory whose basic constituents are the doctrine of accommodation, the Platonic theory of Ideas, and Christian humanism.

In *Paradise Lost* the principle of analogy is based on the fact that in the epic world which Milton gives us there are definite ways in which earthly experience "may compare with

[3] "Milton and Critical Re-Estimates," *PMLA*, LXVI (1951), 1053.
[4] Ben F. Kimpel, *Language and Religion* (New York, 1957), p. 18.

Heaven" (V, 432). Heaven and Earth, Raphael asserts, may be "Each to other like, more then on earth is thought" (V, 576); and even if the correspondence should turn out to be figurative rather than literal, it is still possible to depict the transcendental realm by "lik'ning spiritual to corporal forms" (V, 573), and by "measuring things in Heav'n by things on Earth" (VI, 893). This principle explains, too, why Milton can employ epic similes to portray apocalyptic reality through earthly parallels.

Commentary on Milton's use of analogy as an apocalyptic technique has been overwhelmingly evaluative in approach. Perhaps the presence of the analogical principle in the poem has seemed so obvious that critics have felt justified in proceeding at once to judgment. The present discussion, eschewing evaluation in favor of description, is designed to trace the areas of analogy which the poem postulates between the apocalyptic and earthly realms. In this section I shall be concerned with sketching the categories of scenic details which both realms share, reserving for later chapter divisions the topics of the anthropomorphism of heavenly agents and the humanistic portrayal of Adam and Eve before the Fall.

The urban aspects of Heaven have frequently been noted by commentators, one of whom has called Heaven a city.[5] The emphasis has not been misplaced, for the image of the city is an important one in the description of Heaven in *Paradise Lost*. There are numerous references to the gates of Heaven,[6] and the impression of Heaven as an urban enclosure

[5] Brooks, *PMLA*, LXVI (1951), 1047, speaks of Eden as "a garden poised between two cities, Pandemonium and the City of God."

[6] I, 171, 326; II, 996; III, 515, 541; V, 198, 253, 254; VII, 206, 565, 575, 618; X, 22, 88; references to Heaven's doors appear at VII, 566; XI, 17.

is reinforced by descriptions of its walls.[7] References to Heaven's "Towrs"[8] and "Battlements" (II, 1049) complete the picture of its urban skyline. Further evidences of Heaven's urban character can be seen in such details as "Heav'ns pavement" (I, 682), "th' Empyreal road" (V, 253), "the rode of Heav'n" (IV, 976), "Pavilions" (V, 653), and "Gods Eternal house" (VII, 576), situated on "A broad and ample rode" (VII, 577). There is, finally, a set of ecclesiastical terms which constitute analogies between the earthly and heavenly realms—analogies which include such phenomena as a "Temple" (VI, 890; VII, 148), "Ministries" and "Rites" (VII, 149), "Censers" (VII, 600; XI, 24), and an "Alter" (II, 244; XI, 18).[9]

A specific facet of Heaven's civilized quality is the regal and courtly trappings which are in evidence there.[10] We

[7] II, 343, 1035; III, 71, 427, 503; VI, 860. The question of the exact shape of the heavenly enclosure has been disputed. The statement that Satan, viewing Heaven at a distance, sees "Farr off th' Empyreal Heav'n, extended wide / In circuit, undetermind square or round" (II, 1047–1048), is usually taken as evidence of Milton's uncertainty on the matter. Walter Clyde Curry, *Milton's Ontology, Cosmogony, and Physics* (Lexington, 1957), p. 156, pictures Heaven as circular. But H. F. Robins, "Satan's Journey: Direction in *Paradise Lost*," *JEGP*, LX (1961), 699–711, presents conclusive evidence that Heaven is square, with the ambiguity of description in Book II, 1047–1048, reflecting Satan's indistinct vision at so great a distance.

[8] I, 749; II, 62, 129, 1049; XII, 52.

[9] Malcolm M. Ross, *Poetry and Dogma* (New Brunswick, 1954), p. 224, regards these ecclesiastical images as evidence that Milton has given us "a sacramental Catholic heaven." J. B. Broadbent, *Some Graver Subject* (London, 1960), p. 157, counters the thesis of Ross with the correct conclusion that these images "come from the Jewish temple direct, not via a Roman cathedral."

[10] Heaven's regal structures and accoutrements have sometimes been criticized adversely. For some examples see H. A. Taine, *History*

read, for example, about "the Courts of God" (V, 650), and there are more than twenty references to the throne of God. When Satan views Heaven from afar he sees, atop the golden stairs, "The work as of a Kingly Palace Gate" (III, 505). We read also of God's "regal Scepter" (III, 339, 340; V, 816), and the angels wear "Crowns" (III, 352). The courtly trappings, in short, are a dominant strand in our impression of the heavenly scene, just as God's role as king is among the salient traits of his characterization, as we shall see presently.

Analogues between Heaven and earthly civilization become especially evident during the scenes depicting the war in Heaven. Rejecting the method of Thomas Heywood, who in his work entitled *The Hierarchie of the Blessed Angels* (1535) pictured a celestial battle in which such abstractions as insolence, spleen, humility, and reverence constituted the weapons, Milton gives us a battle conducted in consistently physical terms and often patterned on the details of epic battles found in his classical predecessors. His method has frequently been censured, and it is interesting to note that favorable criticism of Milton's handling of the war in Heaven has usually attempted its defense by allegorizing the concrete details of the account—by finding thematic ideas in the story rather than by remaining content to analyze the physical images themselves.[11] In the present context I am more con-

of English Literature, trans. H. Van Laun (New York, 1872), I, 447–449; Malcolm M. Ross, *Milton's Royalism: A Study in the Conflict of Symbol and Idea in the Poems* (Ithaca, 1943); Mark Van Doren, *The Noble Voice* (New York, 1946), p. 133; and R. J. Zwi Werblowsky, *Lucifer and Prometheus* (London, 1952), pp. 68–78.

[11] Helen Gardner's view, stated in *A Reading of Paradise Lost* (Oxford, 1965), p. 67, that "the War in Heaven itself is to be read as a fiction or parable shadowing truths" has been the assumption of most critics who discuss the battle sympathetically. The following studies all attempt, in one way or another, to establish the metaphoric or

cerned with the nature of the actual physical correspondence which exists between war as conducted in Heaven in *Paradise Lost* and on Earth.

The "Celestial Armourie" is composed of such recognizable earthly objects as "Shields, Helmes, and Speares" (IV, 553). When Satan is accosted by Gabriel's forces on the eve of his arrival in Paradise, the angelic squadron "began to hemm him round / With ported Spears" (IV, 979–80). Similarly, with the coming of morning in Heaven after the night of Satan's initial rebellion, the sun illuminates a battle scene replete with "Squadrons" (VI, 16), "Chariots" (VI, 17), and "Steeds" (VI, 17). As battle becomes joined the physical nature of the conflict is wholly dominant:

> Arms on Armour clashing bray'd
> Horrible discord, and the madding Wheeles
> Of brazen Chariots rag'd; dire was the noise
> Of conflict; over head the dismal hiss

thematic meaning of the episode: James Holly Hanford, "Milton and the Art of War," *SP*, XVIII (1921), 258–9; G. Wilson Knight, *Chariot of Wrath* (London, 1942); Dick Taylor, Jr., "The Battle in Heaven in *Paradise Lost*," *Tulane Studies in English*, III (1952), 69–92; Arnold Stein, *Answerable Style* (Minneapolis, 1953), pp. 17–37; J. H. Adamson, "The War in Heaven: Milton's Version of the *Merkabah*," *JEGP*, LVII (1958), 690–703; Joseph Summers, *The Muse's Method* (Cambridge, Mass., 1962), pp. 115–137; and B. A. Wright, *Milton's Paradise Lost* (New York, 1962), pp. 128–137.

If defenses of the celestial battle stress its metaphoric qualities, critical attacks usually center on the physical aspects. These include Samuel Johnson, *Lives of the English Poets*, ed. L. Archer-Hind (London, 1946), I, 108–109; Van Doren, *The Noble Voice*, pp. 122–147; A. J. A. Waldock, *Paradise Lost and Its Critics* (Cambridge, Eng., 1947), pp. 109–112; John Peter, *A Critique of Paradise Lost* (New York, 1960), pp. 63–84; and Wayne Shumaker, *Unpremeditated Verse* (Princeton, 1967), pp. 119–132.

> Of fiery Darts in flaming volies flew,
> And flying vaulted either Host with fire
> [VI, 209–214].

Michael brandishes a destructive metal "Sword" (VI, 250, 320) and bears "his ample Shield" (VI, 255). At the end of the first day of battle the scene in Heaven could as well describe an earthly battlefield:

> all the ground
> With shiverd armour strow'n, and on a heap
> Chariot and Charioter lay overturned
> And fierie foaming Steeds   [VI, 388–391].

The analogy between earthly and heavenly warfare reaches its most conspicuous point—and for many readers its nadir—with the introduction of gunpowder into the celestial conflict. The invention of gunpowder, while not a Renaissance achievement, was commonly adduced as an argument in favor of modern civilization in the Renaissance debate over the question of whether the ancients or the moderns were superior. Milton, then, could hardly have chosen a more contemporary phenomenon to attribute to Heaven.[12] It is the demonic host, of course, which first designs the cannon and gunpowder, and the event represents Milton's dramatization of another Renaissance commonplace, that the invention of such a weapon could belong only to Satan. Raphael makes the analogical principle in the account of the cannon clear when, in describing how the fallen angels rifled Heaven's soil for "Mineral and Stone" (VI, 517), he states regarding Eden, "nor

[12] Hanford, *SP*, XVIII, 232–266, demonstrates that Milton incorporates many elements of the theory and practice of contemporary warfare into his account. Harold H. Scudder, "Satan's Artillery," *N & Q*, CXCV (1950), 334–337, suggests further parallels between *Paradise Lost* and accounts of Renaissance battles.

hath this Earth / Entrails unlike" those of Heaven (VI, 516–517). The weapons which the demons devise are essentially those which belong to earthly warfare, being comprised of "Engins" (VI, 518, 586, 650) which are mounted "On Wheels" (VI, 573) and which eject "Balls / Of missive ruin" (VI, 518–519). On the climactic third day of the battle Christ rides forth in his apocalyptic chariot, which, despite all its nonempirical qualities, is still an analogue to earthly experience; it is a chariot, it contains wheels (VI, 750, 755, 832), and it is constructed of tangible minerals and stones (VI, 756–759). The battle in Heaven, it is obvious, furnishes numerous and consistent points of analogy between Earth and Heaven.

The civilized aspects of Heaven, seen in its urban character, courtly trappings, and military operations, are complemented by natural and geographic analogies to earthly experience. The heavenly terrain, for instance, contains much besides a city skyline. Heaven possesses "Plains" (I, 104), "Vales" (I, 321), and "fields" (II, 768). There are "Trees" (V, 426) and "vines" (V, 427), as well as a "wide Champain" (VI, 2). Heaven likewise has "hill" (VI, 25) and "soile" (VI, 510), minerals (VI, 511–512, 517), and "Mountains" (VII, 201). The celestial landscape also includes "Rocks, Waters, Woods" (VI, 645), and in mentioning the hills of Heaven Raphael explicitly states the actual analogy which exists between Heaven and Earth: "For Earth hath this variety from Heav'n / Of pleasure situate in Hill and Dale" (VI, 640–641).

Other natural phenomena are also shared by both Heaven and Earth. There are many references to thunder in Heaven.[13] In Raphael's narrative about events which occurred in Heaven

[13] I, 93, 258, 601; II, 166, 294; III, 393; V, 893; VI, 632, 713, 854; VII, 606.

he states, "Eevning now approach'd / (For wee have also our Eevning and our Morn . . .)" (V, 627–628). There are also "Clouds" (V, 642), "Dews" (V, 646), and "coole Winds" (V, 655) in Heaven. And the most salient characteristic of Heaven, its light, is one of the most significant of all analogues between Heaven and Earth. Even after we have distinguished heavenly from earthly light because of the former's greater intensity and because it is pure essential light rather than visible earthly light, the presence of light in Heaven keeps the celestial realm firmly rooted in the earthly experience which we know and which alone is intelligible to us.

When we shift our focus from Heaven to Eden we find a world which is as analogous to daily experience as Heaven was. The flora and fauna of the garden are essentially those of our own experience. Among the animals of Paradise are "the Lion" (IV, 343), "the Kid; Bears, Tygers, Ounces, Pards" (IV, 344), "th' unwieldy Elephant" (IV, 345), and "the Serpent" (IV, 347). In the Creation scene, too, we read about such specific animals as "the Moale" (VII, 467), "the swift Stag" (VII, 469), "The River Horse and scalie Crocodile" (VII, 474), and the "Bee" (VII, 490). It is a much more frequent technique of the narrator to name whole classes of animals rather than specific kinds. We read, for example, about "Foul . . . , / Cattel and Creeping things, and Beast of the Earth" (VII, 451–452), and about "Fowl, Fish, Beast" (VII, 503). The poet's technique here is simply to remind the reader of the general analogy which exists between the animal world before and after the Fall. Indeed, the animals of our own experience find their archetypes in the prelapsarian garden; as a result, we know already that the animals inhabiting the garden are those of ordinary reality, and in order to make his descriptions complete the poet needs do no more than mention such generalities as "Beast, Fish, and Fowle" (VIII, 341).

The analogy between vegetation in the garden and in our daily experience is likewise so evident that it requires no extensive comment here. Paradise has "Trees" (IV, 421), "fruit" (IV, 422), and "Flours" (IV, 438). Sometimes the descriptions become more specific, as when we read of "Laurel and Mirtle" (IV, 694), "*Iris* all hues, Roses, and Gessamin" (IV, 698), and "Violet, / Crocus, and Hyacinth" (IV, 700–701). Usually, however, the poet is content to name only the broad categories of flora, leaving the reader to fill in the picture with the details from empirical reality which he knows were present in Paradise.

Other natural phenomena in the garden are also, as we expect, much as those we observe every day. The geography includes "Groves" (V, 126) and "Field" (V, 136), "Hill" and "Lake" (V, 186). There are "Plains" (V, 143) and "Streams" (IV, 233), as well as "Lawns, or level Downs" (IV, 252). Also present in Paradise are "dew" (IV, 645, 653), "soft showers" (IV, 646), "Clouds" (V, 189), and "Winds" (V, 192). References to the sun, moon, and stars are too many to require specific mention here, as are references to day and night and the seasons. The garden is a totally recognizable locale; it could be nothing else. Like Heaven, Paradise adheres consistently to the principle of analogy, which constitutes one of Milton's chief apocalyptic techniques. The critical disparagement of this technique has been rather irrelevant and misguided. To argue that in the portrayal of apocalyptic reality "analogies between Heaven and Earth should be avoided" [14] is to say virtually that we should have no poem at

[14] Peter, *A Critique of Paradise Lost*, p. 17.

all. The poet who is portraying apocalyptic reality can qualify, negate, and distance the empirical images which he uses, but unless there is first a foundation of analogy established between the known and unknown worlds the apocalyptic vision ceases to be intelligible.

ANTHROPOMORPHISM

Milton's introduction of God into his apocalyptic vision as a speaking character has, along with the portrayal of Satan in the poem, received more critical attention than any other aspect of *Paradise Lost*. The commentary on the subject has usually considered, in one way or another, the question of whether Milton's God is portrayed as a character with whom the reader can sympathize. This kind of evaluative criticism has long plagued Milton scholarship; from the time of Samuel Johnson to the present day Milton's poetry has been judged, sometimes favorably but more often adversely, on the basis of the reader's personal response to the content of the poetry. Instead of attempting to record my satisfactions and dissatisfactions regarding the portrayal of God and the angels in *Paradise Lost*, I wish to describe the human physical traits, mental qualities, and roles which characterize the heavenly agents in Milton's apocalyptic world.

Although Paradise Lost contains no single descriptive passage depicting God as a total physical being, there are many ascriptions of individual human parts to the Deity. Beelzebub, for example speaks of God's "Potent arm" (II, 318). References to God's hand are much more frequent. The Son's position at the Father's "right hand" is mentioned at least six times,[15] and the Son's hand is specifically named twice (VI, 683, 762). In speaking of God's bounty Adam reminds Eve

[15] III, 279; V, 606; VI, 747, 892; X, 64; XII, 457.

that they "at his hand / Have nothing merited" (IV, 417–418), while Raphael speaks of the gifts which the angels receive from God's "copious hand" (V, 641). Similarly, Adam thanks God that he "with hands so liberal / . . . hast provided all things" (VIII, 362–363). During the war in Heaven Abdiel thwarts Satan with the assertion that God could have defeated him "with solitarie hand" (VI, 139). God's hand is also mentioned several times in connection with his Creation of the world. In circumscribing the universe the Creator "in his hand / . . . took the golden Compasses" (VII, 224–225), and the motions of the heavens are said to have begun when "the great first-Movers hand / First wheeld thir course" (VII, 500–501). Adam speaks of God's "creating hand" (IX, 344), while Satan, in viewing Adam and Eve, mentions "The hand that formd them" (IV, 365). We read, too, about how God "with his hands" formed Eve from Adam's rib (VIII, 469), and about how "Under his forming hands a Creature grew" (VIII, 470). Yet another function of God symbolized by the image of his hand is his providential guidance of all that happens. Thus Adam speaks of the decrees which God's "hand" executes (X, 772), and he states his willingness to submit "to the hand of Heav'n" (XI, 372). In such references to God's hand, as with many of the references to other bodily members, Milton's anthropomorphism takes the form of the rhetorical figure of synecdoche, in which a whole person is designated by one of its parts or aspects.[16]

There are also a number of references to God's face. Regarding the Son we read that "in his face / Divine compassion visibly appeerd" (III, 140–141). Similarly, the Son looks for-

[16] Shumaker, *Unpremeditated Verse*, pp. 91–103, undertakes a comprehensive analysis of the figures of synecdoche and metonymy in Books III and IV of the poem in terms of the affective attitudes embodied in these figures.

ward to the time when he, after his incarnation and final conquest of evil, can "return, / Father, to see thy face" (III,
261–262), while the angels sing to the Father about how
Christ's offer to redeem fallen man ended "the strife / Of
Mercy and Justice in thy face discern'd" (III, 406–407). In
his soliloquy of despair after the Fall Adam speaks of how his
sin hides him "from the face / Of God" (X, 723); and when
contemplating his expulsion from Paradise he laments that he
from God's "face . . . shall be hid, deprivd / His blessed
count'nance" (XI, 316–317). Elsewhere the Son predicts that
the Father "out of Heaven shalt look down and smile" (III,
257), and Adam speaks of "the Brow of God" (XI, 880).

Other bodily members are also attributed to God. His ability to speak is dramatized many times in the poem. On one occasion God's speech is preceded by the narrator's statement
that the Father "to his Son audibly spake" (VII, 518), and
there are seventeen references to the "voice" of God.[17] God's
ear is mentioned when the Father states that his "ear shall not
be slow" (III, 193) and when Raphael describes how the harmony of Heaven is so pleasing "that Gods own ear / Listens
delighted" (V, 626–627). The Son implores the Father to
"bend thine eare / To supplication" (XI, 30–31), and later
Adam asserts that he thought he saw God "placable and
mild, / Bending his eare" to Adam's prayer (XI, 151–152).
God's olfactory sense is established when we read that in the
morning in Paradise

> all things that breath,
> From th' Earths great Altar send up silent praise
> To the Creator, and his Nostrils fill
> With grateful Smell [IX, 194–197].

[17] III, 9, 710; VI, 27, 56, 782; VIII, 486; IX, 653; X, 33, 97, 116, 119,
146, 615, 729, 779; XI, 321; XII, 235.

Yet another physical member is attributed to God when Adam states that he fell in adoration at God's "feet" (VIII, 315).

The most frequently mentioned of God's physical parts is his eye. Belial, in arguing against Moloch's proposal to attack Heaven, states that force or guile cannot be perpetrated against a God "whose eye / Views all things at one view" (II, 189-190). In Book III we read that God "bent down his eye / His own works . . . to view" (III, 58-59), and the Father states that his "eye" will not be shut to man's prayer, repentance, and obedience (III, 193). The "unsleeping eyes of God" (V, 647) are all that do not rest at night in Heaven, while his "Eternal eye" (V, 711) sees the rebellion of Satan unfold. After the Fall of man the event "Was known in Heav'n; for what can scape the Eye / Of God All-seeing" (X, 5-6); and when Sin and Death invade the Earth the action is surveyed by "th' Almightie seeing" (X, 613). And in Michael's vision we read that God, wearied by the sins of men, averts "His holy Eyes" (XII, 109).

Taken together, the passages referring to God's physical parts would yield a rather complete composite human figure. As they appear in the poem, however, the allusions to individual human parts in any given passage tend to concentrate on separate physical members, never encouraging us to visualize God as a total human form. Adam speaks of God's having often "Stood visible" (XI, 321) among the trees of Paradise, but despite the consistent portrayal of God in anthropomorphic images we are not intended to respond to Adam's description with a visualized conception of God as a human being. References to individual physical parts are designed to describe concretely and symbolically specific functions of God; a reference to his hand depicts vividly his bestowal of bounty or his creative craftsmanship, just as a reference to his eye conveys a sense of his omniscience and an allusion to his ear expresses with immediacy his response to man's prayers or to events on Earth. References to individual body members also act as instances of synecdoche, in which a physical part stands for the whole divine person. The effect of the portrayal of God in human terms is not a composite human form but a series of anthropomorphic fragments, each describing concretely a function of the Deity or suggesting his whole being.

By contrast, a unified physical conception of the angels is to a much greater extent forced upon us, largely because the battle in Heaven requires warriors which we can visualize and because Milton was at pains to dramatize his view of angels as substantial beings. Let us look first at the warring angels in Heaven. The physical nature of the angels is implied in the description of the event which prompted Satan's rebellion, the appointment of the Son as head of the heavenly host. At the time of the appointment the Father states that to the Son "shall bow / All knees in Heav'n" (V, 607–608). The sensory qualities of the angels emerge also from the statement that at night they "slept / Fannd with coole Winds" (V, 655), and the anthropomorphic picture is continued when Satan, instigating the rebellion, asks a companion, "what sleep can close / Thy eyelids?" (V, 673–674). Abdiel predicts that Satan can expect to feel God's thunder "on thy head" (V, 893). Our visualization of the angels as complete bodies is strengthened by descriptions of their military armor, which is comprised of such recognizable items as "Swords" (VI, 304), "Helmets . . . and Shields" (VI, 83), and "Plate and Maile" (VI, 368).

In actual combat the warring spirits raise their weapons and deliver strokes (VI, 189, 317) much as human warriors have done. A physical conception is also borne upon us by the account of how Michael's sword wounded Satan's "right side" (VI, 327), as well as by the description of "humor issuing . . . / Sanguin" from the wound (VI, 332–333). Moloch becomes "Down clov'n to the waste" (VI, 361), while the presence of angelic facial features can be inferred from Nisroc's "cloudie . . . aspect" (VI, 450) and Satan's "look compos'd" (VI, 469). "Innumerable hands" (VI, 508) dig up the soil in Heaven, and the cannon balls shot by the rebel angels knock their opponents off balance, so that "none on thir feet might stand" (VI, 592). The faithful angels retaliate by taking uprooted hills "in thir hands" (VI, 646) and throwing them at Satan's forces. Unlike the anthropomorphic portrayal of God, then, where the human images are limited to a few basic physical members embodying specific divine functions, the physical descriptions of the warring angels include a greater variety of bodily traits; and since these bodies are visualized in action, the result is a visual perception of the angels as bodies approximating human form.

The same kind of comprehensive correspondence between the forms of angels and men emerges from Raphael's discourse to Adam about the precise nature of angelic substance, diet, and digestion. The heavenly visitor first broaches the subject when, upon his arrival in Paradise, Adam is somewhat apologetic about offering Raphael a dinner of earthly fruits because of his uncertainty whether his guest is accustomed to such a diet. The angel relieves his host of embarrassment by explaining that earthly food

> may of purest Spirits be found
> No ingrateful food: and food alike those pure
> Intelligential substances require

> As doth your Rational; and both contain
> Within them every lower facultie
> Of sense, whereby they hear, see, smell, touch, taste,
> Tasting concoct, digest, assimilate,
> And corporeal to incorporeal turn   [V, 406–413].

This exposition of angelic composition and sustenance is later dramatized when Raphael and Adam both

> to thir viands fell, nor seemingly
> The Angel, nor in mist, the common gloss
> Of Theologians, but with keen dispatch
> Of real hunger   [V, 434–437].

To an even greater extent than with the portrayal of God, then, the angels are presented as beings who possess many physical analogies to humans.

Human mental qualities and emotions are also attributed to the heavenly agents in *Paradise Lost*. Satan, for example, speaks of God's "excess of joy" (I, 123) after having vanquished the rebel angels. When God speaks in Heaven he diffuses "Sense of new joy ineffable" among the angels (III, 137). The angels are pictured as "uttering joy" (III, 347) and spending "Thir happie hours in joy" (III, 417). They are also said to be "rejoycing in thir joy" (V, 641), and when Christ's chariot appears in battle the angels experience "unexpected joy" (VI, 774).

Love, too, is an emotion shared by men and celestial beings alike. The Son demonstrates "Divine compassion" (III, 141) and "Love without end" (III, 142), and his "Heav'nly love" (III, 298) is said to be "unexampl'd love, / Love no where to be found less then Divine" (III, 410–411). Even Satan acknowledges "Heav'ns free Love dealt equally to all" (IV, 68). So, too, with the angels. The Father states that he created the angels with free choice so that they might give "proof . . . sincere / Of . . . Love" (III, 103–104). The angels are also said to perform "acts of Zeale and Love" (V, 593), and they celebrate "Festivals of joy and love" (VI, 94). Raphael tells Adam that the faithful angels "freely love, as in our will / To love or not" (V, 539–540). And there is the well known matter of the angels' love making (VIII, 618–629), which constitutes an analogy to human romantic love.[18]

There is also anger in Heaven. References by the fallen angels to God's wrath are numerous. Satan boasts that God's "wrath or might" (I, 110) will never extort submission from him, and elsewhere he speaks of God's "rage" (I, 95, 175), "his vengeful ire" (I, 148), and "the angry Victor" (I, 169). After causing the Fall of man Satan fears what God's "wrauth / Might suddenly inflict" (X, 340–341). Moloch speaks of the demons as "Vassals of his anger" (II, 90), while Belial mentions the "rage" (II, 144), "ire" (II, 155), and "anger" (II, 158, 211) of the demons' "angry Foe" (II, 152). It is true, of course, that the statements of the fallen angels in Hell are enveloped in irony, so that their version of the war in Heaven cannot be accepted as the truth unless it is corroborated by details elsewhere in the poem. In regard to the anger of God such corroboration appears in remarks which both God and the faithful angels make.

---

[18] E. L. Marilla, "Milton on Conjugal Love Among the Heavenly Angels," *MLN*, LXVIII (1953), 485–6, argues that the romantic love which the angels enjoy must be understood in terms of Renaissance Platonism and that such love consists of a spiritualized union of the lovers, such as we find in Donne's "The Extasie." Don Cameron Allen, "Milton and the Love of Angels," *MLN*, LXXVI (1961), 489–490, supports Marilla's thesis by citing a Renaissance statement which attributes this type of love to angels.

In the inter-trinitarian dialogue in Book III the Son asks that the Father let his "anger fall" on him (III, 237). After his vicarious satisfaction for the sins of men the Son anticipates returning to Heaven and seeing the Father's face,

> wherein no cloud
> Of anger shall remain, but peace assur'd,
> And reconcilement; wrauth shall be no more
>
> [III, 262–264].

The Father replies by commending the Son for having offered to save "mankind under wrauth" (III, 275). The angels, too, praise the Son for undertaking to appease God's "wrauth" (III, 406). When Christ embarks upon the defeat of the rebel angels his face becomes "full of wrauth bent on his Enemies" (VI, 826). After the Fall Adam is fully conscious of God's wrath upon his sin (X, 795, 802, 834; XI, 878; XII, 478), and the epic narrator likewise speaks of God's wrath (I, 220; IX, 10). The angels exhibit the same kind of "inextinguishable rage" (VI, 217) against the forces of evil, and during the war in Heaven "Rage prompted" the good angels to retaliation (VI, 635). The righteous anger of God and his angels emerges as one of their dominant emotions. Their anger is retributory in nature; it is not, however, a desire for personal revenge, but is rather the working out of divine justice. It is not selfishly vindictive anger but the operation of a general moral order which the evildoer sets in motion through desert of punishment.[19]

[19] Although not specifically concerned with Milton, Edwyn Bevan's discussion of the topic of "The Wrath of God" in *Symbolism and Belief* (Boston, 1957; first pub., 1938), pp. 206–251, is relevant to a consideration of *Paradise Lost* and should be required reading for critics of the poem. Without enlisting religious dogma or revelation as support, Bevan argues that retributive anger need not be personally

Laughter constitutes yet another emotion which the celestial agents share with humans. Heavenly laughter is scornful rather than joyous. When Satan, enroute to Paradise, is accosted by the allegorical figure Sin, the latter pictures God as one "who sits above and laughs the while" (II, 731). In the altercation in Eden between Gabriel and Satan, Gabriel "Disdainfully half smiling . . . repli'd" to Satan's taunts (IV, 903). Zephon, too, answers "scorn with scorn" while arguing with Satan (IV, 834). During the war in Heaven the Son says to the Father:

> Mightie Father, thou thy foes
> Justly hast in derision, and secure
> Laugh'st at thir vain designes   [V, 735–737].

And when Adam in his vision of fallen history sees the confusion at the Tower of Babel we read that "great laughter was in Heav'n" (XII, 59).

Heaven is recognizably empirical, not only because of the human physical traits and emotions which we find there, but also because of the roles of celestial agents which are analo-

---

vindictive but is ideally the operation of the justice which a moral order imposes upon evil desert. Both the good and bad kinds of punitive anger "imply a desire that someone should suffer or should go without some kind of good; they may imply the will actually to inflict the suffering, as when a strong man seeing a child ill-treated might strike the ill treater; only in one case the desire is based on the perception of appropriateness in justice; and in the other case, it is a desire for personal revenge" (p. 216). Although this thesis would not settle the question of what kind of anger God exhibits in *Paradise Lost*, it at least has the value of correcting the popular misconception that retributive anger is perforce bad.

For good discussions of wrath in Heaven in *Paradise Lost*, see Irene Samuel, *Dante and Milton* (Ithaca, 1966), pp. 176–184; and Dennis H. Burden, *The Logical Epic* (Cambridge, Mass., 1967), pp. 34–40.

gous to human roles. These roles are embodied in the poem both in the characteristic actions of the agents and the titles or epithets which are applied to them. The relationship between the Father and the Son, for example, is expressed in terms of human familial roles. These roles are established in the poem by the Son's obedience to the Father's authority and by the approximately one hundred references to the titles "Father" and "Son." Similarly, God's role as king is dramatized by references to his courtly trappings, such as a throne, scepter, and court. We hear also about God's "Empire" (I, 114), "his Regal State" (I, 640), and his "Kingdom" (VI, 815). There is also a whole cluster of epithets denoting God's kingship, including more than thirty references to him as "King" and over fifteen as "Lord." [20]

Military roles furnish another point of similarity between human and apocalyptic experience. Heaven is replete with "Squadrons" (VI, 16, 251), "Legions" (VI, 64, 142, 230), and "Watches" (VI, 412). There are "Bands / Of Angels under watch" (V, 287–288), and the very role of "Warriours" (VI, 537) names an essentially human military role. A kind of celestial military hierarchy is implied when the Father sends his forces to battle with the words:

> Go *Michael* of Celestial Armies Prince,
> And thou in Military prowess next
> *Gabriel*, lead forth to Battel these my Sons
>
> [VI, 44–46].

[20] For further comment on epithets denoting kingship applied to God, see Kester Svendsen, "Epic Address and Reference and the Principle of Decorum in *Paradise Lost*," *PQ*, XXVIII (1949), 200–205. Svendsen concludes that "the dozens of king-images and power-images in the epithets for the Son and the Father" confirm kingship as one of the dominant elements in their characterization.

When Christ appears in his chariot *"Michael* soon reduc't / His Armie" under Christ's conduct (VI, 777–778), and the Son subsequently returns "Sole Victor from th' expulsion of his Foes" (VI, 880). All of these passages give evidence that Heaven possesses a military complex which is in many ways analogous to earthly experience.

The anthropomorphism of heavenly agents in *Paradise Lost,* consisting of physical traits, emotions, and roles which are analogous to our own experience, has been variously judged by readers of the poem. Samuel Johnson evaded discussion of the topic with the excuse that God is "such as it is irreverence to name on slight occasions." [21] Coleridge believed that Milton "was very wise in adopting the strong anthropomorphism of the Hebrew Scriptures at once," [22] and Thomas Macaulay likewise felt that "Of all the poets who have introduced into their works the agency of supernatural beings, Milton has succeeded the best." [23] The dominant critical tradition, however, has been one of derogation of Milton's depiction of God as a character and his bold use of anthropomorphism.[24]

While it is outside the scope of this study to evaluate the aesthetic success of anthropomorphism in *Paradise Lost,* our

---

[21] *Lives of the English Poets,* l, 101.

[22] "Lecture on Milton and the Paradise Lost," in *Coleridge on the Seventeenth Century,* ed. Roberta Brinkley (Durham, 1955), p. 591.

[23] *Essay on Milton,* ed. Herbert A. Smith (Boston, 1898), p. 21.

[24] For some representative unfavorable remarks on the anthropomorphism of *Paradise Lost,* see the following critics: C. S. Lewis, *A Preface to Paradise Lost* (New York, 1961; first pub., 1942), pp. 130–131; Van Doren, *The Noble Voice,* pp. 131–140; Waldock, *Paradise Lost and Its Critics,* pp. 97–106; Peter, *A Critique of Paradise Lost,* pp. 17–18; Roy Daniells, *Milton, Mannerism and Baroque* (Toronto, 1963), p. 174; and Marjorie Nicolson, *John Milton: A Reader's Guide to His Poetry* (New York, 1963), pp. 223–227.

understanding of its place in Milton's design will be fuller if we grasp the reasons for Milton's use of anthropomorphism in presenting his supernatural agents. In the first place, Milton's basic themes demanded that he present the Deity as acting directly in the story. Since Milton's concern was to tell how evil first entered a world which God had created good, he could not, as Pope did in the *Essay on Man*, postulate God as the first cause and conduct his theodicy as an exposition about evil as it exists in the world now; and since his theme revolved around God's active Providence in the world, he could not, as Dante did in *The Divine Comedy*, present God as the object of spiritual devotion by a protagonist who is the poet himself.[25] A second cause underlying the anthropomorphism of *Paradise Lost* is the epic tradition itself, which included among its generic characteristics the inclusion in the story of supernatural agents who operate at least partly under human laws.[26] But the main reason for the anthropomorphism of *Paradise Lost* is the theological tradition of analogy, a tradition based on biblical example and developed through centuries of theological and exegetical writing. The *via negativa* has

[25] John M. Steadman, "The God of *Paradise Lost* and the *Divina Commedia*," *Archiv fur das Studium der Neueren Sprachen*, CXCV (1959), 273–289, discusses Milton's portrayal of God as being answerable to his theme of Providence. Mr. Steadman's essay is in every way one of the most satisfactory discussions of Milton's God that I have seen.

[26] Douglas Bush, *John Milton* (New York, 1964), has emphasized that Milton's anthropomorphism is conditioned by epic demands, attributing his technique to "the concrete heroic mold" of his fable (p. 153) and to "epic anthropomorphism" (p. 156). Allan Gilbert, "Form and Matter in *Paradise Lost*, Book III, *JEGP*, LX (1961), 51, likewise argues that "Little else than human conduct is possible when divine beings become actors in epic poetry." On generic considerations see also the article by Steadman cited in the preceding note.

always been balanced by the way of affirmation. John Donne speaks of the two ways of approach to God in this manner: "Sometimes we represent God by Subtraction, by Negation, by saying, God is that, which is not mortall, not passible, nor moveable: Sometimes we present him by Addition; by adding our bodily lineaments to him, and saying, that God hath hands, and feet, and eares, and eyes; and adding our affections, and passions to him, and saying that God is glad, or sorry, angry, or reconciled." [27] Milton, in *De Doctrina Christiana*, likewise speaks of describing God "partly in an affirmative, partly in a negative sense" (*Works*, XIV, 53). The theological tradition of knowing God through analogy to human experience appears in its most specific form, of course, in the doctrine of accommodation. If Milton's epic embodies anthropomorphism to an unusual extent, it is a reflection of his version of the theory of accommodation; for as noted in the analysis of the theoretic considerations underlying Milton's apocalyptic vision, his view of biblical accommodation was extraordinarily literal. Since in Milton's view man is like God "not only as to his soul, but also as to his outward form" (*Works*, XIV, 35), his portrayal of supernatural agents in *Paradise Lost* could not possibly have escaped reflecting his thorough embracing of anthropomorphism.

[27] *The Sermons of John Donne*, ed. Evelyn M. Simpson and George R. Potter (Berkeley, 1956), VIII, 54. For a discussion of the views of Aquinas on knowing God through analogy, see Robert L. Patterson, *The Conception of God in the Philosophy of Aquinas* (London, 1933), pp. 227–257. Bevan, *Symbolism and Belief*, pp. 25–26, argues that all religions, including those which "deny that God is an individual person in the way a man is, . . . form their idea of God out of elements which we know only as constituents of a human personality, and can imagine only as belonging to a personality analogous to man's."

HUMANISM

The depiction of Adam and Eve in their prelapsarian condition conforms in many ways to human existence after the Fall. Physically there is a nearly total similarity between unfallen and fallen experience. Although descriptions of Adam and Eve in the poem tend to be conceptual in nature, a visual picture of the human pair does emerge, and it is a wholly recognizable portrait of humanity. In the first description of the couple we read:

> His fair large Front and Eye sublime declar'd
> Absolute rule; and Hyacinthin Locks
> Round from his parted forelock manly hung
> Clustring, but not beneath his shoulders broad:
> Shee as a vail down to the slender waste
> Her unadorned golden tresses wore
> Dissheveld, but in wanton ringlets wav'd
> [IV, 300-306].

The physical aspect of prelapsarian humanity is portrayed again in Eve's description of her awakening after Creation. In this scene Adam tells Eve that she has been made from "His flesh, his bone" (IV, 483), and a few lines later we read that Eve

> half imbracing leand
> On our first Father, half her swelling Breast
> Naked met his under the flowing Gold
> Of her loose tresses hid   [IV, 494-497].

As with the natural phenomena in the garden, the physical nature of Adam and Eve is so much a part of the reader's expectations that it is largely taken for granted rather than established in frequent or extended descriptive passages.

When we move from the human physical characteristics of Adam and Eve to matters of emotions and roles, we are at once struck by the relative absence of analogues to fallen experience. As noted in the earlier discussion of negation as an apocalyptic technique in the poem, prelapsarian life in the Garden of Eden is devoid of many of the emotions and activities of civilized life as we know it. William Hazlitt stated that before the Fall "there are none of the every-day occurrences, contentions, disputes, wars, fightings. . . . There is none of the fierceness of intemperate passion, none of the agony of mind and turbulence of action." [28] What we find, I believe, is that Adam and Eve are involved in three basic relationships—with God, with each other, and with the Creation as it appears in the Garden of Eden. The emotions or attitudes which correspond to these roles are worship of God, love of each other, and governance of the garden.

The marital relationship of Adam and Eve is consistently presented in terms similar to those used to describe the institution of marriage in human civilization. We read, for example, about "wedded Love" (IV, 750), "the Nuptial Bowre" (VIII, 510), Eve's "nuptial Bed" (IV, 710), and "the bridal Lamp" (VIII, 520). When God first presents Eve to Adam she is not "uninformed / Of nuptial Sanctitie and marriage Rites" (VIII, 486–487). Together the human partners are "Man and Wife" (X, 101), a "Fair couple, linkt in happie nuptial League" (IV, 339). Adam is Eve's "Husband" (VIII, 52), just as Eve is called Adam's "fair Spouse" (IV, 742). In

[28] "On Shakespeare and Milton," in *Milton Criticism: Selections from Four Centuries*, ed. James Thorpe (New York, 1950), pp. 111–112.

keeping with biblical precept and Puritan belief, Adam is the
"Head" of the marriage (IV, 443), and Adam wins Eve by a
process of wooing (IV, 304–311, 465–491).[29]

Milton's humanistic bent is nowhere more in evidence than
in his attribution of physical love to the prelapsarian marriage
relationship. Going counter to a long patristic tradition which
viewed sexual consummation as a result of the Fall,[30] Milton
makes it a norm of perfect marriage. As a result, *Paradise
Lost* contains a number of passages describing the "endearing
smiles" (IV, 337) and "youthful dalliance" (IV, 338) of
Adam and Eve. We read about "soft imbraces" (IV, 471),
"conjugal attraction" (IV, 493), and "kisses pure" (IV, 502).
When narrating Adam and Eve's night in the bower the narrator insists on unfallen sexuality at some length:

> nor turnd I weene
> *Adam* from his fair Spouse, nor *Eve* the Rites
> Mysterious of connubial Love refus'd:
> Whatever Hypocrites austerely talk
> Of puritie and place and innocence,
> Defaming as impure what God declares

[29] The passage in Book IV, 465ff., in which the newly created Eve
is more attracted by her own reflection in the water than by the
appearance of Adam, is regarded by many critics as evidence of Eve's
narcissism and vanity. Burden, *The Logical Epic*, pp. 83–85, offers the
best interpretation of the episode which I have seen, arguing that
"what Milton establishes with the episode is that since Adam proceeded to follow her and of his own will claimed her as his wife,
and since Eve . . . accepted him as her husband, their marriage was
based on consent which was a necessary part of marriage. . . . Dramatizing the idea of the helpmeet and defining the institution of
marriage, it shows Eve's . . . need for instruction."

[30] The tradition is discussed by Mary Irma Corcoran, *Milton's
Paradise with Reference to the Hexameral Background* (Washington,
D.C., 1945), p. 76; and by Arnold Williams, *The Common Expositor*
(Chapel Hill, 1948), p. 88.

Pure and commands to som, leaves free to all,
Our Maker bids increase, who bids abstain
But our destroyer, foe to God and Man?
Haile wedded Love, mysterious Law. . . . .
Farr be it, that I should write thee sin or blame,
Or think thee unbefitting holiest place,
Perpetual Fountain of Domestic sweets,
Whose bed is undefil'd and chaste pronounc't,
Present, or past, as Saints and Patriarchs us'd
[IV, 741–750, 757–762].

Prelapsarian love receives additional emphasis in the poem by being presented as the psychological motivation for Adam's fall, with the susceptibility to uxoriousness which Adam evinces in his conversation with Raphael (VIII, 521–559) culminating in the statement at the time of Adam's fall that he ate of the fruit "fondly overcome with Female charm" (IX, 999). The prelapsarian relationship of Adam and Eve, then, is essentially humanistic in its portrayal, both in its insistence on the presence of physical love and its portrayal in images taken from the institution of civilized marriage.[31]

The dominion which Adam and Eve exercise over the rest of the Creation takes the form of their role as keepers of the garden. It is their only vocation, undertaken in a honeymoon mood and differing from postlapsarian labor in being wholly

[31] William and Malleville Haller, "The Puritan Art of Love," *HLQ*, V (1942), 235–272, place Milton's views of marriage in a context of contemporary Puritan thought, concluding that "Milton was merely presenting in the poetic idiom of *Paradise Lost* what most men and women in his day, certainly most Puritans, thought about marriage, had often heard from the pulpit, and could have read in a large number of edifying books." Cf. also the two articles by Dudley R. Hutcherson, both published in *University of Mississippi Studies in English*, entitled "Milton's Eve and Other Eves," I (1960), 12–31; and "Milton's Adam as a Lover," II (1961), 1–11.

pleasurable—a "delightful task" (IV, 437) and "pleasant labour" (IV, 625), as Adam calls it. This role is Milton's dramatization of another Puritan conviction, the dignity of performing the work to which God calls people, and a great deal of Puritan sentiment is summed up in Adam's statement that "Man hath his daily work of body or mind / Appointed, which declares his Dignitie" (IV, 618–619). As Adam's statement suggests, the work of gardening is not only physical but mental, a means of praising the God who has given them the ability to work and of demonstrating their love to God by obeying his mandate to subdue the Earth.

Slight and unvaried as the role of tending the garden may seem, the importance that Adam and Eve ascribe to it is considerable. In one of our first glimpses of the human pair, we see them resting at the end of the day, "after no more toil / Of thir sweet Gardening labour" remained (IV, 327–328). As they sit conversing after their supper, Adam says to Eve:

> But let us ever praise him, and extoll
> His bountie, following our delightful task
> To prune these growing Plants, and tend these Flours,
> Which were it toilsom, yet with thee were sweet
> [IV, 436–439].

Later Adam suggests that they retire for the night, reminding Eve that they need "repose, since God hath set / Labour and rest" (IV, 611–612). "Other Creatures," Adam continues, "all day long / Rove unimployed, and less need rest" (IV, 616–617). By contrast, Adam states:

> To morrow ere fresh Morning streak the East
> With first approach of light, we must be ris'n,
> And at our pleasant labour, to reform

> Yon flourie Arbors, yonder Allies green,
> Our walk at noon, with branches overgrown
>   [IV, 623–627].

And as they stand in front of their lodge before retiring,
Adam and Eve praise God for having made

>   the Day,
>   Which we in our appointed work imployd
>   Have finisht happie in our mutual help
>   And mutual love   [IV, 725–728].

Daily work in the garden, as in fallen experience, influences
not only the time of retirement but also the time of rising, for
Adam rouses Eve with the words:

>   Awake, the morning shines, and the fresh field
>   Calls us, we lose the prime, to mark how spring
>   Our tended Plants.   [V, 20–22].

Later Adam urges that they "to our fresh imployments rise"
(V, 125), and subsequently "On to thir mornings rural work
they haste / Among sweet dewes and flours" (V, 211–212).
On the day of the Fall, too, the couple

>   commune how that day they best may ply
>   Thir growing work: for much thir work outgrew
>   The hands dispatch of two Gardning so wide
>   [IX, 201–203].

And efficiency of labor constitutes the subject matter in the
ensuing debate (IX, 205ff.). The vocation of gardening, then,
represents the second role attributed to Adam and Eve, and its
importance in the poem exceeds what the lack of variety
might lead us to expect.

The relationship between the human pair and their Creator
yields a picture of worship which is basically similar to post-

lapsarian religious experience. In one of the more fruitful approaches to the poem, one commentator has suggested that its entire theme is "the epic spectacle of the Human-Divine relationship," by which he means "the poet's sustained and ordered awareness in his Poem of man's inescapable connections with Deity." [32] The implications of this thesis touch upon many aspects of *Paradise Lost;* in the present discussion I wish to observe only that the prelapsarian relationship between the human couple in Paradise and God is presented in images and terms which are often analogous to postlapsarian religious experience. Paradisal religious devotion for example, is described in an essentially ecclesiastical and devotional idiom in passages which speak of the "Rites" (IV, 736), "Orisons" (V, 145), "contemplation" (V, 511), and "vocal Worship" (IX, 198) of Adam and Eve. In the mornings in Paradise all of the creatures breath "Thir morning incense" (IX, 194), and "From th' Earths great Altar send up silent praise" (IX, 195). We know, too, that before the Fall Adam was accustomed to raise "grateful Altars . . . / Of grassie Terfe" (XI, 323–324) and "thereon / Offer sweet smelling Gumms and Fruits and Flours" (XI, 326–327). In such passages both the worship and the idiom in which it is described constitute an experience analogous to religion in human experience.

Prelapsarian devotional experience centers in the act of praise to God. "Let us ever praise him, and extoll / His bountie" (IV, 436–437), Adam enjoins Eve. Eve responds by acknowledging that they "To him indeed all praises owe, / And

[32] Charles Monroe Coffin, "Creation and the Self in *Paradise Lost,*" *ELH*, XXIX (1962), 1–2. Corcoran, *Milton's Paradise with Reference to the Hexameral Background*, pp. 109–111, also has a good discussion of prelapsarian religious experience, concluding that "Milton gave first place among the special duties of man to those pertaining directly to his relations to God."

daily thanks" (IV, 444–445). Adam and Eve, before retiring at night, assert that they extol God's "goodness infinite, both when we wake, / And when we seek, as now, thy gift of sleep" (IV, 734–735). The religious response of the human pair consists of the "adoration pure / Which God likes best" (IV, 737–738). The dominant theme of Adam and Eve's well known morning hymn (V, 153–208) is the praise which the whole Creation owes to God, with the word "praise" appearing in the song no fewer than eight times. Adam's first response to his awakening consciousness after his creation is to ask how to "adore" his Creator (VIII, 280), and later he falls "In adoration" at God's feet (VIII, 315). Prelapsarian worship differs from that after the Fall chiefly by the absence of those elements of religion which deal with repentance, redemption, and forgiveness. In matters of praise, however, religious experience before the Fall is the same as that after the Fall, as the idiom of the poem suggests. Along with their physical traits and the roles of marriage and gardening, the religious worship of Adam and Eve in Paradise reflects the basic humanistic similarity between fallen and unfallen experience which Milton postulates in *Paradise Lost*.

❧ 6

Apocalypse through Distance

TECHNIQUES OF REMOTENESS

Milton's apocalyptic vision has often been assailed on the grounds that it is presented in a manner which is too direct and mundane. Milton, we are told, should have kept the apocalyptic realm veiled, should have suggested it obliquely instead of presenting it frontally. It is the burden of the present chapter to show how Milton achieved some of his most remarkable triumphs in precisely the area where critics have so grudgingly conceded even partial success, the area of distancing the apocalyptic vision from our direct view and maintaining the remoteness of the vision throughout *Paradise Lost*.

The response of critics to the presence of God as a speaking character in *Paradise Lost* is a typical example of how readers of the poem have seized upon Milton's anthropomorphic technique without observing how skillfully Milton distances the anthropomorphism after he has introduced it into his apocalyptic vision. Throughout the poem God's speaking is frequently portrayed as issuing, not from a person, but from a "voice." A representative instance of the technique occurs early in Book VI when Abdiel, after having deserted the camp of Satan and returned to God, is led to "the sacred hill" (VI, 25), where he stands "Before the seat supream" (VI, 27). God proceeds to speak words of commendation to Abdiel, but the anthropomorphic effect of God's speaking from his throne is significantly muted when the speech is preceded by the statement that from "the seat supream . . . a voice / From midst a Golden Cloud thus milde was heard" (VI, 27–28). God is not portrayed here as a person but as a disembodied voice, with the golden cloud veiling the Deity further in mystery. The veiled effect is heightened when the words of God to Abdiel are followed by the statement:

> So spake the Sovran voice, and Clouds began
> To darken all the Hill, and smoak to rowl
> In duskie wreathes, reluctant flames   [VI, 56–58].

The motif of God as a transcendent voice is maintained consistently throughout the poem. During God's act of Creation "*Confusion* heard his voice, and wilde uproar / Stood rul'd" (III, 710–711), and in a later account of the same event we read that "*Chaos* heard his voice" (VII, 221). In the invocation to light in Book III the epic narrator employs a similar idiom when he speaks of how light

>   at the voice
> Of God, as with a Mantle didst invest
> The rising world of waters dark and deep
>   [III, 9–11].

When Christ rides forth in his chariot on the third day of the celestial battle the dominant impression of him is not that of a person but of an unvisualized voice, as evidenced by the way in which the uprooted hills return to their accustomed places "At his command" (VI, 781), when "they heard his voice"

(VI, 782). Elsewhere in the poem we read that God to the angels "uttered thus his voice" (X, 615), and Michael informs Adam that "the voice of God / To mortal eare is dreadful" (XII, 235–236).

God's presence in the Garden of Eden is habitually portrayed in veiled fashion by representing him as an invisible voice. When Eve is first brought to Adam after her creation she is "Led by her Heav'nly Maker, though unseen, / And guided by his voice" (VIII, 485–486). God's command not to eat of the Tree of Knowledge is called "Sole Daughter of his voice" (IX, 653). After the Fall Adam and Eve are said to hear "the voice of God . . . / Now walking in the Garden" (X, 97–98), with the remoteness of the voice suggested by the statement that the sound is "by soft windes / Brought to thir Ears" (X, 98–99). Several lines later Adam explains his hiding from God on the grounds that "I heard thee in the Garden, and of thy voice / Affraid, being naked, hid my self" (X, 116–117). The response is not to a person but to a "voice." Christ answers Adam in the same terminology: "My voice thou oft hast heard, and hast not fear'd, / But still rejoyc't" (X, 119–120); and he reprimands Adam for having disobeyed God, for having obeyed Eve "Before his voice" (X, 146). After the Fall Adam recalls the "voice once heard / Delightfully, *Encrease and multiply*" (X, 729–730), and he remembers how "among these Pines his voice / I heard" (XI, 320–321). In similar manner, Adam soliloquizes in despair that death would be welcome, since then God's "dreadful voice no more / Would Thunder in my ears" (X, 779–780).

When God the Father dispatches the Son to judge Adam and Eve after the Fall, his speech is preceded by a description of God which is distanced and veiled in several ways at once; we read,

> the most High
> Eternal Father from his secret Cloud,
> Amist in Thunder utter'd thus his voice
>
> [X, 31-33].

We note, first of all, the familiar motif of presenting God as a voice rather than a person. The voice, moreover, is veiled from the angels as well as us by a "secret Cloud;" and our knowledge that the voice comes from the cloud couched "in Thunder" puts an additional veil between us and the voice. The final detail of remoteness in the description is the epithet "most High" applied to God, since in *Paradise Lost* height denotes not only a position on a moral and emotional scale, but a physical position as well, so that God's high position—"High Thron'd above all highth" (III, 58), in fact—is a suggestion of his physical remoteness from all his creatures.

The frequency with which Milton portrays God as a transcendent voice standing remotely behind all that occurs suggests the care with which he has sought to distance the Deity. The repetitions in God's speeches in the celestial dialogue in Book III are usually interpreted as God's arguing like a person, an unwelcome intrusion of human personality into a context which demands an absence of all that is human. But as I suggested earlier, a more tenable interpretation of the verbal repetitions in the speech would be to regard them as part of Milton's attempt to dramatize the principle of God as an impersonal voice by making patterns of sound, depending ultimately on oral reading for their effect, the basic ingredient of the poetic texture in the passage.

Very similar to the portrayal of God as a remote voice is the presentation of him as a "presence," sensed but not located precisely in space. When, for example, we read of the seven angels who stand "in Gods presence" (III, 649) we are aware of God's existence in a definite part of Heaven, but the Deity finally remains at an indistinct distance from us so far as any precise visualization is concerned. When Adam, recalling the occasion when God first placed him in the garden, speaks of how "among the Trees appeer'd / Presence Divine" (VIII, 313–314), we again sense God as a general presence rather than as a localized person. When God the Judge appears in Paradise to pass sentence on Adam and Eve after the Fall it is "from his presence" that they hide (X, 100); and when the Judge speaks to Adam we read that "the sovran Presence thus repli'd" (X, 144). Adam laments that after his expulsion from Paradise he will be absent from the place where God had "voutsaf'd" his "Presence Divine" (XI, 318–319), although Michael assures Adam that in the world outside of Paradise God is also present, "and of his presence" gives "many a signe / Still following thee" (XI, 351–352). And in the preview of history which Adam receives he sees the time when God withdraws "His presence" from among men (XII, 108). As with references to God as a voice, passages which describe him as a "presence" create a sense of God's active participation in the events of the poem without ever delineating him completely as a person.

A similar technique of distancing God from the reader's perspective consists of describing God as one who is seen by other characters in the poem—as a "sight" viewed by the angels or Adam. When we read, for example, about the "Spirits that stand / In sight of God's high Throne" (III, 654–655) and "th' Angelic Host that stand / In sight of God enthron'd" (V, 535–536), we are aware of the presence of God while any direct view of him is kept at a remote distance from us; for to be told that angels can see God is totally different from our seeing God directly. The same technique of presenting God as a "sight" perceived by others but only suggested to us as an indistinctly apprehended presence is repeated when we read that at God's "sight all the Starrs / Hide thir diminisht heads" (IV, 34–35), and when the rebel angels are said to be driven "from his sight" (VII, 185), with the latter passage implying the angel's sight of God as well as his sight of them. Adam, too, conveys to us a sense of God rather than a direct picture when he calls God "the Heav'nly vision" (VIII, 356). Along with the portrayal of God as a "voice" and a "presence," references to him as a "sight" experienced by other characters give us an impression of the existence of a Deity far removed from ordinary reality, and all three types of descriptions constitute individual ways by which Milton portrays the veiled God of *Paradise Lost*.

Another aspect of Milton's technique of indirection is his use of the traditional theological idea that God can be known through his Creation, which is a kind of extension of many of his qualities. Adam and Eve mention this principle of seeing God indirectly in his works in their morning hymn, where they assert that God

> sitst above these Heavens
> To us invisible or dimly seen
> In these thy lowest works   [V, 156–158].

Adam and Eve proceed to apply this principle in the hymn. They find that the universe is "wondrous fair" (V, 155) and believe this fairness to furnish a glimpse of "how wondrous then" God himself is (V, 155). The works of nature also "declare / Thy goodness beyond thought, and Power Divine" (V, 158–159). Similarly, God's Providential care over all his creatures named in the hymn is adduced as evidence that he is "bounteous" (V, 205). The indirectness of these descriptions of God's attributes stems from their being viewed not directly in God but in his Creation, which reflects in significant ways the qualities of God himself.

The entire role of God as Creator of the universe adheres to the technique of defining him through his works. The principle is stated explicitly in several passages. After Adam has asked about the nature of the movements of the heavenly bodies Raphael tells him that

> Heav'n
> Is as the Book of God before thee set,
> Wherein to read his wondrous Works, and learne
> His Seasons, Hours, or Dayes, or Months, or Yeares
> [VIII, 66–69].

Uriel, too, commends the desire

> to know
> The works of God, thereby to glorifie
> The great Work-Maister   [III, 694–696].

Statements that man is created "in the Image of God / Express" (VII, 527–528) and therefore bears the "resemblance" of the "Maker faire" (IX, 538) also imply the principle that by knowing man we know something of God. And Adam mentions the doctrine that God has revealed himself in his works when he says to Raphael:

> Well hast thou taught the way that might direct
> Our knowledge, and the scale of Nature set
> From center to circumference, whereon
> In contemplation of created things
> By steps we may ascend to God   [V, 508–512].

Applications of the principle that man can receive an oblique view of God's character by observing his Creation are as frequent as are the statements of the principle. Raphael, for instance, tells Adam,

> for the Heav'ns wide Circuit, let it speak
> The Makers high magnificence, who built
> So spacious, and his Line stretcht out so farr
> [VIII, 100–102].

"The swiftness of those Circles," Raphael continues, "attribute, / Though numberless, to his Omnipotence" (VIII, 107–108). Adam, in turn, describes to Raphael how after his creation he first knew of God's existence, goodness, and power by deducing the knowledge from the fact of his own existence. In the recollected experience Adam asks the Creation about him,

> fair Creatures, tell,
> Tell, if ye saw, how came I thus, how here?
> Not of my self; by some great Maker then,
> In goodness and in power praeeminent
> [VIII, 276–279].

Elsewhere Adam, in speaking to Eve, observes certain characteristics of God in the Paradisal surroundings:

> needs must the power
> That made us, and for us this ample World
> Be infinitly good, and of his good
> As liberal and free as infinite,
> That rais'd us from the dust and plac't us here
> In all this happiness [IV, 412–417].

The twenty-five epithets denoting God's role as "Maker" and the seventeen titles which speak of him as "Creator," as well as references to him as "Author of all being" (III, 374), "the great Architect" (VIII, 72), and "Author of this Universe" (VIII, 360), all characterize God indirectly by speaking of his attributes as they are discerned at a distance in the things which he has made. At one point or another in the poem, then, we learn about God's goodness, liberality, magnificence, power, and creativity by hearing characters in the narrative observe these qualities in God's created works.

A technique closely related to that of describing God through his works consists of portraying apocalyptic experience in terms of its effect on other characters in the story. When, for example, we read that the angels in Heaven from God's "sight receiv'd / Beatitude past utterance" (III, 61–62), our impression of the Deity is distanced from us by being located in the subjective experience of those who stand in God's presence. Similarly, when we hear that at the sight of God "all the Starrs / Hide thir diminisht heads" (IV, 34–35) our glimpse of God's glory and power is suggested indirectly by being conveyed to us through the response of God's Creation to his presence. During the war in Heaven, too, Christ's "Power Divine" (VI, 780) is exhibited by its effect on the surroundings as Christ approaches:

> At his command the uprooted Hills retir'd
> Each to his place, they heard his voice and went
> Obsequious, Heav'n his wanted face renewd,
> And with fresh Flourets Hill and Valley smil'd
>
> [VI, 781–784].

When Raphael and Michael descend from Heaven to visit Adam and Eve in Paradise their arrivals in the garden are introduced by descriptions of the responses of the human agents to the presence of their celestial visitors. We view Raphael's arrival in Paradise from Adam's perspective, and the angel first comes into his view at a distance:

> Him through the spicie Forrest onward com
> *Adam* discernd, as in the dore he sat
> Of his coole Bowre   [V, 298–300].

Our impression of Raphael as someone known to us remotely through another character's perception of him is continued in Adam's subsequent words to Eve:

> Haste hither *Eve*, and worth thy sight behold
> Eastward among those Trees, what glorious shape
> Comes this way moving   [V, 308–310].

And the appearance of Raphael is distanced from us even further when we learn that Adam himself has derived his impression of Raphael from the effect of the angel's brightness on the surroundings, from the observation that there "seems another Morn / Ris'n on mid-noon" (V, 310–311). The illusion that Raphael is gradually approaching from an indistinct distance is reinforced by the later statement that Adam approached "Neerer his presence" (V, 358). The approach of Raphael to Adam's bower thus represents something of a drama in miniature, with our initial impression of Raphael as a presence remotely apprehended by Adam only gradually assuming distinctness as the angel approaches the bower and begins to converse with Adam.

The arrival of Michael in Paradise is also presented as the gradual unveiling of a remote figure. Adam is first alerted to Michael's approach by observing the increased brightness in the garden—by observing

> in the East
> Darkness ere Dayes mid-course, and Morning light
> More orient in yon Western Cloud that draws
> O're the blew Firmament a radiant white,
> And slow descends, with something heav'nly fraught
> [XI, 203–207].

Images of gradual descent and approaching brightness are repeated in the narrative summary which follows Adam's statement:

> Down from a Skie of Jasper lighted now
> In Paradise, and on a Hill made alt,
> A glorious Apparition [XI, 209–211].

Several lines later the narrative point of view shifts back to Adam's perspective, and once again we see Michael's approach through the mediation of Adam's consciousness. Adam tells Eve:

> I descrie
> From yonder blazing Cloud that veils the Hill
> One of the heav'nly Host [XI, 228–230].

All that Adam can discern with certainty at such a distant remove is that the "apparition" is

> None of the meanest, some great Potentate
> Or of the Thrones above, such Majestie
> Invests him coming. [XI, 231–233].

Suddenly the distance between Michael and Adam, who still represents the reader's perspective, is shortened, for we read that "th' Arch-Angel soon drew nigh" (XI, 238). The illusion of remoteness is not mitigated, however, for we quickly learn that Michael has come "Not in his shape Celestial, but as Man / Clad to meet Man" (XI, 239–240), with the veiled effect heightened by the fact that "over his lucid Armes / A militarie Vest of purple flowd" (XI, 240–241). We do not, after all, see the angel as he really is, even after he has arrived in Paradise. The arrival of Michael in the garden emerges as one of the most sustained examples of veiled anthropomorphism in *Paradise Lost*, and it represents another instance of how Milton has skillfully contrived to suggest the apocalyptic vision obliquely rather than directly.

Once the angelic visitors have arrived in Paradise the impression of apocalyptic remoteness is maintained by the responses of the human listeners to the account of apocalyptic events. A typical instance of such a response occurs when Adam, in asking Raphael to relate the story of the war in Heaven, lends an aura of strangeness to the whole event by asserting that the story "must needs be strange, / Worthy of Sacred silence to be heard" (V, 556–557). After Raphael has completed his account of the celestial battle the illusion of remoteness is again established by Adam's response to the narrative. He tells Raphael, "Great things, and full of wonder in our eares, / Farr differing from this World, thou hast reveal'd" (VII, 70–71). The story, Adam continues, has been one "which human knowledg could not reach" (VII, 75); Raphael has spoken of "Things above Earthly thought" (VIII, 82). By thus framing the account of the war in Heaven with such responses by Adam, Milton has created the dramatic illusion that the apocalyptic vision is something strange and different from empirical reality, with Adam's response serving as the normative human response to heavenly events.

The awe-filled reaction of Adam to supernatural events elsewhere in the poem also places the apocalyptic vision at a remote distance from ordinary reality. After Raphael's account of God's Creation of the world Adam, recovering from the spell of the narrative as though he were "new wak't" (VIII, 4), thanks Raphael for

> This friendly condescention to relate
> Things else by me unsearchable, now heard
> With wonder   [VIII, 9–11].

In Adam's own account of conversing with God after his creation he records a similar response to the Deity. In addressing God, Adam says,

> O by what Name, for thou above all these,
> Above mankinde, or aught then mankinde higher,
> Surpassest farr my naming   [VIII, 357–359].

On the same occasion Adam tells God,

> To attaine
> The highth and depth of thy Eternal wayes
> All human thoughts come short, Supream of things
> [VIII, 412–414].

And after the conversation with the Deity Adam falls into sleep from the exertion of speaking with a divine being:

> Hee ended, or I heard no more, for now
> My earthly by his Heav'nly overpowered,
> Which it had long stood under, strained to the highth
> In that celestial Colloquie sublime,
> As with an object that excels the sense,
> Dazl'd and spent, sunk down, and sought repair
> Of sleep, which instantly fell on me   [VIII, 452–458].

Such human responses to divine beings and events function dramatically to distance the apocalyptic realm from mortal view.

The same dramatic function is served when the narrators of apocalyptic events speak of the transcendental happenings as something strange and remote from human experience. Before telling Adam about the war in Heaven, for example, Raphael distances the whole account by lamenting that it is a "Sad task and hard" (V, 564) to speak of such "High matter" (V, 563). There is even an element of secrecy in the account, as evidenced by the angel's assertion that he will

> unfold
> The secrets of another world, perhaps
> Not lawful to reveal   [V, 568–570].

The impression that Raphael has given a revelation of hidden things is increased when he concludes his narrative with the statement that he has "reveal'd / What might have else to human Race bin hid" (VI, 895–896). The notion that the ways of God sometimes surpass human comprehension is repeated by Raphael several times when he gives Adam a discourse on the movements of the heavenly bodies. There are some things, Raphael asserts, which

> From Man or Angel the great Architect
> Did wisely to conceal, and not divulge
> His secrets to be scann'd by them who ought
> Rather admire   [VIII, 72–75].

The spaciousness of the firmament, Raphael states, is evidence that man's Earth represents only a limited part of the universe, the rest of which is "Ordain'd for uses to his Lord best known" (VIII, 106). Adam's duty, Raphael tells him, is to "Sollicit not thy thoughts with matters hid, / Leave them to God above" (VIII, 167–168). Such statements by the internal narrator Raphael to the effect that he is telling of celestial beings and events which are hidden and remote from human comprehension are further instances of the distance between the apocalyptic vision and the reader of *Paradise Lost*.

The very presence of internal narrators in the poem is a significant part of the apocalyptic distancing which Milton maintains throughout the poem. The principle involved in such narration, a principle which might be called indirect reportage, has been formulated by one commentator in this manner: "As a rule, the further one retreats into an imaginary and idealistic land, the better it is to report extraordinary events and objects through the medium of additional characters, i.e., at second or third hand rather than at first." [1] The importance

[1] Edward Surtz, ed., *The Complete Works of St. Thomas More*, IV (New Haven, 1965), cxxxv.

of this principle in Milton's apocalyptic technique is obvious. For one thing, the entire poem represents the vision of the epic narrator. It is one of the advances of recent criticism of *Paradise Lost* to have insisted on the dramatic function of the epic narrator. The conclusions stated in the definitive study of the role of the epic narrator in the poem will suffice to explain the narrator's dramatic function: "Nothing takes place in the poem which is not first spoken, or heard and retold by the narrative voice." "We cannot simply respond to" the characters in the story "directly because in the poem without the aid of the inspired narrator we could neither see nor hear them; it is his vision which determines ours and we listen only to what he recites for us." [2] The various invocations in which the narrator asks for vision to "see and tell / Of things invisible to mortal sight" (III, 54–55) are thus more than Milton's decorous bow to epic tradition; these invocations serve the dramatic function of establishing the narrator as a mediator between the story and his audience. With each invocation the illusion of reality is deliberately broken, and we are reminded anew that the vision is one which is being presented at second hand.

Within the epic narrator's account further dramatic distance is achieved by having various aspects of the story told by internal narrators. The large middle section of the poem, telling of the war in Heaven and the Creation of the world, is narrated by Raphael, fulfilling at once the apocalyptic function of distancing the events and the epic demand of beginning the poem *in medias res* and narrating the antecedent action later in the poem. Equally important is the fact that Raphael's story is addressed, not directly to the reader, but to

[2] Anne Davidson Ferry, *Milton's Epic Voice: The Narrator in Paradise Lost* (Cambridge, Mass., 1963), pp. 45, 15.

Adam, as we are reminded whenever the angel addresses Adam in the second person. When we read the account of Creation, then, the epic narrator's invocation (VII, 1–39) places the story at one remove by reminding us that it is his vision which we are seeing, and we later discover further that we are reading the narrator's version of an overheard story told by an angel to the first mortal.

Other apocalyptic events are also narrated by characters within the story. The account of Eve's creation and awakening consciousness (IV, 440–491) is narrated as part of Eve's address to Adam. Similarly, the story of Adam's creation and his asking God for a mate (VIII, 250–451) are presented, not directly, but in Adam's conversation with Raphael; and the account of Eve's creation is presented in the same conversation (VIII, 452–520), this time from Adam's point of view.

Descriptions of Eden, too, are presented obliquely within the epic narrator's account. Our first view of the Garden of Eden, though described by the epic narrator in his own voice, is presented from the point of view of Satan, as though it were his vision which we observe. The objects of Paradise are first described in the order in which Satan meets them in his gradual approach to Eden (IV, 131ff.). We are introduced to the pure air of Eden only as it "Meets his approach" (IV, 154), just as we do not notice the odors of Paradise until "now" they "entertaind . . . the Fiend" (IV, 156, 166). Once Satan is inside the garden, we are told about the things which he, atop the Tree of Life, "Beneath him with new wonder now . . . views" (IV, 205). There follows an extended description of Paradise and its inhabitants (IV, 205–355), and although the description is stated directly by the epic narrator, it is intended to represent Satan's roving view, as evidenced by the fact that the description ends with the statement that Satan is "still in gaze" (IV, 356). The subsequent conversation between Adam and Eve (IV, 408–502) is likewise presented directly by the epic narrator, but once again the passage is framed by reminders that the account describes what Satan is viewing (IV, 395–408, 502–504), giving the dramatic illusion that we are seeing the events as they affect the consciousness of Satan. The "Argument" to Book IV, if it was written by Milton, furnishes further evidence of Milton's intention to place the description of Eden in Satan's consciousness, for we read there that it is Satan who is "now in prospect of Eden," that the book gives us "Satan's first sight of Adam and Eve; his wonder at thir excellent form and happy state," and that it is Satan who "overhears thir discourse."

Other details in the apocalyptic vision are distanced by being described indirectly in the conversations or songs of internal characters. Adam, for example, gives us an oblique description of the garden in his reminder to Eve that they must tend the garden (IV, 610–633). Similarly, Eve's love song, which catalogues the natural phenomena in the garden which she finds pleasant in Adam's company and undelightful in his absence (IV, 635–656), manages to give us a fairly comprehensive description of the garden. Eve's question about why the stars shine when all the Earth is at its nightly rest (IV, 657–658) prompts Adam's reply (IV, 661–688) that the stars are observed by the "Millions of spiritual Creatures" which "walk the Earth / Unseen" (IV, 677–678), whose "Celestial voices" (IV, 682) they have often heard. Dramatically, then, the exchange of question and answer is an exhibition of Adam's superior knowledge, but in the meantime we have caught another indirect glimpse of life as it exists in Paradise. The same method of indirect reportage appears in Adam and Eve's morning hymn (V, 153–208), whose ostensible purpose is to enjoin all God's creatures to praise the Creator but which indirectly serves the function of giving us a full picture of life in the garden. Satan's soliloquy (IX, 99–178) in which he laments how "all good to me becomes / Bane" (IX, 123–124) likewise contains an extended description of the beauty of the earthly surroundings, supporting Satan's exclamation "O Earth, how like to Heav'n, if not preferr'd" (IX, 99). Many of the descriptions which we have of God's attributes are likewise presented, not directly, but as the subject matter of the angels' hymns of praise.[3] Even such qualities as the power and anger which the fallen angels attribute to God represent their view of the Deity, so that the picture of God's character which emerges from the passages is for us an indirect view.

The use of various techniques of indirect reportage thus constitutes an important part of the dramatic illusion of distancing which is built into *Paradise Lost*. Everything which occurs in the apocalyptic world of the poem is at least once removed from the reader by virtue of the narrator's mediating position between us and the vision. But most of the apocalyptic vision is distanced further. The apocalyptic parts of the poem are concentrated in Books III through IX, where the setting is either in Heaven or Paradise before the Fall. If we take into account all of the techniques of indirect reportage—use of internal narrators, observing through the consciousness of an internal character, and description obliquely through the songs or conversations of characters—well over two-thirds of the scenes and events which occur in Heaven and Paradise

[3] Examples include III, 372–415; VI, 886–888; VII, 180–192, 601–632.

in these books of the epic are removed from the reader in ways beyond the single step of distancing represented by the epic narrator.[4]

Milton's attempt to dramatize the Christian doctrine of the Trinity, with the Persons of the Deity functioning as separate agents while at the same time retaining their identity within the Godhead, posed some of the most difficult problems in the entire story.[5] One of the ways in which Milton portrayed the paradoxical unity and differentiation of the divine Persons was to confuse and blur the reader's distinction regarding who is acting, the result being to create the illusion that the apocalyptic state is at an indistinct distance from human perception.

One of the clearest examples of this blurring technique occurs in the account of Creation (VII, 131ff.). God the Father, in decreeing the Creation, tells the Son,

> And thou my Word, begotten Son, by thee
> This I perform, speak thou, and be it don:
> My overshadowing Spirit and might with thee
> I send along   [VII, 163–166].

This accords with the "Argument" to Book VII, which states that God "sends his Son . . . to perform the work of Crea-

---

[4] Helen Gardner, *A Reading of Paradise Lost* (Oxford, 1965), p. 33, considers the proportion of indirect reportage in the poem as a whole and concludes that "well over a third of *Paradise Lost* is thus related, not direct, action."

[5] F. E. Hutchinson, *Milton and the English Mind* (New York, 1948), p. 163, goes so far as to state, "The difficulties involved in dramatizing the Persons of the Trinity . . . make any representation of the Unity in Trinity impossible, even if Milton was concerned to do so." C. A. Patrides, in an important but not wholly conclusive article entitled "The Godhead in *Paradise Lost:* Dogma or Drama?" *JEGP,* LXIV (1965), 29–34, argues that the Father and Son are differentiated only during verbal dialogues in Heaven, and that in any action occurring beyond the confines of Heaven the Godhead is portrayed as a unity.

tion." We are led to expect, then, that the Son will perform the Creation, accompanied by the Spirit of the Father, and this expectation is confirmed when we read that the Father's "Word, the filial Godhead, gave effect" to his Creation decree (VII, 174–175), and that "the Son / On his great Expedition now appeer'd" (VII, 192–193).

Several lines later, however, the designation of who is performing the Creation becomes uncertain. We are told that the gates of Heaven opened

> to let forth
> The King of Glorie in his powerful Word
> And Spirit coming to create new Worlds
> [VII, 207–209].

The lines can plausibly be read as referring to all three Persons of the Trinity, for the concepts of kingship and glory are especially associated with the Father in *Paradise Lost*, the Son has been identified as the Father's "Word" in lines 163 and 175, and the reference to the divine "Spirit" completes the tripartite Godhead.[6] The fusion of identities is continued when we read that "th' Omnific Word" (VII, 217) rode "in Paternal Glorie" (VII, 219). Elsewhere we read that it is "the Spirit of God" (VII, 235) who infuses life into created matter; and the presence of the Father at the time of Creation is implied by the statement that "th' Almightie spake" (VII, 339), since earlier in the same scene the Father's speech to the Son is concluded with the formula, "So spake th' Almightie" (VII, 174). With the account of the Creation of man the simultaneous operation of the Father and the Son becomes explicit, for the event is prefaced by these words:

[6] Patrides, *JEGP*, LXIV, 32–33, takes the passage as a reference to "the triune Godhead."

> the Omnipotent
> Eternal Father (For where is not hee
> Present) thus to his Son audibly spake.
> Let us make now Man in our image, Man
> In our similitude . . . [VII, 516–520].

This plurality of persons is immediately dropped, however, when Raphael tells Adam,

> This said, he formd thee, *Adam*, thee O Man
> Dust of the ground, and in thy nostrils breath'd
> The breath of Life; in his own image hee
> Created thee, in the Image of God
> Express [VII, 524–528].

Just who the creative agent is at this point is unclear; since the Father has been speaking, the syntax would seem to place the action with him ("This said, he formd thee"), but the fact that "his own Image" is equated with "the Image of God" makes it equally possible that the third person singular references are intended to designate the composite Godhead. The impression that the Godhead is performing the Creation is strengthened by the fact that Raphael's account attributes the act to "God" no fewer than sixteen times. Joint action by Father and Son is also suggested when we read about the Son's arrival in Heaven after completing the Creation:

> The Filial Power arriv'd, and sate him down
> With his great Father, for he also went
> Invisible, yet staid (such priviledge
> Hath Omnipresence) and the work ordain'd,
> Author and end of all things [VII, 587–591].

Several lines later the angels hymn the Creator with the words, "Great are thy works, *Jehovah*, infinite / Thy power" (VII, 602–603), and the reference would seem to be either to the complete Godhead or to the Father, since the Old Testament concept of "Jehovah" often has particular reference to the Father or a unified Deity.[7] Paternal activity in the Creation is also implied later in the poem when the Father refers to himself as "Maker" (X, 43).

What, then, should be our final conclusion regarding the identity of the Creator? The answer is far from clear. The text, by variously attributing the act to the Son, the Father, and the Spirit individually and to the composite Godhead blurs our awareness of who is acting. The dramatic illusion is that the divine agents and their actions are too remote to yield a clear and definite impression to human view.

If we look to other parts of the poem there would appear to be some evidence that the Son can be identified as the Creator. The divine agent who creates Adam and places him in Paradise (VII, 524–538) is the same agent who converses with Adam and creates Eve from Adam's rib (VIII, 295–499). We know, too, that the divine agent who comes to judge Adam and Eve after the Fall is the Creator, for Adam speaks to him about "This Women whom thou mad'st to be my help" (X, 137). If the Judge can be identified as the Son, we can infer that he was active in the act of Creation, though even here Adam's statement would not indicate explicitly that the Son was the only Person of the Godhead who participated in the creative act. There is some evidence that the Judge of Book X is the Son. The Father states his inten-

---

[7] Thomas Newton, *Paradise Lost*, 5th ed. (London, 1761), II, 61, regards the name as a reference to the unified Deity: "In this hymn the Angels intimate the unity of the Son with the Father, singing to both as one God, Jehovah." The Old Testament concept of Jehovah is often that suggested by Deut. 6:4, where we read, "Hear, O Israel: Jehovah our God is one Jehovah" (American Standard Version).

tion to send as Judge his "Vicegerent Son" (X, 56). The Son replies that he will go "to judge / On Earth" (X, 71–72), and later he rises from his seat and descends to the Earth (X, 85–90). The impression that the Son is performing the act of Judgment is strengthened by the presence of epithets which in Christian tradition have always been applied to the work of the Son: "Judge and Intercessor" (X, 96), "both Judge and Saviour" (X, 209). Moreover, during the conversation with Adam the judging agent speaks of the Father's prohibition regarding the Tree of Knowledge in the third person, as the command of "his voice" (X, 146); and after pronouncing the punishment the Judge ascends back to his Father (X, 223–226). The Judge is also identified as the Son when we read that the Jesus who was born of Mary is "Eeven hee who now foretold" Satan's final defeat and who "to the Woman thus his Sentence turn'd" (X, 183–192).

As in the account of Creation, however, there are other details in the story of the Judgment of Adam and Eve which seem to controvert the identification of the Son as the Judge. The same divine agent who speaks of the prohibition pronounced on the Tree of Knowledge as issuing from "his voice" also tells Adam,

> Because thou hast heark'nd to the voice of thy Wife,
> And eaten of the Tree concerning which
> I charg'd thee, saying: Thou shalt not eate thereof
>
> > [X, 198–200].

Moreover, once the Son has left the confines of Heaven he is never specifically identified as the Son, being rather referred to only by epithets. The Judge is identified by the general title "God" five times, and several of the other epithets refer to attributes which are generally more appropriate to the Father: "the sovran Presence" (X, 144), "the Lord God" (X, 163). Again, the Judge states that he has often spoken with Adam in the garden (X, 119–120), and later in the poem there is a suggestion that this Person is the Father; Adam identifies the "Presence Divine" (XI, 319) who has often spoken in the garden as the divine agent who has pronounced "his absolute Decree" (XI, 311) that Adam must leave Paradise (in *Paradise Lost* it is the Father who decrees), and Michael alleviates Adam's fears about leaving God's presence in Paradise by assuring him that the same God will be present outside of Eden to surround him with "paternal Love, his Face / Express" (XI, 353–354).

The episode of the pronouncement of God's Judgment on Adam and Eve thus follows the same pattern as does the account of Creation. Before the event occurs, its execution is assigned by the Father to the Son, but when the event actually takes place there are details which contradict the ascription of the action to the Son only. Instead of concluding that the acts of Creation and Judgment are definitely the work of the Son or that they are explicitly the work of the entire Godhead,[8] a third alternative suggests itself—that the whole issue is left in doubt and ambiguity, with some passages indicating the Son's activity and other passages referring to the participation of other Persons of the Deity. All that happens is too remote to furnish a clear vision.

In view of the large number of distancing techniques which remove the apocalyptic vision of *Paradise Lost* from direct

[8] These two views are those respectively of Kester Svendsen, "Epic Address and Reference and the Principle of Decorum in *Paradise Lost*," *PQ*, XXVIII (1949), 199, and Patrides, *JEGP*, LXIV, 34.

view, it is not surprising that there are a number of instances in the poem where veiled images are used in connection with apocalyptic events. Mammon, for example, speaks of how God often resides "admidst / Thick clouds and dark" (II, 263–264), and of how "with the Majesty of darkness round / Covers his Throne" (II, 266–267). The angels around God's throne likewise give us a picture of the veiled God of *Paradise Lost* when they sing to the Father:

> when thou shad'st
> The full blaze of thy beams, and through a cloud
> Drawn round about thee like a radiant Shrine,
> Dark with excessive bright thy skirts appeer,
> Yet dazle Heav'n, that brightest Seraphim
> Approach not, but with both wings veil thir Eyes
>
> [III, 377–382].

That any agent which is less than divine cannot behold the Father directly is also implied by the statement of the angels that the Son is the only celestial being who can behold the Father "without cloud" (III, 385–387). Elsewhere the voice of God speaks "From midst a Golden Cloud" (VI, 28) and "from his secret Cloud" (X, 32), while in Heaven "incense Clouds / Fuming from Golden Censers hid the Mount" of God (VII, 599–600). We also read that on one occasion when God spoke "Clouds began / To darken all the Hill" (VI, 56–57). The same veiled quality is associated with the angels, as evidenced by the fact that Raphael "stood / Vaild with his gorgeous wings" (V, 249–250) and by the description of how, when Michael arrives in Paradise, he is accompanied by a "blazing Cloud that veils the Hill" (XI, 229). Such images of veiling are simply the most explicit of a whole host of techniques by which Milton has distanced his apocalpytic vision from ordinary reality.

SPATIAL DISTANCE

One of the means by which the apocalyptic vision of *Paradise Lost* is given the illusion of remoteness is through the placing of the transcendental realm at a spatial distance from the reader and from various characters within the poem. Ultimately this kind of spatial distancing is rooted in the cosmology of the poem, which is arranged vertically with Heaven at the top, the Earth in the middle, and Hell at the bottom of the universe. The whole network of vertical imagery in the poem, based on a vocabulary of rising and falling, high and low, is not only metaphoric, suggesting moral and emotional gradations, but is first of all physical and spatial.[9] The universal human archetype which expresses the inaccessible transcendence of the supernatural by ascribing to it the quality of height draws upon what is in its essence a spatial concept.

Spatial distance depends, of course, on the vantage point of the observer. It is most significant, therefore, that *Paradise Lost* begins in Hell, at the lowest point in the universe and at the point farthest removed from Heaven. Specifically, we know that the distance between Heaven and Hell is so immense that it is identified not in spatial units but in temporal units; we are told that the demons, upon their expulsion from heaven, fell for nine days and nights (I, 50; VI, 871). Once the reader is aware of this fact, any allusion to the height of Heaven carries definite impressions of its remoteness. The suggestion of Heaven's distance thus appears when Satan,

[9] The topic of spatial imagery in *Paradise Lost,* both in its literal and metaphoric aspects, has been discussed by Isabel MacCaffrey, *Paradise Lost as "Myth"* (Cambridge, Mass., 1959), pp. 44–73; and Jackson Cope, *The Metaphoric Structure of Paradise Lost* (Baltimore, 1962), pp. 72–148.

speaking of Beelzebub's fall from Heaven, mentions "From what highth" his compeer has "fall'n" (I, 92). Beelzebub, in turn, speaks of how the demons have "fall'n such a pernicious highth" (I, 282), and during the infernal council he asserts that they are "thus far remov'd" from Heaven (II, 321). Elsewhere we hear about "him who rules above" (II, 351), and again we are reminded of the position of the heavenly realm far above Hell. As Satan journeys upward toward Paradise from Hell, Heaven is still "farr off" (II, 1047) and "farr distant" (III, 501).

Heaven's remote position relative to the Earth is of particular importance in the poem, not only because most of the action of the poem is told from a terrestrial viewpoint, but also because the earthly perspective is the normal one for the reader of the poem. The spatial remoteness of the transcendental realm is suggested when the epic narrator speaks of the angels "in heav'n, above the starry Sphear" (III, 416), with the remoteness increased when we keep in mind Raphael's assertion that the stars themselves are "from human sight / So farr remote, with diminution seen" (VII, 368–369). Satan, standing in Paradise, likewise talks about the angels who "serve thir Lord / High up in Heav'n" (IV, 943–944). Adam and Eve praise God "who sitst above these Heavens / To us invisible" (V, 156–157), while the epic poet, ready to describe the Creation of the world after having completed the account of the war in Heaven, states that he will now confine his vision "Within the visible Diurnal Spheare; / Standing on Earth, not rapt above the Pole" (VII, 22–23). Raphael tells Adam that after the Creation the Creator "up returned / Up to the Heav'n of Heav'ns his high abode" (VII, 552–553). Elsewhere Raphael is more explicit about the distance which separates Heaven from Earth. He informs Adam that it is a "distance inexpressible / By Numbers that have name" (VIII, 113–114). The angel goes on to state:

> God to remove his wayes from human sense,
> Plac'd Heav'n from Earth so farr, that earthly sight,
> If it presume, might erre in things too high,
> And no advantage gaine   [VIII, 119–122].

Raphael also instructs Adam that "Heav'n is for thee too high / To know what passes there" (VIII, 172–173). Throughout the poem, then, Heaven's remoteness from earthly experience is presented in terms of the spatial distance between the two realms, with the physical transcendence of Heaven suggesting also its inaccessibility to human comprehension and experience.

Even within Heaven itself some parts of apocalyptic reality are portrayed as being spatially higher than other aspects of the transcendental realm. Usually it is God who is removed from other apocalyptic agents in this manner. Thus the Deity is seated on a hill in Heaven (V, 604, 619, 732; VI, 25, 57). That the hill of God represents the highest point in Heaven can be inferred from Raphael's description of "the holy mount / Of Heav'ns high-seated top" (VII, 584–585). It is easy to understand, then, that God can see all things "from his prospect high" (III, 77) and that he can be said to be "High Thron'd above all highth" (III, 58).

Since the prelapsarian garden belongs to the same earthly perspective to which the reader is accustomed, it could not be distanced by being presented as a realm removed spatially from empirical reality. But because *Paradise Lost* opens in Hell, which represents the reader's initial vantage point in the poem, Milton is able to distance Paradise by making it physically remote from our opening point of view. The reader's gradual introduction to Paradise corresponds to Satan's flight toward the garden from outer space, the effect being to make Eden seem spatially distant. The gradual approach to Paradise in *Paradise Lost* is, indeed, one of the exciting events not only in the poem but in English literature.[10]

The gradual approach to Eden begins with Satan's exit through the gates of Hell in Book II. Satan travels through the chaotic "Illimitable Ocean without bound, / Without dimension" (II, 892–893), with our sense of his continual progress through space strengthened by such statements as that "on he fares" (II, 940), that he "wins his way" (II, 1016), and that he "Springs upward . . . / Into the wilde expanse" (II, 1013–1014). The voyage has many obstacles, and we are told that Satan "with difficulty and labour hard / Mov'd on" (II, 1021–1022). After Satan has passed through Chaos he

> with less toil, and now with ease
> Wafts on the calmer wave by dubious light
> And like a weather-beaten Vessel holds
> Gladly the Port, though Shrouds and Tackle torn
>
> [II, 1041–1044].

By the time we come to the end of Book II Satan has journeyed through the "spacious Empire" of Chaos (II, 974), but despite the great distance which he has traversed the Earth is still so far away that it is "in bigness as a Starr / Of smallest Magnitude" (II, 1052–1053).

---

[10] Two especially superb analyses of the approach to the garden in *Paradise Lost* are those by C. S. Lewis, *A Preface to Paradise Lost* (New York, 1961; first pub., 1942), pp. 49–51; and Arnold Stein, *Answerable Style* (Minneapolis, 1953), pp. 51–62. In my discussion the phrases "images of gradual approach" and "the theme of serialism" come from Lewis.

Following the interlude of the dialogue in Heaven in the opening lines of Book III our perspective returns to Satan's flight. We read that Satan "Looks down with wonder at the sudden view / Of all this World at once" (III, 542–543). Later he

> Down right into the Worlds first Region throws
> His flight precipitant, and windes with ease
> Through the pure marble Air his oblique way
> Amongst innumerable Starrs, that shon
> Stars distant . . .   [III, 562–566].

Subsequently we follow Satan's progress past the stars and planets, past the sun, and "toward the coast of Earth beneath" (III, 739). With his arrival on Earth the images of gradual approach become even more prominent, beginning with the statement, "So on he fares, and to the border comes, / Of *Eden*" (IV, 131–132). By the time we reach the next line Paradise is "Now nearer" (IV, 133). The fact that Paradise is located on top of a mountain yields a whole series of images suggesting gradual ascent: the trees on the hill are "over head" (IV, 137), their ranks "ascend / Shade above shade" (IV, 140–141), the wall of Paradise is "Yet higher then thir tops" (IV, 142), and "higher then that Wall" (IV, 146) stand the trees of Paradise itself. The theme of serialism is resumed when in later passages we read that "now purer aire / Meets his approach (IV, 153–154), "now gentle gales / . . . dispense / Native perfumes" (IV, 156–158), and "Now to th' ascent of that steep savage Hill / Satan had journied on" (IV, 172–173). In each instance the repetition of the word "now" reinforces the impression that we are witnessing an on-going progression toward the garden. Only with Satan's bound over the wall of Paradise have we finally completed the long journey from Hell to Paradise. The chief dramatic function served by the extended account of Satan's voyage, which occupies substantial parts of Books II, III, and IV, is to create the impression that Paradise is spatially remote from the reader.

The spatial distancing of apocalyptic reality thus involves two major motifs in Paradise Lost—the inaccessible height of Heaven and the physical remoteness of Paradise from the reader's initial perspective. This spatial remoteness of the apocalyptic realm is a measure of its inaccessibility to our own experience. It is an important part of Milton's technique of portraying the "otherness" of apocalyptic reality.

TEMPORAL DISTANCE

Paradise Lost is concerned preeminently with first things —with events which occurred before history and with happenings which mark the beginnings of human existence on Earth. This quality of the poem is borne upon us by the opening phrase of the epic, which identifies the poet's theme as one which tells "Of Mans First Disobedience." The prehistoric nature of the subject matter is also emphasized in the "Argument" to Book I, where we are told that the angels "were long before the visible Creation" and that Hell is not located in the center of the Earth in the poem "for Heaven and Earth may be suppos'd as yet not made." Because the story of the epic belongs to prehistory, Milton's apocalyptic vision is removed temporally from the reader's experience, and this temporal distance appears in many details in the poem.

Raphael begins his reconstruction of the war in Heaven by emphasizing its temporal remoteness from earthly experience:

As yet this world was not, and *Chaos* wilde
Reignd where these Heav'ns now rowl, were Earth now rests
Upon her Center pois'd   [V, 577–579].

When describing the actual combat Raphael, in trying to
make the uproar vivid to Adam by describing its effects in
earthly terms, is forced to postulate the hypothetical existence
of the Earth at the time of the battle:

all Heav'n
Resounded, and had Earth bin then, all Earth
Had to her Center shook   [VI, 217–219].

The story of Creation, too, belongs to the remote past, even
for Adam, the first man, as evidenced by his desire to hear
from Raphael

how this World
Of Heav'n and Earth conspicuous first began,
When, and whereof created, for what cause,
What within *Eden* or without was done
Before his memorie   [VII, 62–66].

Several lines later Adam requests his angelic visitor to instruct
him regarding "How first began this Heav'n which we behold" (VII, 86); and Raphael concludes his story of Creation
with these words, addressed to Adam:

And thy request think now fulfill'd, that ask'd
How first this World and face of things began,
And what before thy memorie was don
From the beginning   [VII, 635–638].

For the reader of the poem, even more than for Adam, the
apocalyptic events are distanced by vast ages of time.
  Once the rebellious angels and Adam and Eve have fallen,

their earlier state of perfection is spoken of as a past condition —as their "first" state, or as a situation which prevailed "then" rather than "now." Such references are another way by which the epic poet distances his apocalyptic vision temporally. When we read about the perfection which "once" belonged to the demons (I, 316), we are reminded that from a fallen perspective the apocalyptic state is a distant event. The same impression is conveyed by statements regarding the "Powers that earst in Heaven sat on Thrones" (I, 360), the glory which Satan possessed "then" as opposed to "now" (IV, 838–839), and the angels who were "glorious once" (V, 567). We read also about the angels who were "once upright / And faithful, now prov'd false" (VI, 270–271), about how bright Satan "once" shone (VII, 132), and about the angels who were "Purest at first, now gross by sinning grown" (VI, 661). The same kind of time differentiation distances Adam and Eve from their apocalyptic state after they have fallen. Adam recalls that he "earst with joy / And rapture so oft beheld" God in the garden (IX, 1081–1082), while the impassioned minds of Adam and Eve after the Fall are said to have been "calm Region once / And full of Peace" (IX, 1125–1126). Similarly, Adam states that if he and Eve had worked together on the day of the Fall they "had then / Remaind still happie" (IX, 1137–1138).

The temporal distance which removes Adam and Eve from the reader of Paradise Lost is established largely through a group of epithets which are based on the principle that Adam and Eve are the first parents of the long succeeding line of the human race. Beelzebub, for example, calls Adam the "Original" of his human "Sons" (II, 373, 375). The epic narrator likewise identifies Adam and Eve as the distant predecessors of the human race, calling them "Our two first Parents, yet the onely two / Of mankind" (III, 65–66). Elsewhere he again speaks of them as "our first Parents" (IV, 6). Adam alludes to their status as the original ancestors of the human line when he tells Eve about the "Nations yet unborn" (IV, 663). And after the expulsion of the fallen angels from Heaven the Father tells the Son of his intention to create "Another World, out of one man a Race / Of men innumerable, there to dwell" (VII, 155–156).

Adam and Eve, when mentioned individually, are similarly distanced from the reader by the presence of epithets placing them at the head of their human descendents. We read, for instance, that "*Adam* first of men" spoke "To first of women *Eve*" (IV, 408–409). In other passages Eve is called "Mother of human Race" (IV, 475) and "our general Mother" (IV, 492). Raphael greets Eve with the words:

> Haile Mother of Mankind, whose fruitful Womb
> Shall fill the World more numerous with thy Sons
> Then with these various fruits the Trees of God
> Have heap'd this Table   [V, 388–391].

Similarly, Adam says to Eve:

> Haile to thee,
> *Eve* rightly call'd, Mother of all Mankind,
> Mother of all things living, since by thee
> Man is to live   [XI, 158–161].

In like manner Adam is referred to as "our first Father" (IV, 495), "our general Ancestor" (IV, 659), and "our Primitive great Sire" (V, 350). Elsewhere Adam is called "the Patriarch of mankind" (V, 506), "our great Progenitor" (V, 544), and "our Ancestor" (XI, 546). The "shape Divine" (VIII, 295) who created Adam tells him:

> *Adam*, rise,
> First Man, of Men innumerable ordain'd
> First Father   [VIII, 296–298].

Such epithets for the human agents in the epic represent one of several ways in which the apocalyptic vision is distanced temporally from the reader of *Paradise Lost*. The prehistoric nature of the events, the identification of the state of perfection as something existing "at first" or "then" and the presentation of Adam and Eve as the distant ancestors of the succeeding human line all serve to make the apocalyptic vision temporally remote from historical reality.

❦ 7

Apocalyptic Imagery

Most critical discussion of Milton's apocalyptic imagery has been characterized above all by its impressionistic nature. The result of this impressionistic orientation has been a huge body of criticism, sometimes controversial, which has been concerned with the recurrent concepts of "mystery" and "vagueness," or synonyms of these terms. Let us look first at the question of the "mystery" or "suggestiveness" of Milton's apocalyptic imagery.

Writers who have commented on the question of whether Milton is suggestive or mysterious in his portrayal of apocalyptic reality have most often centered their remarks on the presentation of God and the angels. Charges of Milton's lack of mystery in presenting the celestial scenes of his epic are numerous, and they often involve comparison with Dante. Raleigh believed that there is "nothing mysterious, except in name, throughout the whole poem," and that for Milton "the ultimate mysteries . . . were no mysteries." [1] A similar sentiment is conveyed by the statement that Milton had "a mind

[1] Walter Raleigh, *Milton* (London, 1909), pp. 113, 126.

insensitive to mystery,"[2] while other commentators argue that Milton "tends toward a rationalistic absence of mystery,"[3] and that "there are no mysteries for Milton, no reticence before the Ineffable."[4] Similar critical verdicts are that "Milton has . . . missed the higher mysteries of divinity,"[5] that there "was a lack of the sense of mystery in Milton,"[6] and that "Milton's God is . . . not a mystery."[7] In like fashion John Peter opines that Milton's "God could have been allowed much more of mystery than he is,"[8] while another Milton detractor, A. J. A. Waldock, repeats the charge that Milton lacks "the tactful, prudent method of Dante with God—to keep him hidden."[9] Even C. S. Lewis believed that Milton's God "would escape criticism if only He had been made sufficiently awful, mysterious, and vague," with Milton's failure stemming from the fact that he is too rarely "content to suggest."[10]

Opposed to critics who deny the element of mystery to

[2] R. E. Neil Dodge, "Theology in *Paradise Lost*," *University of Wisconsin Studies in Language and Literature*, II (1918), 15.

[3] William J. Grace, "Orthodoxy and Aesthetic Method in *Paradise Lost* and the *Divine Comedy*," *CL*, I (1949), 175.

[4] F. E. Hutchinson, *Milton and the English Mind* (New York, 1948), p. 124.

[5] Paul Elmer More, "The Theme of 'Paradise Lost,'" *Shelburne Essays*, Fourth Series (Cambridge, Mass., 1922), p. 251.

[6] John Bailey, *Milton* (London, 1915), p. 160.

[7] William Haller, "Order and Progress in *Paradise Lost*," *PMLA*, XXXV (1920), 218.

[8] *A Critique of Paradise Lost* (New York, 1960), p. 17.

[9] *Paradise Lost and Its Critics* (Cambridge, Eng., 1947), p. 98.

[10] *A Preface to Paradise Lost* (New York, 1961; first pub., 1942), p. 130. For additional statements of the thesis that "Milton's mind was neither mystical nor metaphysical" and that Milton's major defect was "his lack of a sense of the inexplicable, of a feeling for . . . mystery," see, respectively, Sir Herbert J. C. Grierson, *Milton and Wordsworth* (New York, 1937), p. 110, and John H. Collins, "Milton and the Incomprehensible," *SAQ*, XXIV (1925), 377.

Milton's apocalyptic vision are many readers who believe that Milton did achieve suggestiveness. This is the tradition headed by Thomas Macaulay, who stated that Milton's images depend "less on what they directly represent than on what they remotely suggest." [11] Later critics have agreed that Milton possessed "the spirit of true art—he suggests," [12] and that "the art of his description lies in its suggestiveness." [13] Still other writers share this view: "in *Paradise Lost* . . . there is no lack of . . . suggestiveness;" [14] "that . . . Milton is mysterious, Dante picturesque, everyone now knows;" [15] Milton's God "remains a mystery." [16]

This brief survey reveals two things—that the concept of suggestiveness or mysteriousness has been a recurrent theme in critical discussions of Milton's apocalyptic vision, and that commentators have divided sharply on the question whether Milton manages to achieve an effect of mystery. It should be equally obvious that both views cannot be correct; *Paradise Lost* cannot be both mysterious and not mysterious, although a few critics are bent on having it both ways, with Milton being at the same time guilty of saying too much and leaving too much to mere suggestion.[17] It is possible, of course, that

[11] *Essay on Milton,* ed. Herbert Augustine Smith (Boston, 1898), p. 19.

[12] A. H. Strong, *The Great Poets and Their Theology* (Philadelphia, 1897), p. 248.

[13] Elbert N. S. Thompson, *Essays on Milton* (New Haven, 1914), p. 205.

[14] J. B. Leishman, *"L'Allegro* and *Il Penseroso* in Their Relation to Seventeenth-Century Poetry," *Essays and Studies,* n. s., IV (1951), 18.

[15] Elmer E. Stoll, *Poets and Playwrights* (Minneapolis, 1930), p. 271.

[16] B. A. Wright, *Milton's Paradise Lost* (New York, 1962), p. 45.

[17] Mark Van Doren, *The Noble Voice* (New York, 1946), states that Milton "decides too soon that the things he must tell us about

one group of critics is simply wrong in its reading of *Paradise Lost*. But it is also possible that there is something wrong with the whole critical issue which is being raised here, and this is what I believe to be the case. Is Milton's portrayal of apocalyptic reality mysterious and suggestive? No clear cut, yes or no answer can be given to the question, although critics have assumed that the question will yield such an answer.[18] The question is not a descriptive one but an affective one; its answer is not a comment on the data of the poem but on the effect which the poem has on the reader. Mystery depends on certain prior qualities, and there are issues which exist logically prior to the matter of suggestiveness. If criticism is to be a contribution to knowledge it must ask descriptive rather than impressionistic questions. What causes mystery in poetry? What is the exact nature of Milton's apocalyptic imagery? What kinds of phenomena do his words name? These are the relevant questions if we are to describe the data of the poem, and the present discussion is an attempt to discuss Milton's imagery on such a basis.

The stock critical judgment about the "vagueness" of Mil-

are things that cannot be seen" (p. 130), but on the next page he argues that Milton "should have stared still longer into this abyss, till he grew mute" and subsequently complains of the fact that Milton made a speaking character of God, who "is by definition one who does not think or speak." John Peter, *A Critique of Paradise Lost,* is at equal pains to contradict himself; on the one hand, "Milton's general approach, when it errs, errs usually in the direction of particularity, of saying too much," but, on the other hand, "when his style is weak it is often because it is too vague, too unrealized" (both quotations are from p. 159).

[18] On the matter of the necessity to distinguish between criticism which is concerned with verifiable, true or false statements and criticism which is not concerned wih such statements, I am indebted to Morris Weitz, *Hamlet and the Philosophy of Literary Criticism* (Cleveland, 1966).

ton's transcendental imagery is as common as are references to his suggestiveness. Critics have claimed that Milton's style "is too vague," [19] that "in Milton the theology is clear, the images vague," [20] and that there is a "relative vagueness of Milton's Hell and Heaven." [21] A basic objection to the use of the term "vague" to describe Milton's imagery is that the designation itself is too imprecise and as a result means different things to different critics. Vagueness usually denotes indefiniteness and indistinctness, and a number of commentators make it clear that they view Milton's alleged vagueness in this manner. We read, for example, about "the vast indefiniteness of Milton's pictures," [22] about the "indistinctness" and "ambiguity" of his images,[23] and about "the vague terms" and "indistinct quality" of the descriptions of Paradise.[24] Similar critical views state that Milton "characteristically and felicitously avoids definiteness and precision," [25] and that "the topography of *Paradise Lost* seems, of course, indistinct." [26] To other readers, however, Milton's vagueness is not first of all a matter of indistinction, but rather of the use of particular types of images. This was the approach of F. R. Leavis, who

[19] Peter, *A Critique of Paradise Lost,* p. 159.

[20] C. S. Lewis, *English Literature in the Sixteenth Century Excluding Drama* (Oxford, 1954), p. 387.

[21] Phyllis MacKenzie, "Milton's Visual Imagination: An Answer to T. S. Eliot," *UTQ,* XVI (1946–1947), 21.

[22] James Holly Hanford, *A Milton Handbook,* 4th ed. (New York, 1961), p. 196.

[23] F. Joseph Kelley, "Milton and Dante: A Few Points of Contrast," *Catholic World,* CXXXII (1930), 172.

[24] M. M. Mahood, *Poetry and Humanism* (New Haven, 1950), pp. 180–181.

[25] Stoll, *Poets and Playwrights,* p. 280.

[26] W. J. Courthope, "A Consideration of Macaulay's Comparison of Dante and Milton," *Proceedings of the British Academy,* III (1907–1908), 267.

spoke of Milton's "sensuous poverty,"[27] and of T. S. Eliot, who believed that Milton's apocalyptic effects were achieved through the use of nonvisual imagery.[28]

As a critical term, then, "vagueness" is weak because, as with the concept of mystery, there are prior considerations. What kind of imagery yields vagueness? Does vagueness involve something not seen distinctly, or does it arise from something which is not seen at all? Is vague imagery completely nonsensory, or only nonvisual? Questions such as these, if left unanswered, result in an imprecise critical analysis. Moreover, if Milton's vagueness is equated with indistinctness and lack of clarity, the thesis is largely inaccurate when applied to the apocalyptic scenes of Paradise Lost, as this study is designed to demonstrate.[29]

It is the conclusion of the present study that, in addition to techniques of imagery touched upon in earlier chapters, Milton's apocalyptic imagery depends on three major techniques. These are the frequent use of conceptual imagery rather than sensory imagery, the use of generic terms rather than specific images, and, within the area of sensory imagery, frequent use of nonvisual images. Although some of these conclusions are by no means original, the remarkable thing is the scarcity of demonstrations supporting critical generalizations (even accurate ones) about Milton's imagery. My own view is that

[27] *Revaluation: Tradition and Development in English Poetry* (New York, 1947; first pub., 1936), p. 47.

[28] See his two essays on Milton in *On Poetry and Poets* (New York, 1957).

[29] Indistinctness and imprecision of outline are much more a part of Milton's technique in describing the demonic scenes in Hell. One of the values of separating the apocalyptic and demonic aspects of Milton's vision is that it allows for a more accurate description than is usually achieved when both aspects are discussed together under the heading of Milton's supernatural technique.

general impression is a dangerous guide for a literary critic, and I have accordingly attempted to support my generalizations at some length with specific examples.

CONCEPTUAL IMAGERY

In his outline for a "rhetoric of motives" Kenneth Burke suggests that a distinction should be made regarding the kinds of terms used to name phenomena on the basis of the ontological nature of the phenomena which are named. Burke distinguishes two main types of terms, which he calls "positive terms" and "dialectical terms." [30] Positive terms "name par excellence the things of experience, the *hic et nunc*. . . . The imagery of poetry is positive to the extent that it names things having a visible, tangible existence. . . . A positive term is most unambiguously itself when it names a visible and tangible thing which can be located in time and place. . . . And whatever else it may be in its ultimate reaches, such a terminology of perception is 'positive' in its everyday, empirical availability." The other kind of vocabulary, the dialectical terms, "have no such strict location as can be assigned to the objects named in words of the first order. . . . Here are words for *principles* and *essence*. . . . Here are 'titular' words. Titles like 'Elizabethanism' or 'capitalism' can have no positive referent, for instance." Such dialectical terms "refer to *ideas* rather than to *things*. Hence they are more concerned with *action* and *attitude* than with *perception*." This distinction between terms which name things and objects on the one hand and ideas and concepts on the other is an extremely useful one in the analysis of *Paradise Lost,* though I

[30] *A Grammar of Motives and A Rhetoric of Motives* (Cleveland, 1962), pp. 707–710. Cf. also pp. 608–614.

wish to substitute the terms "sensory imagery" and "conceptual imagery" for Burke's terms.

The very term "image" has been so customarily used by critics to refer only to words which name tangible objects that to speak of "conceptual imagery" requires a broader definition of imagery than is usually given. In the present discussion an "image" is any word which names a phenomenon existing in human experience. The phenomenon may be part of the physical world but can also be an abstract quality. Considered in this manner, any noun, and any adjective, adverb, or verb expressing a quality or action which can be formulated as a noun, would constitute an image. A prominent recent theorist who has argued that the definition of the poetic image must be extended to include concepts is Northrop Frye, who writes perceptively, "We are accustomed to associate the term 'nature' primarily with the external physical world, and hence we tend to think of an image as primarily a replica of a natural object. But of course both words are for more inclusive: nature takes in the conceptual or intelligible order as well as the spatial one, and what is usually called an 'idea' may be a poetic image also." [31] This is the principle which I propose to apply to an analysis of *Paradise Lost*.

The lack of an adequate critical vocabulary to deal with nonsensory imagery is in part a product of the twentieth-century bias, both poetic and critical, against any kind of poetic language which is not concrete and sensory. Because of this demand for the sharply perceived sensuous image, the usual critical procedure has been to deny the status of an image to a concept or idea. Instead of distinguishing between sensory and conceptual images, there has been a tendency to label any nonsensory image as a vague sensory image. The error in such

[31] *Anatomy of Criticism* (Princeton, 1957), p. 84.

a procedure is, of course, that it fails to grasp that a conceptual image names a phenomenon which is just as real and definite as a sensory image. The difference between imagery which is vague and imagery which is distinct lies in the way in which the image is handled in description, involving the difference, for example, between the presentation of a visual object with blurred outline and lack of precise descriptive detail or with clear outline and color. The difference between a sensory and conceptual image, on the other hand, is not a matter of how the image is handled by the poet. Instead, such a distinction lies in the ontological difference between the phenomena being named. Whereas vagueness depends on the poet's descriptive technique, then, conceptual imagery depends on the nature of the thing being described. In the pages which follow I wish to demonstrate the manner in which conceptual images frequently constitute the poetic texture in descriptions of apocalyptic reality in *Paradise Lost*. Such an analysis will show that conceptual terms, as used in Milton's poem, fulfill the same descriptive function that sensory images do in other poetic contexts.

T. S. Eliot has written that in reading *Paradise Lost* he was "happiest where there is least to visualize."[32] Analysis of the conceptual nature of the apocalyptic imagery will contribute to an understanding of such a response, and the famous initial description of Adam and Eve will provide a good point of departure. When Satan arrives in the garden he sees, among the other creatures,

> Two of far nobler shape erect and tall,
> Godlike erect, with native Honour clad
> In naked Majestie seemd Lords of all,
> And worthie seemd, for in thir looks Divine

[32] *On Poetry and Poets*, p. 162.

> The image of thir glorious Maker shon,
> Truth, wisdome, Sanctitude severe and pure,
> Whence true autoritie in men . . .   [IV, 288–295].

This is the first extended description of the two human agents in Milton's apocalyptic vision, and the most apparent characteristic of the description is its heavy reliance on conceptual images. No fewer than fourteen conceptual terms comprise the poetic texture of the description: nobleness, Godlikeness, honor, majesty, lordship, worthiness, glory, truth, wisdom, sanctitude, severity, purity, freedom, and authority. Each of the terms names a quality which is no less real and distinct than a tangible object perceived through the senses, and although many modern critics would deny the statement, such conceptual images possess all the multiplicity of associations and complexity of connotations that a concrete physical image does. Like the sensory image, the conceptual image is a "potential of meaning, a nexus or cluster of meanings." [33]

The initial view of Adam and Eve in conceptual terms is maintained throughout the middle books of the epic, with the patterns of conceptual images consistently complementing the sensory descriptions of the human pair. Adam's description of his first view of Eve is no less conceptual than Satan's first view of Adam and Eve was:

> On she came
> Led by her Heav'nly Maker, though unseen,
> . . . Grace was in all her steps, Heav'n in her Eye,
> In every gesture dignitie and love   [VIII, 484–489].

This accords also with Eve's first view of herself as reflected in the water, since her description of what she saw is likewise

---

[33] This is Cleanth Brooks's famous description of the poetic image, stated in *The Well Wrought Urn* (New York, 1947), p. 210.

phrased in abstractions: the reflection "returnd as soon with answering looks / Of sympathie and love" (IV, 464–465).[34] When Adam narrates to Raphael the story of his first wooing of Eve, the account again depends for much of its impression on conceptual rather than physical images:

> She heard me thus, and though divinely brought,
> Yet Innocence and Virgin Modestie,
> Her vertue and the conscience of her worth,
> . . . Wrought in her so, that seeing me, she turn'd;
> I follow'd her, she what was Honour knew,
> And with obsequious Majestie approv'd
> My pleaded reason   [VIII, 500–502, 507–510].

The key images in the passage are such intangible qualities as innocence, modesty, virtue, worth, honor, and majesty. The visual image counts for very little in such a description, but that is inherent in the nature of an apocalyptic vision, which seeks to transcend the world of the senses.

Elsewhere Eve is also imagined in conceptual terms. Adam affirms that Eve is "pure" (V, 100), and he beholds her "Beautie, which whether waking or asleep, / Shot forth peculiar Graces" (V, 14–15). Similarly, the epic narrator describes Eve in images which name qualities and defy us to search for a tangible referent when he tells us that she retired "With lowliness Majestic . . . And Grace" (VIII, 42–43), and that she went "With Goddess-like demeanor" (VIII, 59). Qualities such as lowliness, majesty, and grace are of course not capable of being located precisely in time and place, but

---

[34] The fact that the description of Eve's reflection in the water is phrased in conceptual images has significant implications for the interpretation of the scene, since it is not as readily apparent as critics have claimed that it is a sign of vanity and sinfulness to be attracted by the qualities of "sympathie and love."

they are no less real and richly connotative for their being intangible. Even the erotic account of Adam and Eve's embraces (IV, 429ff.) moves from the physical to the conceptual; Eve's "swelling Breast" (IV, 495) leans on Adam's, but Adam, instead of viewing erotic physical details, is said to see such intangibles as "Beauty" and "submissive Charms" (IV, 498). Adam's parting view of Eve on the fatal day is a view comprised of her "native innocence" (IX, 373) and "vertue" (IX, 374). In like manner, the change which Satan hopes to effect in Eve involves her intangible, spiritual qualities, since he wishes to despoil her "of Innocence, of Faith, of Bliss" (IX, 411).

The same kind of cumulative conceptual image emerges from the descriptions of Adam and Eve as a pair of human creatures. Satan asserts that he could admire and even love the couple,

> so lively shines
> In them Divine resemblance, and such grace
> The hand that formd them on thir shape hath pourd
> [IV, 363-365].

Satan is also moved by the "harmless innocence" (IV, 388) which he observes in the human pair, and it is such ideas as "joy" (IV, 369) and happiness (IV, 534) which he identifies as the qualities which differentiate unfallen human experience from fallen experience. Similarly, as Adam clearly realizes, the very characteristics which make perfect human beings different from the rest of God's creatures are certain abstract qualities: God has

> so many signes of power and rule
> Conferrd upon us, and Dominion giv'n
> Over all other Creatures . . .   [IV, 429-431].

The narrator tells us that of all the creatures in Paradise, only the "wedded love" of Adam and Eve was "Founded in Reason, Loyal, Just, and Pure" (IV, 755), that only the human pair are "endu'd / With Sanctitie of Reason" (VII, 507–508). Another example of how the narrator describes our first parents in conceptual rather than visual terms occurs when he tells us that they prayed "innocent" (V, 209) and in so doing recovered "peace" and "calm" (V, 210). The narrator later apostrophizes the couple's "innocence / Deserving Paradise" (V, 445–446). God likewise describes the apocalyptic condition in conceptual images when he states that he created man with "Happiness / And Immortalitie" (XI, 58–59). As all these passages illustrate, the recurrent images used to describe the apocalyptic state of Adam and Eve frequently turn out to be conceptual images, such as innocence, grace, happiness, power and rule, reason, and immortality.

Many of the retrospective views of prelapsarian humanity from the vantage point of fallen experience also conduct the description in conceptual terms. Thus the epic narrator contrasts fallen love with the "simplicitie and spotless innocence" (IV, 318) which was lost. Where, asks the narrator, "meet now / Such pairs, in Love and mutual Honour joyn'd?" (VIII, 57–58). In the latter parts of Book IX the picture which we get of the apocalyptic state which was lost by the Fall is largely a conceptual picture:

> innocence, that as a veile
> Had shadow'd them from knowing ill, was gon,
> Just confidence, and native righteousness
> And honour from about them   [IX, 1054–1057].

> They destitute and bare
> Of all thir vertue . . .   [IX, 1062–1063].

> . . . Which leaves us naked thus, of Honour void,
> Of Innocence, of Faith, of Puritie [IX, 1074–1075].

> O how unlike
> To that first naked Glorie [IX, 1114–1115].

The lost apocalyptic state, in short, is a state consisting primarily of abstract concepts and qualities, not physical objects.

There are a number of instances in which a sensory image is combined with a conceptual image. The technique is similar to that of personification, though the effect is somewhat different.[35] Whereas personification tends to make the abstract appear concrete, the passages which I have in mind present a movement from the concrete to the abstract, from the world of the senses to a world which transcends the senses. For example, the apocalyptic state is recovered in the epic when Christ, after the Fall, covers Adam and Eve "with his Robe of righteousness" (X, 222), with the conceptual image of righteousness canceling out the sensory expectation set up by the robe image. Similarly, God promises to encompass Adam and Eve, not with a physical phenomenon, but "With goodness and paternal Love" (XI, 353). When Adam goes forth to greet Raphael he is of course accompanied with his "train," but any expectation of a visual spectacle is denied when his accoutrements turn out to be such conceptual entities as "his own compleat / Perfections" (V, 352–353). Eve,

---

[35] The topic of personification in *Paradise Lost* has been less discussed than might be expected. The fullest study is that by A. L. Keith, "Personification in Milton's *Paradise Lost*," *The English Journal*, XVII (1928), 399–409. Keith relates Milton's frequent use of personification to the apocalyptic nature of his subject, noting that "Abstract ideas and qualities and conditions are personified far oftener than concrete objects. We are prepared for such a distribution because of the nature of the subject which removes the reader largely from earthly contact."

too, is "Not unattended, for on her as Queen / A pomp of winning Graces waited still" (VIII, 60–61). In such instances the sensory world is transcended before our eyes, with the physical image giving way to the conceptual image.

It becomes clear that the description of Adam and Eve in their apocalyptic state of perfection depends for much of its effect on a poetic texture of conceptual images. If, as T. S. Eliot has claimed, we can derive pleasure from the account of the human couple in Paradise "only by the deliberate effort not to visualize Adam and Eve," [36] the present analysis suggests that Milton has done much to insure a successful reading of his poem. For in passage after passage the visual image is not simply blurred and vague but wholly denied, with the images which describe the apocalyptic state naming qualities which have no sensory object as their referent.

We tend to think of Paradise as a place of sensuous fulfillment, and so it is. But even here there is a consistent motif of conceptual imagery running through the descriptions of profuse vegetation, fragrance, and harmony. The first description of Paradise occurs early in Book III as God looks down from above. What he sees is two human beings inhabiting, not a physical place, but a conceptual universe, with Adam and Eve

> in the happie Garden plac't,
> Reaping immortal fruits of joy and love,
> Uninterrupted joy, unrivald love
> In blissful solitude   [III, 66–69].

It is not a sensory description at all, being characterized rather by happiness, immortality, joy, love, and bliss.

The initial description of Paradise is a good summary of the conceptual images used to describe the garden later in the poem. The motif of happiness, for example, is repeated a num-

36 *On Poetry and Poets*, p. 162.

ber of times. Beelzebub tells the infernal council about "another World, the happy seat / Of some new Race" (II, 347–348), and eventually Satan directs his flight toward "Paradise the happie seat of Man" (III, 632). Adam remarks to Eve God's goodness in placing them "In all this happiness" (IV, 417), while later they sing their morning hymn on "Edens happie Plains" (V, 143). Before we have finished reading about Paradise we have had it described as "A happy rural seat of various view" (IV, 247), "this happie Place" (IV, 562; XI, 303), "these happie Walks and Shades" (XI, 270), and "thir happie seat" (XII, 642). It is interesting to note also that when Milton in *Paradise Regained* alludes to Paradise as the theme of his former epic, he speaks of "the happy Garden" (I, 1).

The related concepts of joy and delight recur as frequently as does the image of happiness. As Satan first approaches Eden, for example, he meets "Vernal delight and joy" (IV, 155), and subsequently "the Fiend / Saw undelighted all delight" (IV, 285–286). When Satan contemplates the Fall of Adam and Eve he again equates the life in Paradise with delight and joy:

> Your change approaches, when all these delights
> Will vanish and deliver ye to woe,
> More woe, the more your taste is now of joy
>
> [IV, 367–369].

Again, Adam describes the garden as a place "of manifold delights" (IV, 435) and as "this delightful Land" (IV, 643, 652). And God, about to decree the Creation of the world, states that it will be a place of "Joy . . . without end" (VII, 161).

Another pattern of conceptual images describing Paradise

centers around the concept of bliss. We read that "blissful Paradise / Of God the Garden was" (IV, 208–209), and that in Eden Adam and Eve "enjoy thir fill / Of bliss on bliss" (IV, 507–508). Gabriel accuses Satan of designing to destroy the "dwelling God hath planted here in bliss" (IV, 884), while the narrator sums up his description of the garden with the phrase "enormous bliss" (V, 297). Elsewhere Paradise is described as "that new world of light and bliss" (II, 867), "a place of bliss" (II, 832), "the blissful seat" (III, 527), and the "room of bliss" (IV, 359).

Although Paradise is primarily a place of sensory objects, of trees and fruits and brooks, of stars and sunlight, it is also a conceptual world filled with such unmistakable intangibles as happiness, joy, and bliss. In this respect the Paradise in Eden corresponds to the "paradise within," which consists of such concepts as "knowledge . . . , Faith, / . . . vertue, Patience, Temperance, . . . Love" (XII, 582–583). As with the other apocalyptic scenes in the poem, Milton does not remain in the realm of the physical but transcends the world of sense impressions by entering a conceptual realm of qualities and essences.

Conceptual images are used even more frequently in the depiction of Heaven and its agents than in descriptions of Eden and its inhabitants. This is especially true of the portrayal of God, as we might expect from Milton's statement in *De Doctrina Christiana* that God can be described only in terms of his qualities: "But though the nature of God cannot be defined . . . , some description of it at least may be collected from his names and attributes" (*Works*, XIV, 39). Since many of the epic epithets and forms of address involve the process of basing a name on a quality or characteristic of the person being named, the matter of conceptual imagery is integrally related to the epithets applied to God and the angels in *Paradise Lost*. Moreover, many epithets refer to positions or roles, such as king, judge, or creator, and since such titles name abstractions having no tangible referent, they, too, usually constitute conceptual images.[37] Keeping in mind, then, the many ways in which Milton's epic style is linked to the whole topic of conceptual imagery, let us observe how inaccurate are many of the complaints about the excessive concreteness of Milton's portrayal of God.

In the first two books of *Paradise Lost* Satan talks frequently about God, and, as we might expect, in speaking of the supreme apocalyptic being he often attributes conceptual qualities to God. He attributes to God the qualities of "high Supremacy" (I, 132), "supernal Power" (I, 241), sovereignty ("he / Who now is Sovran"—I, 245–246), and "majesty" (II, 266). Although none of these characteristics are tangible, they are completely real to Satan, and there is no warrant for our concluding that they are vague or indistinct.

The view which the angels in Heaven have of God is likewise largely conceptual, since the most dominant visible characteristic of God, his light, is too intense for them to behold (cf. III, 380–387). Thus when they view God they receive "Beatitude past utterance" (III, 62), as well as observing "Divine compassion . . . , / Love without end, and without measure Grace" (III, 141–142). The angels hear the Son speak of the Father's "goodness" (III, 165) and "greatness" (III, 165), and they attribute "Mercie and Grace" to him (II, 401).

[37] The definitive study of Milton's use of epithets in *Paradise Lost* is that by Kester Svendsen, "Epic Address and Reference and the Principle of Decorum in *Paradise Lost*," PQ, XXVIII (1949), 185–206, which I regard as one of the most significant analyses of Milton's epic style to appear and to which the present discussion is indebted.

Conceptual images abound in the song which the angels sing in praise of God:

> Thee Father first they sung Omnipotent,
> Immutable, Immortal, Infinite,
> Eternal King; thee Author of all being,
> Fountain of Light, thy self invisible   [III, 372–375].

The description is totally nonsensory, and yet it manages to connote as many values and emotional overtones as any descriptive passage can. To say that "Milton's style is not heavenly" and that Milton "cannot make his preferences poetically inevitable" is somewhat wide of the mark, founded on the assumption that we should grant poetic validity only to sensory imagery.[38]

Adam and Eve, like the angels, speak of God in terms of his qualities. Adam, for example, refers to him as "the power / That made us" (IV, 412–413), and Adam and Eve together praise him as "Power Divine" (V, 159) in their morning hymn. In asking God for a partner Adam also addresses God as the "Heav'nly Power" (VIII, 379). The concept of power is reiterated by other characters in the poem and becomes a leading characteristic of God. He is referred to as "the Almighty Power" (I, 44) and as "th' acknowledg'd Power supream" (IV, 956). We read also that "all Regal Power" (V, 739) is given to the Son, and that "All power" (VI, 678) is transferred to him. Again, Christ is called "The Filial Power" (VII, 587), and his appearance at the end of time will be "With glory and power" (XII, 460).

The attribution of power to God is only one example of

---

[38] The quoted remarks are by B. Rajan, *Paradise Lost and the Seventeenth Century Reader* (London, 1947), p. 129.

how a single conceptual image forms a recurring image pattern throughout the epic. One of the most frequently used of such terms is the concept of "glory." In the opening book the epic narrator speaks of the "invisible / Glory" of God (I, 369–370), and he subsequently repeats the conceptual image when stating that the demons' "spite still serves / His glory to augment" (II, 385–386). The plotting demons in Hell also conceive of God in terms of glory, as evidenced by Mammon's acknowledgment that God's residing in clouds leaves "his Glory unobscur'd" (II, 265). The conceptual image of glory is also frequently applied specifically to the Son of God, who is "The radiant image of his Glory" (III, 63). Similarly, on the Son "Impresst the effulgence of his Glorie abides" (III, 388), and the Father affirms that in the Son "my glory I behold / In full resplendence" (V, 719–720), addressing him elsewhere as the "Effulgence of my Glorie" (VI, 680). The Creator is described as "The King of Glorie" (VII, 208), riding "in Paternal Glorie" (VII, 219). When the Redeemer goes on the mission of judging Adam and Eve after the Fall he is said to rise from his seat "Of high collateral glorie" (X, 86). And the Son's position near the Father in Heaven is several times described conceptually as a proximity to glory, as when the Son rises "From the right hand of Glorie where he sate" (VI, 747) and when the Father, in turning toward the Son, is said to turn "Toward the right hand" of "his Glorie" (X, 64). The concept of glory thus becomes, by a cumulative process, one of the chief identifying characteristics of the Deity, and as with many other terms used to describe God, the images employed are conceptual rather than sensory.

A number of conceptual descriptions are applied specifically to the Son. The Father, for instance, uses three conceptual images in addressing the Son as "My word, my wisdom, and effectual might" (III, 170). The narrator informs us that in the Son "the fulness dwels of love divine" (III, 225), and Christ is destined to receive "all Power" (III, 317) from the Father. The Father associates such qualities as "glory," "might," and "Omnipotence" with the Son (V, 719–722). Again, Christ is hailed as "Second Omnipotence" (VI, 684), and in the Creation scene he is "Girt with Omnipotence, with . . . / Majestie Divine, Sapience, and Love" (VII, 194–195).

Titles and forms of address, whether they name qualities or roles, usually constitute conceptual images. A typical example occurs when the angels hail Christ as

> Victorious King,
> Son, Heir, and Lord, to him Dominion giv'n,
> Worthiest to Reign   [VI, 886–888].

The angels here name phenomena which have no tangible referent in the world of things but which nonetheless refer to such real entities as victory, kingship, sonship, dominion, and worth. This technique of describing the Deity conceptually through the use of epithets is one of the most consistently used techniques in *Paradise Lost*. In the opening hundred lines of the poem, for example, epithets employing conceptual images to describe God occur seven times: "Creator" (I, 31), "the most High" (I, 40), "The Almighty Power" (I, 44), "th' Omnipotent" (I, 49), "Eternal Justice" (I, 70), "the Potent Victor" (I, 95), and "the mightiest" (I, 99).

The frequency with which conceptual epithets occur is perhaps sufficiently obvious to preclude the necessity for extensive illustration. Consideration of some of the most frequently recurrent epithets, however, has a special relevance to the present argument. There are no fewer than twenty-nine epithets for God which include the term "almighty," and titles which attribute the identical concept of omnipotence to God number ten. In addition, God is called a "power" seven times in the poem, while the related concept of sovereignty is applied to him about ten times. Several related epithets identifying God by his role as Creator are also numerous: the title "Creator" is applied to him seventeen times, "Maker" twenty-four, and "Author" eight. Descriptions of God in terms of his role of kingship form another dominant conceptual motif in *Paradise Lost*, with the title "King" applied to him at least thirty-three times and "Lord" more than fifteen times. God is identified by the title "Deity" seven times and by the related epithet "Godhead" five. As might be expected, references to the inter-trinitarian roles of Father and Son are frequent; the title "Father" is used over forty times and the title "Son" appears more than forty-five times. All of these titles, and many others besides, give us a description of God comprised of conceptual images.

The important point which this summary of specific instances allows us to perceive is that the epic device of epithets and periphrastic titles was answerable to the apocalyptic nature of Milton's subject matter as well as to the problem of epic style. If, as theologians have said, God can be described by naming his qualities and roles but cannot be precisely located in space and time, the technique of applying epic titles to the Deity becomes an especially meaningful way of presenting God as a character in the poem. As Verity correctly stated regarding Milton's use of epithets, "An abstract expression for a concrete seems specially appropriate when divine persons are spoken of." [39] The commonplace critical view that Milton is excessively anthropomorphic and materialistic

[39] A. W. Verity, ed., *Milton: Paradise Lost* (Cambridge, Eng., 1929), II, 536.

in his portrayal of God needs qualification. Such a view overlooks that the anthropomorphism is consistently balanced by the presence of conceptual, nonmaterialistic images. We will appreciate the remarkable balance which Milton achieved only if we grant the epic epithets the significance which they deserve, only if we are aware that such titles are bona fide images, though of a conceptual rather than sensory nature.

The angels, like God, are frequently presented by means of conceptual images, and the conceptual references to them, too, are often attached to epithets and forms of reference. When, for example, the angels are called God's "Ministers of vengeance and pursuit" (I, 170), the title names a role which has no tangible object as its referent. Similar occurrences of conceptual images appear when the angels are called "the Sanctities of Heaven" (III, 60), "th' Ethereal Powers" (III, 100), "Heav'nly Powers" (III, 213), "th' Angelic Powers" (VI, 898), and "Powers of Heav'n" (VII, 162).[40] There are several passages in which the poet, in presenting a scene filled with celestial beings, multiplies the epithets and conceptual images:

> Hear all ye Angels, Progenie of Light,
> Thrones, Dominations, Princedoms, Vertues, Powers
> [V, 600–601].

> Regions they pass'd, the mightie Regencies
> Of Seraphim and Potentates and Thrones
> In thir triple Degrees   [V, 748–750].

> About his Chariot numberless were pour'd
> Cherub and Seraph, Potentates and Thrones,
> And Vertues, winged Spirits   [VII, 197–199].

[40] Further examples of this type of epithet applied to the angels are found in the following passages: III, 136, 217; VI, 22, 841; VII, 192; X, 615; XI, 221, 230, 232; XII, 577.

> him Thrones and Powers,
> Princedoms, and Dominations ministrant
> Accompanied to Heaven Gate   [X, 86–88].

By thus multiplying the terms the poet effectively gives a sense of vast numbers of angels, but since the images are titular words, the aggregate of images keeps the apocalyptic vision in the realm of concepts which transcends the world of visual objects.

The traditional division of the angels into various orders and ranks, despite Milton's rather loose adherence to such Scholastic distinctions, lent itself readily to speaking of the angels in terms of their intangible but real places in the celestial hierarchy. Thus we hear about archangels, cherub or cherubim, and seraph or seraphim about fifteen times each. Elsewhere we read of "Hierarchs" (V, 587; XI, 220), "Hierarchies" (V, 591, 692; VII, 192), "Degrees" (V, 591, 750, 838), and "Orders" (I, 737; V, 587, 591; VI, 885; X, 615). Even the references to the good angels as "spirits," of which there are more than forty, can be regarded as examples of conceptual images, since in this context the term "spirit" constitutes the title of a certain position in the hierarchy of God's Creation. The effect of all these titles is to give the angels a recognizable identity without ever making the presentation concrete and sensory.

Conceptual images are used to describe the angels in passages other than those involving epithets. They are "Crownd . . . with Glory" (V, 839), a quality which is attributed to them on several occasions (e.g., I, 141; III, 622). Other conceptual qualities associated with the angels in the apocalyptic state include purity (I, 425; IV, 837; V, 407), blessedness (III, 136), joy (III, 137), goodness (IV, 847), and virtue (IV, 848). All of these references represent another part of the general pattern of conceptual images used to describe supernatural beings, whether they be the angels or God.

The scene-agent ratio, Kenneth Burke's term for the consistency which exists between scene and character in a literary situation,[41] would lead us to expect a Heaven which, like its agents, is described in conceptual images. We have already observed how the Garden of Eden, like its inhabitants, is often conceptual in nature, and the descriptions of Heaven furnish further illustration of the same principle. The key conceptual terms used to describe Paradise—joy, delight, and bliss—are also the most frequently used in describing Heaven, suggesting that the apocalyptic state in Heaven is in many ways identical to the apocalyptic state in Paradise.

Descriptions of Heaven as a place of bliss abound. As Satan looks at his fallen cohorts on the burning lake, the narrator reminds us parenthetically that the fallen angels had been "Far other once beheld in bliss" (I, 607), and in the great consult in Hell Moloch laments the fact that the demons have been "driv'n out from bliss" (II, 86). As Satan views the golden stairs joining Heaven and Earth he is reminded of "His sad exclusion from the dores of Bliss" (III, 525), while Raphael describes the fall "from Heav'n to deepest Hell" conceptually as a fall "From what high state of bliss into what woe" (V, 543). Again, we are told that the demons have been driven "out from God and bliss" (VI, 52). In Heaven the Son sits by the Father "in bliss imbosm'd" (V, 597), and after triumphing

---

[41] *A Grammar of Motives and A Rhetroic of Motives*, pp. 7–9. Of particular interest in the present context is Burke's observation that "The contents of a divine container will synecdochically share in its divinity."

over the evil spirits he now "sits at the right hand of bliss" (VI, 892). Elsewhere we hear about "Heav'n the seat of bliss" (VI, 273) and about "the Peace of God in bliss" (VII, 55); and when the new Heaven succeeds the dissolution of the world the faithful will be received "into bliss" (XII, 462) and will enjoy "eternal Bliss" (XII, 551).

The apocalyptic region of Heaven is described by means of a number of other conceptual images as well. Heaven is a place where angels utter "joy" (III, 347) and where they spend "Thir happie hours in joy" (III, 417). We read also about "Heav'ns blessed peace" (VI, 267) and about the "Blessedness" (VII, 59) which characterizes the place. Heaven is a region "Founded in righteousness and peace and love" (XII, 550). And just as in the descriptions of Paradise a sensory image is sometimes combined with a conceptual image to form such nonempirical entities as the Tree of Knowledge and the Tree of Life, so, too, Heaven has its "Books of Life" (I, 363), "Fount of Life" (III, 357), and "river of Bliss" (III, 358), while the angels, in addition to drinking nectar, also "Quaff immortalitie and joy" (V, 638). Heaven, in short, is a conceptual world as well as a material one; adverse criticism disqualifies itself by complaining about the concreteness without recognizing the patterns of conceptual images.

The conclusion which the foregoing analysis suggests is that Milton's portrayal of the apocalyptic scenes and agents in *Paradise Lost* draws consistently and significantly upon conceptual images which name phenomena having no substantial, tangible existence. If, as Basil Willey claims, Milton "lived in a moral rather than a physical world," [42] that fact has a special relevance to the imagery which he used to portray apoca-

[42] *The Seventeenth Century Background* (London, 1942), p. 239.

lyptic reality.[43] Critical discussions centering upon the anthropomorphism and concreteness of Milton's apocalyptic technique are not wrong, since they direct attention to data which are clearly in the poem; but such discussions frequently err in their emphasis, overlooking that conceptual image patterns complement the concreteness of the apocalyptic descriptions. Attributing the quality of vagueness to conceptual images is also objectionable, since qualities and concepts are not indistinct simply because they are intangible. Indeed, a convincing case could be made for the impossibility of there being such a thing as an indistinct conceptual image, for although it is possible to describe such tangible objects as trees or people with varying degrees of definiteness, qualities such as bliss or joy do not lend themselves to such variation. It is difficult to see how such concepts, once they have been named, can be made either more or less distinct.

The use of conceptual imagery to present a reality which transcends everyday experience is an archetypal apocalyptic technique. It is the way of Platonic transcendence, since "Plato equated the divine with the abstract, apparently because both transcend the realm of the senses." [44] The ascent to a level of concepts is also a characteristic of Christian mysticism; as Saint Dionysius stated, "in ascribing, to that which is beyond all, attributes which are more fitting to Him, it is proper to ascribe things abstract. . . . For is He not more

[43] Hanford, in discussing Milton's portrayal of Heaven, makes the identical point when he states that Milton "knows, in fact, only a moral Paradise" (*A Milton Handbook*, p. 201).

[44] Burke, *A Grammar of Motives and A Rhetoric of Motives*, p. 253. J. A. Stewart, *The Myths of Plato* (London, 1905), p. 494, similarly states that in the Platonic transcendence "the Wisdom of God is that World of Ideas."

truly Life and Goodness than air and stone?"[45] The fact
that an apocalyptic vision, regardless of where or when it is
written, is likely to be comprised partly of conceptual images,
implies that an inability to grant poetic validity to such images will have a debilitating effect on a reader's response to
apocalyptic literature. When reading apocalyptic poetry such
as *Paradise Lost* we should, I submit, speak not of sensuous
poverty but of conceptual richness.

GENERIC IMAGERY

Milton's propensity for images which name a whole class of
objects has frequently been noted by commentators. Coleridge observed that the difference between his own poem "A
Hymn before Sunrise in the Vale of Chamouny" and poems
on sunrise by Milton, Thomson, and the Psalmist lay in the
fact that he himself addressed *"individual* objects as actually
present to his Senses," while the other poets "apostrophize
classes of things, presented by the memory and generalized by
the Understanding."[46] Many reasons for Milton's habitual
use of generalized imagery have been suggested. His generaliz-
ing habit has been related to his adherence to the classical tradition and its "instinct for rendering the normal and universal,
not the peculiar,"[47] to "the noble dignity of his themes,"[48]
to the generic demand than an epic be rendered in a public, ri-

[45] *The Theologia Mystica of Saint Dionysius,* ed. Alan W. Watts
(West Park, New York, 1944), p. 31.

[46] Samuel T. Coleridge, "Lecture on Milton and the *Paradise Lost,"*
in *Coleridge on the Seventeenth Century,* ed. Roberta F. Brinkley
(Durham, 1955), pp. 599–600.

[47] Douglas Bush, *Paradise Lost in Our Time* (Ithaca, 1945), p. 93.

[48] Walter Graham, "Sensuousness in the Poetry of Milton and
Keats," *SAQ,* XVI (1917), 351.

tualistic style and evoke stock responses,[49] and to the mythical, archetypal nature of Milton's subject matter, which presents images "of representative rather than of singular interest" [50] and images which record "not one experience, but a composite of many experiences." [51] It seems to me that all of these explanations are accurate and important.[52] In the context of the present study still another principle underlying Milton's generalized imagery suggests itself, namely, that generic images are a means of describing an experience which is remote from ordinary experience and which is less amenable to the realistic descriptive details which we associate with the objects of everyday reality. This is the view urged by T. S. Eliot when he says of the descriptions of Paradise that "a more detailed account of flora and fauna could only have assimilated Eden to the landscapes of earth with which we are familiar. As it is, the impression of Eden which we retain is the most suitable." [53]

[49] Lewis, *A Preface to Paradise Lost,* pp. 51–61, argues the relationship between generalized diction and epic expectations.

[50] Wright, *Milton's Paradise Lost,* p. 66. Wayne Shumaker, *Unpremeditated Verse* (Princeton, 1967), p. 115, likewise attributes Milton's generic imagery to the fact that "Milton is intent on the norm, the archetype, rather than on variations from it."

[51] Isabel MacCaffrey, *Paradise Lost as "Myth"* (Cambridge, Mass., 1959), p. 116.

[52] Another consideration is suggested by Kenneth Myrick's analysis of the style of Sidney's *Arcadia* in *Sir Philip Sidney as a Literary Craftsman* (Lincoln, 1965; first pub., 1935), p. 187. In discussing Sidney's habit of naming "only the classes" to which objects belong, Myrick attributes "the generalness of the description" and the lack of "realistic detail" to the fact that Sidney was "a person trained to think in logical categories." Logical training and inclination are equally characteristic of Milton, as has been amply demonstrated by Dennis H. Burden, *The Logical Epic* (Cambridge, Mass., 1967).

[53] *On Poetry and Poets,* p. 178. A similar view is stated by Douglas Bush, *Paradise Lost in Our Time,* p. 97: "A localized sharpness of

Since generic images name classes of things without attempting to delineate the objects further, such images have obvious affinities with conceptual images. The distinction between the two kinds of images is that generic images name things having a visible, tangible existence in the external world, while conceptual pheonomena have no such tangible existence. It is a moot question whether such generic images constitute visual images. To T. S. Eliot generalized images are not primarily visual, and he discusses such images in support of his famous contention that "Milton may be said never to have seen anything." [54] Another commentator asserts with pejorative intent that when reading Milton's description of Paradise in generic terms he does "not *see* these flowers." [55] To other critics, however, generic images are visual in effect. E. M. W. Tillyard, for instance, takes Eliot to task for equating generalized imagery with nonsensuous imagery, since in his view generic imagery can carry full sensory force.[56] J. B. Leishman likewise believes that Eliot errs in assuming that lack of minute detail results in an imprecise visualization,[57] and D. C. Allen speaks of "the visual image suggested by the word *flower*." [58] Presumably, then, whether generic imagery is visual or nonvisual is a question of reader response, and in the interest of keeping the present analysis descriptive in nature I shall speak simply of "generic imagery," differentiating

sensation would have both cramped and dissipated that half-abstract impression of an ideal world."

[54] *On Poetry and Poets*, p. 162.

[55] Laurence Binyon, "A Note on Milton's Imagery and Rhythm," in *Seventeenth Century Studies Presented to Sir Herbert Grierson* (Oxford, 1938), p. 189.

[56] *The Miltonic Setting: Past and Present* (Cambridge, Eng., 1938), pp. 93–94.

[57] *Essays and Studies*, n. s., IV, 18.

[58] *The Harmonious Vision* (Baltimore, 1954), p. 99.

it from conceptual imagery, already discussed, and nonvisual imagery, which I shall take up presently.

Descriptions of the geography of Heaven furnish some typical examples of how Milton employs generic imagery in his depiction of apocalyptic scenes. We are told, for instance, about Heaven's "Fields" (I, 249; II, 768), "Flowers" (II, 245; III, 359), and "Hills" (VI, 528, 639, 644). We know, too, that Heaven possesses "Vale . . . , Wood . . . , Stream" (VI, 70), and "Plant, Fruit, Flour" (VI, 475). The scene includes "Hill and Dale" (VI, 641), as well as "Rocks, Waters, Woods" (VI, 645) and "Hill and Valley" (VI, 784). In all of these instances Heaven is described in images naming tangible objects, but by naming only general classes of objects the poet manages to present his apocalyptic scene as something removed from the everyday world of specific objects and realistic detail.

Heaven has its urban aspects as well, and here, too, generic images frequently constitute the substance of the description. We are told, for instance, that Heaven has "high Towrs" (I, 749; II, 62), but "the Towrs of Heav'n" (II, 129) are not pictured with any additional details. Similarly, there is an "Altar" (II, 244) in the heavenly region, as well as a "high Temple" (VII, 148), but once again we are prevented from locating the objects very specifically in space because of the generality of the descriptive terms. The generic image "gate" is used in descriptions of Heaven fifteen times, and God's "throne" is mentioned more than twenty times, and in most instances there are no specific details added to the generic image. Similar instances of generic imagery include "the wall of Heaven" (III, 503), "a Structure high" (III, 503), "a Kingly Palace" (III, 505), "Mansion" (III, 699), "Sanctuarie of Heaven" (VI, 672), "Battlements" (II, 1049), and "habitations" (VII,

186). The cumulative effect of such images is to portray a realm devoid of the precise colors and shapes which, as D. C. Allen has demonstrated, Renaissance Neoplatonists and poets regarded as "a confession of imperfection" and a result of the Fall.[59]

The greatest concentration of generic images occurs in the descriptions of Paradise, which is perhaps the most substantial of all regions in the cosmos of *Paradise Lost*. The flora of the garden are customarily presented generically rather than specifically. We read of Eden's "loftie shades" (III, 734),[60] "Groves" (IX, 388), "Fruit" or "Fruits" (IV, 219, 331, 422),[61] and "Flour" or "Flours" (IV, 241, 256, 438).[62] Paradise also has "goodliest Trees loaden with fairest Fruit, / Blossoms and Fruits" (IV, 147–148), but aside from their superlative quality we do not know anything very specific about these plants of Paradise. The same principle underlies several descriptions of the trees in Eden, which are described superlatively rather than with precise detail: "Trees of noblest kind" (IV, 217), "goodliest Trees" (VIII, 304), "fairest Fruit" (VIII, 307), "rich Trees" (IV, 248) and "delicious Vines" (V, 635). Other examples of images naming whole classes of objects occur with the descriptions of "the Trees / In Paradise" (IV, 421–422), "Those Blossoms" (IV, 630), "Our tended Plants" (V, 22), "those Trees" (V, 309), "These various fruits" (V, 390), and "each Plant" (IV, 240;

[59] *The Harmonious Vision*, pp. 101–102.

[60] Wright, *Milton's Paradise Lost*, pp. 70–72, presents evidence for concluding that the word "shade" carries the Virgilian meaning "trees" or "shrubery" in many passages in *Paradise Lost*.

[61] Other references to "fruit" include V, 83, 304, 341, 635; VIII, 44, 527; IX, 735, 781.

[62] Futher instances of "flour" occur in IV, 451, 697, 709; V, 212, 636; VIII, 44, 286, 527; IX, 278, 437.

V, 327). Sometimes a whole scene of vegetation is called into being by the naming of several classes of plants, as when we read of the sun's journey over "herb, tree, fruit, and flour" (IV, 644). In all these instances, generic images create for us a scene which is wholly tangible but which is also removed from the world of realistic detail.

The animals which inhabit the prelapsarian garden are also customarily described generically. We hear several times about "Birds" as a group (IV, 264, 642, 651; V, 8; VIII, 265). Similarly, we read about "Flocks" (IV, 252), "the sportful Herd / Of those fourfooted kinds" (IV, 396–397), "Beast and Bird" (IV, 600), "Beast, Bird, Insect, or Worm" (IV, 704) and "Creatures that livd, and movd, and walk'd, or flew" (VIII, 264). Often terms denoting the whole animal kingdom appear: "Animals" (IV, 621), "Beast" or "Beasts" (IV, 177, 341, 704),[63] "Creature" or "Creatures" (III, 230; IV, 287, 431),[64] or simply "all things" (IV, 611; VIII, 265).

We have already observed how the terrain of Heaven is frequently described in generic images, and the geography of Paradise shares the same descriptive technique. The garden, for example, is surrounded by a "Wall" (IV, 182), but the wall is not delineated for us with precise descriptive detail. Eden likewise has its "River large" (IV, 223) and "Mountain" (IV, 226), as well as its "Hill and Dale and Plaine" (IV, 243). There are "Lawns, or level Downs" (IV, 252), "hills" (IV, 261), and "a Lake" (IV, 261). Similar generic images describe Eden's "field and grove" (IV, 265), "Hill or Thicket" (IV, 681), and "this delicious Grove" (VII, 537).

[63] Additional references to "beast" include VIII, 395, 397, 438, 582, 594; IX, 94, 521, 543, 556; X, 94.

[64] More examples of "creature" are found in IV, 616, 703; V, 164; VII, 413, 455, 507.

In several instances a whole scene is evoked simply by naming the objects in the view: [65]

> about me round I saw
> Hill, Dale, and shadie Woods, and sunnie Plaines
> [VIII, 261–262].

Ye Hills and Dales, ye Rivers, Woods, and Plaines
[VIII, 275].

> sweet interchange
> Of Hill, and Vallie, Rivers, Woods and Plaines,
> Now Land, now Sea, and Shores with Forrest crownd,
> Rocks, Dens, and Caves   [IX, 115–118].

There are a few scenes in the poem in which vegetation, animal life, and topography are together described as a composite generic world. The most notable of such passages is the Creation scene. Here "Mountains" (VII, 285), "Hills" (VII, 288), and "Waters" (VII, 290) combine with "Herb . . . / And Fruit Tree" (VII, 310–311) and "copious Fruit" (VII, 325). "Each / Plant of the field" (VII, 334–335) and "every Herb" (VII, 336) are complemented by the animal world, also described in generic terms: "Fowle" (VII, 389, 398), "each / Soul living" (VII, 391–392), and "every Bird of wing" (VII, 394). The topography of "Caves, and Fens and shoares" (VII, 417), "Woods" (VII, 434), and "Fields" (VII, 460) is populated by "Cattel and Creeping things, and Beast of the Earth" (VII, 452), by "Innumerous living Creatures" (VII, 455), and by "flocks" (VII, 461) and

[65] This descriptive technique, recurrent in eighteenth-century nature poetry and in Wordsworth, is technically known as the "prospect" technique, which includes among its characteristics "the tendency to enumerate rather than describe in detail" (Cf. C. V. Deane, *Aspects of Eighteenth Century Nature Poetry* [Oxford, 1935], p. 106.)

"Herds" (VII, 462). The generic entities "Fowl, Fish, Beast" (VII, 503) occupy a generic universe of "Aire, Water, Earth" (VII, 502). A nearly identical world is described when Satan views the prelapsarian garden just before the Fall; the devil sees "Herb" and "Plant" (IX, 111), "Hill, and Vallie, Rivers, Woods and Plaines" (IX, 116), "Rocks, Dens, and Caves" (IX, 118), and "Creatures animate" (IX, 112).

As these passages demonstrate, the technique of employing generic images to present apocalyptic reality is a pervasive stylistic feature of *Paradise Lost*. The presence of this trait is, as I have stated, explicable on a number of complementary grounds. What is claimed here is that the use of generic imagery is appropriate in a special way to the presentation of the apocalyptic vision and that it is consistently used in such a manner in Milton's epic. Form and style serve many simultaneous functions in *Paradise Lost*, and in the present instance one of the ways in which generic imagery adheres to a principle of decorum is to make the apocalyptic vision remote from the ordinary world of realistic details and precise physical and spatial boundaries.

NONVISUAL IMAGERY

The preceding analysis of conceptual and generic imagery suggests that the apocalyptic imagery of *Paradise Lost* often shares the underlying principle of being, in one way or another, less sharply located in space than are the realistic physical objects in the everyday natural experience of man. The patterns of nonvisual imagery in the poem are additional evidence of Milton's attempt to portray apocalyptic reality as something which transcends the world about us. Since the images with which I am concerned here name things which are perceived through the senses, they belong to a different category from the conceptual images, which are totally nonsensory. Yet it is obvious that within the order of sensory imagery, nonvisual images such as those of smell and sound are far less tangible and sharply defined than images naming the concrete, visible objects in the world about us.

It has long been the critical practice to discuss Milton's predilection for nonvisual imagery in connection with the effects of his blindness. T. S. Eliot, for example, prefaces his discussion of the nonvisual nature of Milton's imagery by stating, "The most important fact about Milton, for my purpose, is his blindness." [66] T. H. Banks, in his survey of Milton's imagery, comes to the same conclusion regarding Milton: "His visual sense . . . weakened, but his other senses—smell, hearing, and touch—became more quick and sharp. In so doing, they showed a development characteristic of a man who goes blind." [67]

In the present context I wish to take the view that, whatever the biographical facts of the case may be, there is a significant formal reason for the portrayal of apocalyptic reality in nonvisual terms. Such nonvisual images constitute an archetypal technique for portraying an experience which is at once like and unlike ordinary experience, which is amenable to human understanding but also removed from the tangible world about us. That nonvisual imagery is related in a special way to the presentation of apocalyptic reality has been recognized by several commentators. One writer observes that "the literally unimaginable nature of his subject prevented Milton from appealing at all often or consistently to our visualizing

[66] *On Poetry and Poets*, p. 157.

[67] *Milton's Imagery* (New York, 1950), p. 137. The same conclusion is reached by Sigmund Spaeth, *Milton's Knoweldge of Music* (Ann Arbor, 1963; first pub., 1913), pp. 79, 92; and Eleanor Gertrude Brown, *Milton's Blindness* (New York, 1934), p. 136.

faculty." [68] Similarly, a leading critic of the visionary aspects of romantic poetry equates aural and apocalyptic imagery when he writes, "The art past ripeness and harvest is the art of the ear, apocalyptic." [69] It has also been observed that a particular branch of apocalyptic literature, the mystical garden, includes among its conventions a reliance on images of fragrance.[70] As with so many apocalyptic techniques discussed in this book, there is a long philosophical tradition behind the technique of nonvisual imagery, and Arnold Stein is able to adduce relevant passages from both Plato and Aristotle in which they grant primacy among the senses to the eye but in so doing concede that sight is linked particularly to our knowledge of the physical world, while hearing is in a special way man's avenue to the moral universe and the realm of superior intelligence.[71]

Let us observe some of the ways in which Milton associates apocalyptic reality with nonvisual sensory imagery. The fragrance of the Garden of Eden is a well-known instance. As Satan makes his initial approach to the garden we read,

> now gentle gales
> Fanning thir odoriferous wings dispense
> Native perfumes, and whisper whence they stole
> Those balmie spoiles   [IV, 156–159].

This description is followed by the extended epic simile of spice merchants who sail to regions where they find "*Sabean* Odours" (IV, 162), "spicie shoare" (IV, 162), and "grateful

[68] Donald Davie, "Syntax and Music in *Paradise Lost*," in *The Living Milton*, ed. Frank Kermode (London, 1960), p. 71.

[69] Harold Bloom, *The Visionary Company: A Reading of English Romantic Poetry* (Garden City, New York, 1963), p. 453.

[70] The conventional fragrance of mystical gardens is noted by Marie P. Hamilton, "The Meaning of the Middle English *Pearl*," *PMLA*, LXX (1955), 817–818.

[71] *Answerable Style* (Minneapolis, 1953), pp. 152–153.

smell" (IV, 165). All of these olfactory images are in turn transferred to Satan's approach to Paradise when the simile is specifically applied to his journey toward the garden: "So entertaind those odorous sweets the Fiend" (IV, 166). The sensory and emotional weight of such a description exceeds the space devoted to presenting it, and once Paradise has been established so fully as a place of fragrance we need only be reminded of its odors in subsequent passages in order for its fragrance to remain in our minds as one of the garden's dominant characteristics.

Reminders of the fragrance of Paradise are relatively frequent. The epic narrator describes Eden's "Groves whose rich Trees wept odorous Gumms and Balme" (IV, 248), and he tells about the "vernal aires, / Breathing the smell of field and grove" (IV, 264–265). In Eve's lyric love song addressed to Adam she mentions that after showers the fertile earth is "fragrant" (IV, 645), and later we learn that the bower of Adam and Eve is comprised partly "Of firm and fragrant leaf" (IV, 695) and that on the sides of the bower "each odorous bushie shrub / Fenc'd up the verdant wall" (IV, 696–697). Eve decks her nuptial bed with "sweet-smelling Herbs" (IV, 709). Adam, in expressing his alarm over the rapid growth of the plants in Paradise, mentions "those dropping Gumms" (IV, 630), and although it is perhaps not unavoidable that the image be considered olfactory, we are justified in associating odors with the "Gumms" because the association is made elsewhere in the poem when Adam speaks of "sweet smelling Gumms" (XI, 327).

As the narrative unfolds there are further confirmations of our impression of Paradise as a place of olfactory richness and fulfillment. At the beginning of Book V Adam wakes Eve so that they can mark "how blows the Citron Grove, / What

drops the Myrrhe, and what the balmie Reed" (V, 22–23).
Later Adam again urges his spouse to rise and work

> Among the Groves, the Fountains, and the Flours
> That open now thir choicest bosom'd smells
>
> > [V, 126–127].

As Raphael descends from Heaven to Eden our olfactory impressions are again reinforced as the angel

> **now is** come
> Into the blissful field, through Groves of Myrrhe,
> And flouring Odours, Cassia, Nard, and Balme
>
> > [V, 291–293].

A few lines later we read that the angel proceeded "through the spicie Forrest" (V, 298). Eve, as the queenly hostess of Raphael, "strews the ground / With Rose and Odours from the shrub unfum'd" (V, 348–349), while Adam and Raphael retire to the lodge, which "smil'd / With flourets dek't and fragrant smells" (V, 378–379). After Creation the Earth is said to possess a "bosom smelling sweet" (VII, 319), and the flowers of Eden, we are told, "breathd / Thir morning incense" (IX, 193–194), filling the Creator's nostrils "With grateful Smell" (IX, 197). The fragrance of Paradise becomes so dominant that it finally assumes a kind of substantial quality, as when Satan spies Eve "Veild in a Cloud of Fragrance" (IX, 425).

The Garden of Eden was by tradition and convention a place of sensuous fulfillment, and Milton's garden adheres to that tradition, despite the consistent presence of conceptual image patterns. A great deal of the sensuous density of the garden is olfactory in nature, and this is what we would expect of a realm of experience which is sensory but yet remote from the more tangible, substantial world of everyday reality. This perhaps explains why stressing the odors of Paradise was a theological tradition,[72] and why the use of olfactory imagery recurs in literature which portrays transcendental experience.[73]

The technique of using olfactory images to present a realm which is recognizably sensory but not substantial and visual constitutes a motif in the celestial scenes of the epic also. Our earliest views of Heaven—through the eyes of the fallen angels —draw several times on images of fragrance. Belial recalls that God's "Altar breathes / Ambrosial Odours" (II, 244–245), while Beelzebub instills in his fallen cohorts the desire either to re-enter Heaven or find a mild zone visited by Heaven's influence, where "the soft delicious Air / . . . Shall breathe her balme" (II, 400, 402). After the narrative has carried us from Hell to Heaven we find that "while God spake, ambrosial fragrance fill'd / All Heav'n" (III, 135–136). Similarly, Raphael, enroute to Paradise, "shook his Plumes, that Heav'nly fragrance filld / The circuit wide" (V, 286–287). And later in the poem our impression of Heaven as a place of odors is confirmed when we read that the prayers of Adam and Eve ascend to Heaven "clad / With incense" (XI, 17–18) and "mixt / With incense" (XI, 24–25). As in Para-

[72] The tradition was perpetuated by such writers as Bernardus Sylvestris, Godfrey of Viterbo, Prudentius, Pseudo-Tertullian, and Sidonius Apollinaris. Cf. A. Bartlett Giamatti, *The Earthly Paradise and the Renaissance Epic* (Princeton, 1966), pp. 70–79. Parallel statements are collected by Mary Irma Corcoran, *Milton's Paradise with Reference to the Hexameral Background* (Washington, D.C., 1945), pp. 22–23; and by Howard Rollin Patch, *The Other World According to Descriptions in Medieval Literature* (Cambridge, Mass., 1950), pp. 88, 97, 100, 111, 115, 132, and 137.

[73] One of the most famous instances in English literature of the portrayal of a transcendental realm through nonvisual images of smell occurs in stanza 5 of Keats's "Ode to a Nightingale," where the poet "cannot see" the flowers of the transcendental region but instead perceives the natural objects in the scene through their smells.

dise, then, sensory experience in Heaven is often comprised of odors and fragrance. It should be observed also that the descriptions of smells in *Paradise Lost* tend to be general rather than specific, with the generic nature of the images reinforcing the intangible, unlocalized effect.

The presence of aural imagery in apocalyptic contexts is even more frequent than is the presence of olfactory images. Descriptions of Eden again yield some representative examples. One of the first sensory experiences which Eve had after her creation was hearing the "murmuring sound / Of waters" (IV, 453–454). When Adam first awakes after his creation he likewise is at once attracted by such sounds as the "liquid Lapse of murmuring Streams" (VIII, 263) and "Birds on the branches warbling" (VIII, 265). The nights in Eden are accompanied by the "amorous descant sung" by the nightingale (IV, 603), while Adam and Eve "lulld by Nightingales imbraceing slept" (IV, 771). When Adam led Eve to the nuptial bed "heav'nly Quires the Hymenaean sung" (IV, 711), and during the night it is customary to hear in Eden "Celestial voices . . . / Singing thir great Creator" (IV, 682, 684), and to find bands of angels

> nightly rounding walk
> With Heav'nly touch of instrumental sounds
> In full harmonic number joind, thir songs
> Divide the night   [IV, 685–688].

Adam and Eve awake to "the shrill Matin Song / Of birds on every bough" (V, 7–8), and in the morning hymn of our first parents the music of all Creation becomes a dominant motif:

> Fountains and yee, that warble, as ye flow,
> Melodious murmurs, warbling tune his praise.

> Joyn voices all ye living Souls, ye Birds,
> That singing up to Heaven Gate ascend,
> Bear on your wings and in your notes his praise
> . . . Witness if I be silent, Morn or Eeven,
> To Hill, or Valley, Fountain, or fresh shade
> Made vocal by my Song, and taught his praise
>
> [V, 195–199, 202–204].

The prelapsarian garden, in short, is replete with sounds and music. The aural nature of experience in the garden is reinforced by Adam's decorous compliment to Raphael, when he tells the angel:

> Thy words
> Attentive, and with more delighted eare,
> Divine instructor, I have heard, then when
> Cherubic Songs by night from neighboring Hills
> Aereal Music send   [V, 544–548].

Aural harmony becomes a kind of ritualistic feature of life in the garden, as evidenced by the account of how in the morning "forth came the human pair / And joind thir vocal Worship to the Quire / Of Creatures" (IX, 197–199). Sound is thus one of the dominant sense impressions which we gain from descriptions of the garden, and the intangible nature of aural imagery accords well with the apocalyptic nature of the subject.

The greatest concentration of sound imagery occurs in the presentation of the celestial parts of the poem. In Book III we read:

> No sooner had th' Almighty ceas't, but all
> The multitude of Angels with a shout
> Loud as from numbers without number, sweet
> As from blest voices, uttering joy, Heav'n rung

> With Jubilee, and loud Hosanna's filld
> Th' eternal Regions   [III, 344-349].

After the angels had bowed with reverence toward God

> again thir gold'n Harps they took,
> . . . and with Praeamble sweet
> Of charming symphonie they introduce
> Thir sacred Song, and waken raptures high;
> No voice exempt, no voice but well could joine
> Melodious part, such concord is in Heav'n
>   [III, 365, 367-371].

In praising the Son the individual angels affirm, "never shall my Harp thy praise / Forget, nor from thy Fathers praise disjoine" (III, 414-415). And in case the dramatic presentation were insufficient, the epic narrator summarizes the action as well:

> Thus they in Heav'n, above the starry Sphear,
> Thir happie hours in joy and hymning spent
>   [III, 416-417].

In the first extended scene set in Heaven, then, music and sound are established as the normative response of the angels to God and his apocalyptic acts. With remarkable consistency, high points in the events which occur in Heaven are climaxed by angelic songs and music. The angels with songs

> And choral symphonies, Day without Night,
> Circle his Throne rejoycing   [V, 161-163].

The angels spend "solemn days . . . / In song and dance about the sacred Hill" (V, 618-619), and the "mystical dance" of the celestial spheres gives such "charming tones, that Gods own ear / Listens delighted" (V, 626-627).

When some of the angels in Heaven disperse at night to sleep in tents, others "Melodious Hymns about the sovran throne / Alternate all night long" (V, 656–657). Before the rebellion of Satan's forces all of the angels were

> wont to meet
> So oft in Festivals of joy and love
> Unanimous, as sons of one great Sire
> Hymning th' Eternal Father [VI, 93–96].

Satan scornfully describes the faithful angels as spirits who have been "traind up in Feast and Song" (VI, 167), and he calls them, with malicious intent, "the Ministrelsie of Heav'n" (VI, 168). The Son tells the Father that following the expulsion of the evil angels from Heaven the faithful angels will

> circling thy holy Mount
> Unfained *Halleluiahs* to thee sing,
> Hymns of high praise [VI, 743–745].

And when Christ returns from the overthrow of the rebel angels, "each order bright, / Sung Triumph, and him sung Victorious King" (VI, 885–886). As the Creation drama unfolds in Book VII, angelic song climaxes the Father's decree of the Creation (VII, 182), several of the days of Creation (VII, 256–259, 274–275, 450), and the return to Heaven following the Creation (VII, 558ff., 594–601). After so many scenes of hymning, the narrator's concluding summary is the inevitable one: "So sung they, and the Empyrean rung, / With *Halleluiahs*" (VII, 633–634).

Musical sound thus becomes ritualistic in Heaven, the normative response of angels to apocalyptic events. Because sound imagery appears full-fledged at so many climactic moments in the story, it becomes dominant in our general impression of the celestial region, and the force of such imagery is qualitatively greater than any tabulation of the number of passages containing it could indicate. We know that songs of praise are perpetual in both Heaven and Paradise, and we need only occasional reminders to keep that impression in our consciousness.

The question of the sensuousness of Milton's apocalyptic scenes is not uncommonly raised by commentators. The view expressed by F. R. Leavis that *Paradise Lost* suffers from "a certain sensuous poverty" [74] is in the mainstream of twentieth-century critical theory, with its emphasis on images which convey sharply localized sensations. J. B. Broadbent counters this complaint with a view which my earlier discussion of conceptual imagery would substantiate: "The point surely is that in Paradise the details are not so sensuously rich because sensuousness would have been out of place: these are the riches of God." [75] Yet it is important that we grant full consideration to the sensuous elements in the apocalyptic scenes. These scenes carry more sensuous force than is often realized, but the sensory impressions belong to the apocalyptic senses of smell and hearing rather than to the everyday world of visual details.

[74] *Revaluation,* p. 47.
[75] "Milton's Paradise," *MP,* LI (1954), 171.

❧ 8

The Unified Apocalyptic Vision

The foregoing chapters have isolated the motifs which underlie Milton's apocalyptic vision in *Paradise Lost*. Such a separation of the apocalyptic vision into its constituent parts is necessary if we are to understand the basic principles which determine the nature of that vision. Lest the poem remain a series of fragments, however, it is necessary to emphasize the manner in which the various individual techniques become organically fused in the texture of the poem. The purpose of this concluding chapter is to demonstrate the simultaneous presence of many apocalyptic elements in some representative passages in the poem.

At the end of Book II Satan, enroute from Hell to Paradise, beholds

> Farr off th' Empyreal Heav'n, extended wide
> In circuit, undetermind square or round,
> With Opal Towrs and Battlements adorn'd
> Of living Saphire, once his native Seat;
> And fast by hanging in a golden Chain
> This pendant world, in bigness as a Starr
> Of smallest Magnitude close by the Moon
>
> [II, 1047–1053].

These seven lines represent a tissue of apocalyptic motifs. Heaven's spatial remoteness is indicated by its position "Farr off"—so far off, in fact, that Satan is unable to see the exact shape of the celestial domain. The Earth, too, is so remote, from the reader as from Satan, that it appears to have no more magnitude than a star. Temporal distance is established by the statement that Heaven was "once" Satan's native region, before he fell. The same phrase can be viewed as an example of the technique of contrast, with the apocalyptic state of perfection described as a condition which forms an opposition to postlapsarian experience. There is analogy in the passage as well, as evidenced by the fact that Heaven possesses such recognizably urban characteristics as towers and battlements. Despite the element of analogy, however, the enameled images of "Opal," "Saphire," and "golden" give the heavenly city an aura of supernatural hardness, brilliance, and permanence which transcend the transient world of nature which we know. Finally, the phrase "living Saphire" is a mystic oxymoron, combining two qualities (here vitality and marmoreal hardness) which in empirical reality cannot coexist but which in combination suggest a transcendental realm where earthly laws of contradiction no longer exist.

The invocation to Book III, ending with the poet's prayer for divine illumination to enable him to "see and tell / Of things invisible to mortal sight" (III, 54–55), is followed by this description of God as he looks down from Heaven:

> Now had the Almighty Father from above,
> From the pure Empyrean where he sits
> High Thron'd above all highth, bent down his eye,
> His own works and their works at once to view:
> About him all the Sanctities of Heaven
> Stood thick as Starrs, and from his sight receiv'd

Beatitude past utterance; on his right
The radiant image of his Glory sat,
His onely Son; On Earth he first beheld
Our two first Parents, yet the onely two
Of mankind, in the happie Garden plac't,
Reaping immortal fruits of joy and love,
Uninterrupted joy, unrivald love
In blissful solitude   [III, 56–69].

In reading the passage, one of the first impressions which we gain is the remoteness of the Father, "High Thron'd above all highth" and surveying all things at once. The analogy which exists between the supernatural and human realms is suggested by the inter-trinitarian roles of Father and Son, as well as by the anthropomorphic detail of God's eye and his being localized on a throne. The Deity is distanced from the reader by being portrayed through his effect on the consciousness of the angels, who receive "Beatitude" from his sight. There is a concentration of conceptual imagery in the description, evident in the identification of the angels by a title or role ("Sanctities of Heaven"), in the attribution of the qualities of omnipotence and glory to the Deity, and in the portrayal of the Paradisal state as one comprised of such intangible qualities as happiness, joy, love, and bliss. Empirical reality is negated in the terms "past utterance," "immortal," "uninterrupted," and "unrivald." And the entire vignette is distanced temporally by our awareness that the story concerns the original ancestors of the human race, who are "yet the onely two / Of mankind."

The angels' hymn to the Father in Book III contains an equally rich profusion of apocalyptic motifs. The angels sing thus:

> Thee Father first they sung Omnipotent,
> Immutable, Immortal, Infinite,
> Eternal King; thee Author of all being,
> Fountain of Light, thy self invisible
> Amidst the glorious brightness where thou sit'st
> Thron'd inaccessible, but when thou shad'st
> The full blaze of thy beams, and through a cloud
> Drawn round about thee like a radiant Shrine,
> Dark with excessive bright thy skirts appeer,
> Yet dazle Heav'n, that brightest Seraphim
> Approach not, but with both wings veil thir eyes
>
> > [III, 372–382].

An initial consideration is that this vision of the Deity of *Paradise Lost* is distanced by the fact that it is voiced by characters in the story; it is all reported to us indirectly as the angels' view of God. We do not see directly any of the characteristics ascribed here to the Father. The passage depends heavily on conceptual images, not naming things with a tangible referent but rather such intangible qualities as omnipotence, immutability, immortality, infinity, and glory. The principle of negation, denying to God the qualities of empirical existence, appears in the words "Immutable," "Immortal," "Infinite," "invisible," and "inaccessible." Similarly, the portrayal of God as light suggests the Deity's lack of human personality. The element of analogy between apocalyptic and ordinary reality is present in the ascription of the human roles of "Father" and "King" to God, as well as by the attribution of light to the celestial region. At the same time some of these analogues are modified in such a way as to imply a contrast with human experience; the modifying term in the phrase "Eternal King" implies that God is different from earthly kings, and the light

233

which is God is unearthly in its brightness and intensity. The Deity is veiled from human view in several ways. His brightness is so intense as to be invisible to mortal sight, a cloud is drawn around him like a shrine, and the angels, whose view is ours, do not approach God without first veiling their eyes with their wings. There is, finally, the technique of mystic oxymoron, present in the phrase "Dark with excessive bright," since only in the transcendental realm can darkness and light exist together without contradiction.

Apocalyptic patterns appear with such frequency in the descriptions of Paradise in Book IV that practically any passage can be shown to consist of an amalgam of apocalyptic themes. A typical fusion of several techniques appears in the lines in which the poet strives

> to tell how, if Art could tell,
> How from that Saphire Fount the crisped Brooks,
> Rowling on Orient Pearl and sands of Gold,
> With mazie error under pendant shades
> Ran Nectar, visiting each plant, and fed
> Flours worthy of Paradise which not nice Art
> In Beds and curious Knots, but Nature boon
> Powrd forth profuse on Hill and Dale and Plaine
>
> [IV, 236–243].

The initial protestation by the narrator that his art is inadequate to the task of describing Paradise is a kind of negation —a way of denying that the apocalyptic vision is amenable to portrayal in human terms. Because the passage describes an earthly garden our expectation that it bears many resemblances to empirical reality is confirmed by the recognizable terrain of streams, trees, flowers, hills, and plains. The images describing the scene tend to be generic, naming broad classes of objects without resorting to realistic detail: "Brooks," "each plant," "Flours," "Hill and Dale and Plaine." When we read that the flowers of the garden are "Flours worthy of Paradise" the empirical quality of the flowers is modified somewhat, since the qualifying phrase suggests that the flowers of Eden surpass in worth the flowers of ordinary experience. The narrator's assertion that the arrangement of the flowers is not a product of human art but of nature is part of the general pattern of pastoral negation, with the garden representing an experience characterized by an absence of human civilization. In view of the narrator's explicit exclusion of art from Paradise, as well as the inherently vital, vegetative nature of the garden, it is paradoxical to find the garden described in images of jeweled hardness. Yet we read about the "Saphire Fount," "crisped Brooks," "Orient Pearl and sands of Gold," all of which are part of the enameled, permanent quality which raises Paradise above ordinary nature. Finally, the phrase "mazie error" is an example of how words which were originally positive in meaning but eventually acquired negative connotations can be used to reflect a parallel contrast between unfallen and fallen moral states.

Analysis of several lines from the account of the war in Heaven will illustrate how various apocalyptic strands are combined in a typical passage from yet another part of the poem. On the occasion of the rebel angels' procurement of gunpowder from Heaven's soil Satan asks his followers,

> Which of us who beholds the bright surface
> Of this Ethereous mould whereon we stand,
> This continent of spacious Heav'n, adornd
> With Plant, Fruit, Flour Ambrosial, Gemms & Gold,
> Whose Eye so superficially surveyes
> These things . . . ?   [VI, 472–477].

The anthropomorphic nature of the angels emerges from the presence of Satan as a speaking character and from references to the angels' eyes and to their standing on the ground. Scenic analogies between Heaven and Earth are also present, as evidenced by the totally physical ground and "continent" which are the chief topic of Satan's address, as well as by the catalog of geographic details which Satan gives. The physical objects are described in generic images: "Plant, Fruit, Flour . . . , Gemms & Gold." Empirical images are modified in the phrases "Ethereous mould" and "Flour Ambrosial," where the qualifying terms place the objects in an apocalyptic context. That the celestial region possesses a supernatural permanence which contrasts with the transient world of nature is indicated by the enameled images of "Gemms & Gold," as well as by the allusion to "the bright surface" of Heaven, with its suggestion of a surface brilliance which goes beyond earthly experience. A final apocalyptic technique underlying the passage is dramatic distancing, for the description of Heaven which we have here is the overheard speech by Satan, an internal character, to other characters in the story, and the whole passage is part of Raphael's narrative to Adam and is, in turn, mediated to the reader through the epic narrator.

As this analysis of selected passages illustrates, different strands of apocalyptic technique are fused in the texture of the poem. Various kinds of contrast, negation, analogy, distancing, and apocalyptic imagery are elements in an organic whole. The elements become interrelated and reinforce each other to produce the unified apocalyptic vision of *Paradise Lost.*

Index

Index